Contents

PART ONE

The Barak Years 1999–2001

CONTENTS

PART TWO
Sharon vs Arafat 2001–2004

List of Illustrations

Photographic acknowledgements are given in parentheses.

List of Maps

Acknowledgements

This book, which accompanies the BBC/PBS television series, is in many ways as much the work of my colleagues at Brook Lapping Productions as it is mine. We spent 11 months together on and off aeroplanes and flat sharing in Jerusalem. Between us we interviewed nearly 100 top decision makers and officials, often both off-the-record and on film. Then we each took our piles of transcripts home, they to edit a series of documentaries, I to write this book.

Series Producer Norma Percy led the effort with her typical determination and tenacity, leaving no stone unturned in our efforts to unveil the behind-the-scenes drama in the search for peace in the Middle East. As with her previous television documentaries, Norma leaves behind not only engrossing films but also an impressive archive, mainly a collection of in-depth filmed interviews with world leaders lodged at King's College's Liddell Hart Centre, which will be invaluable to future generations of researchers. Series Producer and Director Mark Anderson brought with him vast experience and ability beneath his unflappable demeanour – teaching me that a glass of Scotch, followed by red wine and a good dinner, is the best inspiration. Producer and Director Dan Edge proved that wisdom is not the prerogative of the older generation, and his charm, investigative mind and energy were critical to our success. Our film researcher Declan Smith quietly scoured the world's archives for those undiscovered snippets, and was a pleasure to work with; Tom Raw, our talented researcher and co-ordinator, was an example of quiet efficiency and modesty; and Carrie Pennifer ensured that we were equipped for all our needs before leaving base. Norma, Mark, Dan and Tom have all read the manuscript and their comments were invaluable. Brian Lapping, head of Brook Lapping Productions, kept an eye on us from afar, but his interventions, when they came, were, as usual, sharp as a nail. I was fortunate to be part of this fantastic group of filmmakers, for which I am both humble and grateful.

Thanks are also due to Nava Mizrahi in Israel, who from her tiny car made sure the show went on despite the often enormous difficulties; Suha Arraf, who worked with us in the occupied territories; our translator Ora Silberstein; and Nili Aslan and Issa Freij, who filmed it all.

The series and, indeed, the book could not have been made without the interviewees, the Israelis, Palestinians, Jordanians, Syrians, Americans, British, French and others, who were the real participants of the Middle East drama. Their willingness to share their experiences with us made it possible to produce the documentary and this book. The list of interviewees is included at the end of the book.

Parts of this book were written at Franklin College in Lugano, where for each of the last four years I have spent a few relaxing weeks teaching summer courses and catching up with unfinished projects. The peaceful atmosphere of this beautiful spot in the foothills of the Swiss Alps, and the warm welcome I always receive there, provided me with the peace of mind I needed to meet the often maddening deadlines. At Franklin, I would like to thank in particular: the Dean, Armando Zanecchia; Andrew Starcher; Morris Mottale; and my larger-than-life friend Mel (Melvin) Schlein.

It has been my good fortune to have Stuart Proffitt as my publisher and editor. Stuart, who commissioned this book, believed in it from the beginning, and it was only his willingness to accept a delay in completing another book I owe him, *A History of the Occupied Territories*, which made it possible for this book to be written. At Penguin I would also like to thank Liz Friend-Smith, Richard Duguid, Elisabeth Merriman and my copy-editor, Charlotte Ridings. Thanks also to my literary agent Elaine Steel in London, Peter Kaufmann in New York, Simon Lawrence, Suzanne Nicholas, and to Ruti Frensdorff for help with the images.

Last, but certainly not least, are my debts to Dana, Daniel, Maya and Adam, all of whom have had to pay the price for one of the busiest years I have ever had. Dana single-handedly ran the show at home – no easy task – while I was absent for weeks on end, often calling in for literally only a few hours while on the Jerusalem–London–Lugano line. I dedicate this book to Dana.

Ahron (Ronnie) Bregman
London
2005

Preface – Elusive Interviews

This is all Bill Clinton's fault. I thought we had finished with the Arab–Israeli conflict. Our BBC series, *The 50 Years War: Israel and the Arabs*, had been broadcast around the world for that anniversary in 1998. We'd spent two years immersed in the story. That, we thought, was that.

We were wrong. Just after President Clinton left office in March 2001, we interviewed him for a series of programmes we were making about Ireland. Afterwards, he showed us round the study of his new home in a leafy New York suburb. Spotting a photo of him with Palestinian leader Yasser Arafat and Israeli Prime Minister Ehud Barak, I couldn't help re-researching the last series. 'Arafat?' Clinton sighed heavily. 'What a great deal he turned down.' Clearly Clinton still woke up in the middle of the night re-living his attempt to broker a peace settlement at the Camp David summit in the summer of 2000. He called himself 'a complete failure' for not having pulled it off.

Clinton whetted our appetite. Here was a very clever politician who had made a serious attempt to solve one of the biggest international conflicts of our time. We wanted to find out the story.

Like everyone else, we were soon distracted by 9/11, and then by President Bush's plan to go to war in Iraq. But the conflict over Israel was a story that didn't go away. The BBC commissioned three more hours on the issue. Penguin then asked Dr Ahron Bregman, whose encyclopaedic knowledge and effective interviewing were the backbone of the original series, to write this book. In May 2004 we were back in the Middle East.

But making a sequel wasn't easy.

*

As with all the history programmes Brian Lapping and I have made together over twenty years, we set out to make viewers feel what it is like to *be there* when really big political decisions are made. These decisions are taken by a handful of people − in private. When the Israeli Cabinet decides to besiege Arafat's West Bank headquarters, or to withdraw from the Gaza strip; when the Palestinian Authority decides to call a ceasefire; when a Hamas activist organizes a suicide bomber, no one is ever let in to film. By their nature such meetings are often so secret that their very existence is known only by those who take part in them. Our task is to pinpoint the key meeting, and then ask the people involved, one by one, to tell us afterwards what they said.

The difficulty we face every time is that sometimes the key decision makers won't talk − because they are afraid it might upset delicate negotiations in progress, or are too busy, or are just plain frightened to speak. If that happens, we are stuck. There are no substitutes. The participants are most likely to speak freely just *after* the story has reached an end point. They can often then be coaxed to reminisce about their own part in the completed jigsaw puzzle. *The 50 Years War* was commissioned in the wake of the 1993 Oslo Agreement, at a time when it looked as though peace in the Middle East really was on its way. And researching back over fifty years allowed us to interview pensioners who had time to sit and reminisce about the 1967 war, and President Sadat's strategy for peace.

Not so with the sequel, which deals only with the very recent past. President Clinton was now touring the world promoting his memoirs and tsunami relief. When our first letter reached him he was recovering from heart surgery, and he said no. Prime Minster Sharon said yes in principle, but that he would give no interviews until the Israeli withdrawal from the Gaza Strip was complete. Prime Minister Barak, though out of office, had just launched his bid to re-enter politics and was a very busy man. A first research meeting on 30 June 2004 didn't lead to a filmed interview until 1 November. Even then, after 40 minutes, his time ran out and we hadn't reached our questions about his amazing offer, made at the Camp David summit, to share Jerusalem with the Palestinians. It took until 9 March 2005 and a special trip to the Middle East – a round trip of 4,640 miles for a one-hour-long interview – to finish it.

In the first series Yasser Arafat had eluded us. His gatekeeper never actually said no, but the interview never happened. It was the week after the series was broadcast that the call came: 'President Arafat would be at our disposal during his forthcoming visit to London.' Surely we wouldn't be so unlucky again. Moreover, the Palestinian leader was now confined to his compound in the West Bank, and the Israeli government was hinting that if he left the occupied territories he would never be allowed to return.

To get the interview, we scrupulously followed the drill his office imposed on journalists. Appointments were not given in advance. The President usually received his visitors in the middle of the night (the Israelis close the checkpoint at sundown). So you book a hotel room, and await the summons. After several fruitless visits we were granted an audience at noon the following day – but only with his press secretary.

We presented ourselves at the entrance, and – our best pressed linen wilting in the heat – picked our way among the rubble, ruined cars and barbed wire, remains of the siege two years before, left to dramatize for visitors what the Israeli tanks had wrought. The press secretary sat impassively through our pitch. Suddenly he asked to be excused for a minute; when he reappeared he announced that President Arafat would like us to join him for lunch.

Our first impression was of a large pile of papers at the end of a long table. A famous black and white *keffiyya* was just visible over the top. He looked, as famous people do, like himself – but smaller. We were seated immediately on his left; he kept on reading and signing. It was an awkward moment. Should we speak? 'Speak, El Rais ["The Head"] can work and listen', we were told. I began to explain the project; he didn't look up.

My colleague Mark Anderson, who delights in unusual social situations, was enjoying my discomfort, but finally decided to help me out. 'Mr President, you have met many of the great men of the century. Who was the most memorable?' It worked; Arafat looked up and raised his finger. 'General de Gaulle, who honoured me with the award of the cross of Lorraine, Nikita Khrushchev, who invited me to Moscow, Fidel Castro, my brother' – a list of the great men of the century poured forth. Ice broken, he spoke, albeit somewhat cryptically, about his first tête-à-tête with Barak who, as a commando, had masterminded an attempt to assassinate him a decade before their meeting.

The table was laid with the usual Arab array of delicious-looking dishes. But Arafat ignored them. Instead he was brought a plate of plain boiled broccoli and small corncobs and proceeded to feed me tidbits with his fingers. Perhaps I was not a complete flop. Then the next supplicant appeared; we were ushered out . . .

Arafat's negotiators and ministers – Mohammed Dahlan, Saeb Erekat, Mohammed Rashid, Salam Fayyad, Nabil Shaath – were almost as hard to catch. Flying around the world, or back and forth to Gaza, they were hardly 'inside' for long – and like many great storytellers their stories take time to tell.

However, in November, one of Arafat's men summoned us to Paris where the Palestinian leader now lay dying. With Mrs Suha Arafat keeping firm guard over his bedside, they kept their vigil in the Intercontinental hotel – finally with time on their hands to talk to our cameras.

Then there was Arafat's successor as President, Mahmoud Abbas, known to everyone in the Middle East as Abu Mazen (literally, 'father of Mazen'). His son, the Mazen in question, explained to me that our problem was that his father was such an unassuming chap. That morning, he said, he had tried to take him out canvassing for votes in the presidential election. 'What?', said Abu Mazen. 'You expect me to go and ask people to vote for me? No, I couldn't do that.' When we finally filmed him, however, Abu Mazen was a star – a twinkly grandfather who demonstrated how he charmed George Bush, and raised the President's enthusiasm for the Palestinian cause.

Interviewing the Palestinian militants of Hamas and the Al-Aqsa Martyrs Brigade presented somewhat different problems. They don't have secretaries, and as the Israelis often use their mobile phones to target assassinations, it is not easy to get their phone numbers.

Only Dan Edge, our young director, was equipped to take on the task. Savvy and security minded from a previous year spent in Gaza, he finally managed an early-morning rendezvous in the notorious Jenin refugee camp. He was directed to the martyrs' graveyard and told to follow a car conspicuously filled with laundry. After driving round in circles he was brought face to face with a Camp Commander. An extract from Dan's diary reads: 'This is basically the first interview I have ever shot. And I'm doing it with a nervous gunman scratching the trigger on his rifle with the ever-present threat of an Israeli assassination. Not ideal conditions.'

Dan's trip back involved a tussle with a bored Israeli soldier, who lobbed what looked like a grenade straight at him (it turned out to be 'only' a stun grenade, but it was a nasty moment); then his passport was confiscated. Only many desperate phone calls by our clever Israeli producer Nava Mizrahi, helped by the Israeli Defence Force HQ who were as exasperated as we were, got him safely home to Jerusalem at midnight.

When we suggested Dan go back into Gaza to interview Hamas, Major Ronnie Bregman, rtd. (like all Israelis, Ahron has served time in the army) was horrified. The Israelis had recently assassinated the Hamas leader Sheikh Ahmed Yassin, and then his successor, Sheikh Abdel Aziz al-Rantissi 26 days later. Did we want Dan to be beside the target when the next assassination came? Nava had an inspired idea. The only safe place to talk to Hamas militants was inside an Israeli jail. As usual the negotiation to get inside took months and, as usual, Nava pulled it off. There were some conditions: we couldn't take a Palestinian crew, in case they smuggled in explosives, and we couldn't ask the prisoners anything about conditions inside the jail, but about how they arranged suicide bombings, well, fine, ask away. These men, who recruited and drove the suicide bombers, told us some chilling tales (see chapter 15).

We finally got the interview with Bill Clinton in June 2005, just days before our deadline. We knew his memory was prodigious − but what if it differed from that of other participants in an almost finished programme?

Seated in the newly opened Clinton Library in Little Rock Arkansas, his recall was as expected. When he spoke about the moment he put

Barak's offer to President Assad of Syria you could see from his expression that he was back in that room with him, and was as surprised and baffled as ever.

I'll never forget what he said: he said, 'It's our Lake too. They don't trust us not to foul the Lake? I want to run my feet in that lake and I want to sit on the shore and have my feet in the Lake. That is all I want, if I can do that, fine, if not we can't continue this conversation.' I mean he totally shut the talk down – I didn't get through the whole presentation.

As Clinton spoke, I got that feeling in the pit of my stomach – that sense of being there while history was being made. That sensation is the reason all of us keep at it, and Ahron's book really captures the best of the moments he and the rest of the team that made *Elusive Peace* lived through together.

Norma Percy, Series Producer
London, August 2005

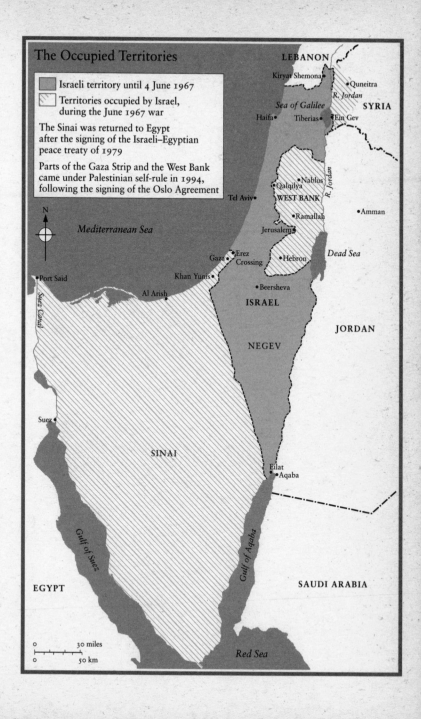

The Occupied Territories

Israeli territory until 4 June 1967

Territories occupied by Israel, during the June 1967 war

The Sinai was returned to Egypt after the signing of the Israeli–Egyptian peace treaty of 1979

Parts of the Gaza Strip and the West Bank came under Palestinian self-rule in 1994, following the signing of the Oslo Agreement

N

LEBANON

Kiryat Shemona

Quneitra

R. Jordan

SYRIA

Sea of Galilee

Haifa

Tiberias

Ein Gev

Mediterranean Sea

Nablus

Qalqilya

WEST BANK

R. Jordan

Tel Aviv

Ramallah

Amman

Jerusalem

Gaza

Erez Crossing

Hebron

Dead Sea

Khan Yunis

Port Said

Beersheva

Al Arish

ISRAEL

JORDAN

NEGEV

Suez

Suez Canal

SINAI

Eilat

Aqaba

EGYPT

SAUDI ARABIA

Gulf of Suez

Gulf of Aqaba

0   30 miles

0   50 km

Red Sea

Introduction

This is the sequel to *The Fifty Years War: Israel and the Arabs*, the companion book to a six-part BBC/PBS documentary of the same name, which I wrote in 1998 with the Egyptian Jihan el-Tahri.[1] *The Fifty Years War* has been translated into several other languages, reprinted twelve times in the UK, and has sold thousands of copies worldwide. As its name clearly implies, the first book was more about war and conflict, while *Elusive Peace* is more about attempts at making peace between Israelis and Arabs. *The Fifty Years War*, both the documentary and book, ended with the coming to power of Benjamin Netanyahu in May 1996. Although Netanyahu was Israel's Prime Minister for nearly three years, his premiership is hardly mentioned in the TV series and in the companion books. This is not a reflection on Netanyahu as a man or as Prime Minister, but results from the simple fact that his tenure in office falls between the two TV series and the books. We should not draw wrong conclusions from this, for the agreement Netanyahu negotiated before he left office in July 1999, the Wye River Memorandum, was critical in shaping the relationship between Israelis and Palestinians, particularly during the tenure of his successor, Ehud Barak.

Brokered by US President Bill Clinton, the Wye River Memorandum was signed by Netanyahu and Yasser Arafat, Chairman of the Palestinian Authority (PA), at the Aspen Institute in the Wye River Plantation, Maryland on 23 October 1998.[2] The purpose of the Memorandum was mainly to facilitate implementation of previous Israeli–Palestinian agreements, notably Oslo 2, signed on 28 September 1995, also known as the Interim Agreement on the West Bank and Gaza Strip. The

Wye River Memorandum called on Israel, among other things, to relinquish 13 per cent of West Bank land occupied in 1967,[3] release 750 Palestinian prisoners, provide the Palestinians with a licence for the operation of Gaza's air and sea ports, and create a safe corridor between the West Bank and the Gaza Strip. In return, the PA should take concrete measures to prevent acts of terrorism against Israel, collect illegal weapons and reduce the Palestinian police by 6,000 to 30,000. Arafat would also reaffirm the letter he sent to President Clinton on 13 January 1998, agreeing to nullify all the provisions of the Palestinian Covenant which were inconsistent with the PLO commitment to recognize and live in peace side by side with Israel.[4]

The summit at Wye was not just intended to facilitate implementation of previous agreements, however. It was also – and this fact has never before been published – the climax of an Israeli–Palestinian plot to impose a deal on Prime Minister Netanyahu, and, should he fail to play ball, to oust him.

Netanyahu was despised not only by Palestinians, who regarded him as an obstacle to peace, but also by the Israeli Left. Hence, in the period just before Wye, senior politicians from the Israeli opposition, including Yossi Beilin and Chaim Ramon, put their heads together with leading Palestinians, such as Saeb Erekat, Abu Mazen (also known as Mahmoud Abbas), Hassan Asfour and Mohammed Dahlan. Meetings took place at the residence of Egypt's ambassador to Israel, Mohammad Bassiouni (giving the group its name – 'The Bassiouni Forum'), and there the plan was hatched. The Israelis advised the Palestinians on how to deal with Netanyahu in general, and at Wye in particular. According to Yossi Beilin, 'We would usually get to the ambassador's house in the evening . . . there would be dinner. After dinner Saeb Erekat would insist on smoking a *Nargileh* . . . then we would talk.'[5] Erekat recalls these meetings as, 'collusion between me and members of the Israeli opposition . . . a cabal of me and my Israeli sympathizers . . . We developed certain ideas about how to deal with Netanyahu and we contacted the Americans with it and gave them something.'[6] The US special envoy to the Middle East, Dennis Ross, and his deputy, Aaron Miller, as Beilin recalls, 'often phoned during the meetings . . . and we would transfer the phone between us . . .

Sometimes the [US] ambassador would join these talks. He lives not far from Bassiouni.' When the package was ready it was given to the Americans and, as Yossi Beilin recalls, they then came back with it and offered it to Netanyahu and Arafat, and 'this in the fall of 1998 became [the draft for] Wye'.[7]

In other words, a secret draft was put together behind the back of the Prime Minister by the Israeli opposition and the Palestinians, in co-ordination with the Americans. This draft was then presented as an 'American' paper to Netanyahu and Arafat, becoming the basis for negotiations at Wye.

Saeb Erekat adds, 'Netanyahu [at Wye] was looking for ways to make us say "No" to the proposal.' But by going along with the paper Erekat knew 'if [Netanyahu] implements we're in business . . . and if he doesn't, he's out [as he will turn both the Americans and many in Israel against him]. We knew that. So we were in a win-win situation.'

The plot worked perfectly and Netanyahu was trapped. He signed the Wye River Memorandum – after all, he did not want to be blamed by the US for blowing the talks – but on his return to Israel he started to backtrack, fearing the wrath of his far Right supporters. Now both Right and Left alike attacked him: the Right because he had betrayed them – after all at Wye Netanyahu was willing to give away parts of *Eretz Yisrael*; while the Left blamed him for dragging his feet, saying the Prime Minister never really intended to live up to promises made at Wye.

The *coup de grâce* came on 4 January 1999, when Left and Right joined forces in the Israeli parliament (the Knesset) to produce an overwhelming majority of 81 in favour of dissolving the Knesset and forcing a new general election.

The election took place on 17 May 1999 and resulted in a stunning victory for Ehud Barak of Labour over Netanyahu.[8] The Left rejoiced as did the Palestinians, and with good reason. 'We felt', the Palestinian Hassan Asfour, one of the pre-Wye plotters, recalls, 'that we had a victory when Barak came to power . . . because we prepared it . . . we . . . the Americans . . . some Israelis. We felt it was a victory for us.'[9] It was a moment of hope for many Israelis and Palestinians.

This book starts with Ehud Barak's election victory. I call this part of the book 'The Barak Years', for it was Barak, his tone and actions, who – for well or ill – dictated the agenda. The book's second part focuses on the period from Ariel Sharon's rise to power in 2001 to the death of Yasser Arafat in 2004. I have called this part 'Sharon vs Arafat', for it is the story of the historical rivalry between these two arch-enemies which lies at the bottom of these dramatic years.

And always in the background was the world's only superpower – the United States. Under President Clinton, from 1999 to 2001 it tried to lend a hand to the parties in brokering peace, but failed disastrously. Then, it simply gave up. When George W. Bush came to power, America stood back, intervening only when faced with no other option. Indeed, in some respects, the Holy Land has defeated America.

PART ONE

The Barak Years
1999–2001

I

Barak's Grand Plan

'WE SEE THE ICEBERG IN FRONT OF US . . .'

As a soldier – and he was Israel's most decorated soldier – Ehud Barak was known as the 'missile which is always locking on one single target'.[1] Now, as the newly elected Prime Minister of Israel, Barak's target was peace. He declared domestic issues would have to come second, and, rather apocalyptically, he added that if peace did not come, another round of violence would begin. 'And then', as Barak put it, 'we will bury our victims, and they will bury their victims, and a generation later, we will sit down once more to the same geography, the same demography, the same problems.'[2] Barak's favourite analogy for the urgency of the situation was that of a ship heading towards an iceberg. As he said in an interview for *Elusive Peace*: 'We see the iceberg in front of us. Should we fail steering the ship away from it then we will crash into it.'[3] In other words, should peace fail then the ship – Israel – would be certain to collide with the Arab-Palestinian iceberg.

Barak's peace strategy was simple, at least on paper. He would first strike a deal with Syria, then get Israeli troops out of Lebanon, where they had been deployed since the 1982 invasion, then – and only then – turn seriously to the conflict with the Palestinians. A Syria-First approach was not Barak's brainchild, but rather an idea that had also been favoured by his predecessors. From the late Yitzhak Rabin, through Shimon Peres, to Benjamin Netanyahu, former Israeli prime ministers – and indeed Bill Clinton, the US President with whom they had worked – all were devotees of a Syria-First approach, preferring a peace treaty with Damascus *before* one with the Palestinians. There were good reasons for this.

First, the main issue separating Israel and Syria was that of the Golan Heights, taken from Syria by Israel in 1967. How much of the Golan should be returned to Syria, and what Israel would receive in return, appeared to be simpler to resolve than the complicated issues dividing Israelis and Palestinians – most notably the future of Jerusalem. As Barak explains, 'the Syrian issue is simpler than the Palestinian. On the Golan Heights there is no Temple Mount [the artificially expanded hill in Jerusalem where King Solomon built the First Temple 3,000 years ago] . . . only some old synagogues.'[4] Second, as Barak and his predecessors acknowledged, Syria, unlike the Palestinians, posed a *strategic* threat to Israel's existence. It had fighter-jets, tanks, missiles – even chemical weapons – and could inflict a severe blow on Israel. The Palestinians, meanwhile, could make life uncomfortable for Israel but did not pose an immediate strategic threat. Third, as Barak rightly assumed, a deal with Syria could help isolate – and this was urgent – two other sworn enemies of Israel, both potential nuclear powers: Iran and Iraq. Finally, and on a more personal level, Barak, like his predecessors, preferred to deal with President Hafez al-Assad of Syria rather than with Yasser Arafat. For while Assad was a tough nut to crack, nonetheless he was regarded in Israel – rightly or wrongly – as someone who could be trusted, a leader who would live up to any agreement he signed with Israel.[5] Arafat, on the other hand, was seen differently. Past experience had taught Israelis that Arafat could not be trusted, as he would often simply pocket offers made to him in the course of negotiations, only to come back later and ask for more. Barak referred to this practice when he said that 'the Palestinians are like crocodiles. The more you give them meat, the more they want.'[6] Barak believed that settling with Syria first would isolate Arafat and make him less inclined to stick to hardline positions. As Barak explained to me, 'I believe that there is strategic logic in making [peace] with Syria [first] . . . a deal with Syria [would] limit Arafat's ability to manoeuvre.'[7]

However, there was a history of peace efforts with Syria. In the summer of 1993, Prime Minister Yitzhak Rabin made an offer to Syria via a third party, US President Bill Clinton, asking him to keep it in his back pocket until the right moment, and then test it on Assad as an *American* idea. Rabin had said:

[He] would be prepared to commit to the United States that Israel would withdraw fully from the Golan Heights provided Israel's needs were met . . . (1) There must be normalization of relations, with full diplomatic relations and an exchange of ambassadors after the first phase of withdrawal. Withdrawal should be spread out over five years; (2) Full normalization required trade and tourism; (3) There must be satisfactory security arrangements, with the United States manning the early-warning sites on the Golan; (4) Israel's water need must be safeguarded.[8]

This became known as the 'deposit', or the 'pocket', in Israel and America, but the Syrians regarded it as a commitment. When US Secretary of State Warren Christopher put it to Assad when they met on 4 August 1993 in Damascus, he ignored Rabin's instruction to put the offer as an American idea and, instead, presented it as an offer to Assad *directly* from Prime Minister Rabin. When Israeli intelligence services (God knows how) intercepted a message showing this, the short-tempered Rabin was so furious he literally screamed at Christopher.[9] But Assad offered only a minimal response. Annoyed by this lukewarm reception, Rabin simply dropped the Syrian track and turned to strike a deal with Arafat in September 1993 (the 'Oslo Agreement').

Rabin's proposal was off the table. But such unofficial offers, even those made via a third party, tend to develop a life of their own. And thus, ever since Christopher's presentation, the Syrians have insisted that a 'commitment' was made to them by Prime Minister Rabin for a full Israeli withdrawal from the Golan Heights to the 4 June lines – the lines on which Israeli and Syrian forces were deployed on the eve of the 1967 Six-Day War before the Golan Heights were seized – and that Rabin's successors, including Barak, must honour this commitment.

What did Rabin's offer really mean? That Israel would withdraw to the 4 June 1967 lines? Or to the line further to the east, the putative international border, the one fixed between British Mandatory

Palestine and French-controlled Syria in 1923? (See map, Golan Heights: Israel–Syria Border Area, p. 20.) The answer is buried with Rabin. Assad certainly viewed all the territory under Syrian control on the eve of the 1967 war as Syrian, and this included land *west* of the 1923 recognized border, all the way up to the edge of the Sea of Galilee. Syria had, in fact, five villages touching the water of the Sea of Galilee and Syrians could swim and fish in the sea.[10] Rabin, on the other hand, might well have thought that any territory west of the recognized 1923 international border should be Israeli. While the difference in territory between these two lines is not particularly great – a mere 66 sq. km – for Assad land held before 1967 was 'sacred', while for Rabin the difference meant that by keeping the Syrians *east* of the 1923 line, he could deny them access to the precious water of the Sea of Galilee – the source of 40 per cent of Israel's fresh water – as the 1923 border ran 10 metres inland from the water's edge.

Barak, of course, knew of Rabin's 'deposit', but thought it had been a grave mistake to offer it. He was particularly annoyed because when the offer was made he was Chief of Staff and Rabin had not consulted him, although it is the practice in Israel to consult the head of the military on such vital issues.

Now, however, confident of his powers of reason and persuasion, Prime Minister Barak thought that, in spite of the 'deposit' or 'commitment', which he was not willing to reaffirm, a Syria-First approach was still preferable. The fact that by that time President Assad was gravely ill (he was suffering from severe heart problems) also meant, Barak believed, that the Syrian President would be keen to conclude a deal, so as to leave a clean slate for his successor – presumably his son.

'WHAT CAN I SAY TO HIM?'

It was then little wonder that Barak was in no hurry to see Arafat, least of all during the sensitive time when he was trying to put together a coalition government composed of seven different parties. Barak rightly assumed that a photo opportunity with Arafat, with the latter attempting one of his famous kissing sessions, could easily frighten off potential coalition partners. 'And, anyway,' said Barak, 'what can I say to him now before my government is in place?'[11] But, pressed by aides to make a gesture, Barak phoned Arafat, telling him that he had almost finalized his coalition and they would meet soon.

On 7 July 1999, Barak presented his government to the Knesset and declared that his supreme goal was to bring peace to the Israeli people, so that 'mothers will be able to sleep peacefully'. Two days later, he went to Alexandria to meet Egyptian President Hosni Mubarak. Only then did his Chief of Staff, Danny Yatom, phone Arafat's Chief of Staff, Nabil Abu Rudeineh, to arrange an official meeting with Arafat. Clearly, Arafat was not the priority.

Barak's sense of Palestinian protocol was shaken as Ami Ayalon, head of Shin Bet, Israel's General Security Service, explained to him that he would have to take a present to give to Arafat on their first meeting. Ayalon recalls: 'Barak didn't understand that if you meet somebody like Arafat, you have to give him a token. I told him, "Ehud . . . you have to bring something." He said, "What should I bring?" So we prepared a beautiful Bible and Koran, in a beautiful wooden case with silver.'[12]

The meeting took place on Sunday, 11 July, at the Erez Crossing, on the northern border between the Gaza Strip and Israel. Barak arrived by helicopter a few minutes before Arafat and went out to meet him in the courtyard. They then went in and exchanged gifts. Arafat gave Barak a silver menorah in the shape of a dove and a tablecloth. Barak pulled out his gift and handed it over to Arafat, who was 'very moved'.[13] They sat together – not face to face as negotiators would often do, for Barak was not there to negotiate, but rather side by side, Barak in his dark suit and Arafat in his ironed uniform and famous chequered *keffiyya*, both sweating in the stifling summer heat. After some smiles to photographers they retired for a twenty-minute tête-à-tête.

Like a conjuror, Arafat pulled a document from his pocket. It detailed those commitments Israel was still due to implement according to the Wye River Memorandum, which Arafat had signed with Barak's predecessor Benjamin Netanyahu the previous October. These included the release of Palestinian prisoners,[14] further Israeli withdrawals from occupied territory, a safe passage between the Gaza Strip and the West Bank, the provision of a licence for the Palestinians to build a deep-water port in Gaza, and more. Barak ignored this. He had his own plan and he would not let Arafat confuse the matter with facts from the past.

For, apart from wanting to deal with Syria first, and he would not divulge *that* to Arafat in their first official meeting, Barak was also determined to change tactics with the Palestinians. He planned to stop giving them territory or other concessions until after *all* stumbling blocks were resolved. He thought that Israel needed to retain all the occupied land, to use as leverage, when facing the Palestinians across the negotiating table to deal with the most complicated issues – Jerusalem, refugees, borders and settlements. Barak understood that he could not simply cancel Wye; instead he wished to renegotiate it in a way which would defer its implementation, thus leaving the bargaining assets in Israeli hands, and in the meantime move rapidly to agree on the final permanent deal. When such a permanent deal was finalized, and as Arafat declared that the conflict was over and that he had no more claims, then, and only then, would Israel pay up, surrendering the assets – mainly land – in a single go.

Thus in Barak's first official meeting with Arafat, as the Palestinian negotiator Saeb Erekat who was in attendance recalls, when Arafat asked for implementation of Wye, 'Barak hastened to say: "We don't need to waste our time on little issues ... we should aim to get the whole thing done in one go."' Mohammed Dahlan, head of Palestinian Preventive Security in the Gaza Strip, recalls the metaphor Barak used: 'We need to cut it out in one go ... just one operation, we could do the surgery.'[15] And, as Barak put it in an interview for *Elusive Peace*, 'Why was it necessary for Israel to go through serial amputations? First, a finger ... then another finger ... then the whole hand ... Do it all in one go!' Giving the land in a single move could also help limit the furious debate that raged within Israel whenever the government announced yet another small withdrawal.

Arafat objected strongly. He said, 'The two have to be done at the same time, implementing Wye [by withdrawing from occupied lands] and starting negotiations on the final status.' Barak replied, 'No, no, think about it.' Arafat: 'That means you want to abrogate the agreements we concluded with Netanyahu.' Barak: 'Give it some thought.'[16]

However, it was difficult for Arafat to 'give it some thought' when his mind was focused on the Wye River Memorandum, which, if implemented, would leave in his hands much of the occupied territories even before the core issues – Jerusalem, refugees, borders and settlements – were discussed. And now Barak was asking him to give this up? 'I've looked at Arafat,' Mohammed Dahlan recalls. 'He was not hearing it . . . He was just not listening . . . He was not there, not in the room. He was angry.' The rapid movement of the foot, a clear sign of a nervous Arafat, was also apparent. 'The left foot was still,' recalls Erekat, 'but the right foot was moving and fast.'[17] That Arafat was unhappy did not escape the Israelis either. Barak's Chief of Staff, Danny Yatom, remembers that, 'Arafat was shocked by Barak's new approach . . . He said, "This is a manipulation. I demand an implementation of previous agreements."'

Thus, the first official summit meeting between the two leaders was a dialogue of the deaf. Whereas Barak kept talking about renegotiating Wye, deferring its implementation, jumping to the endgame and linking any Israeli concessions to the final deal and 'end of conflict', Arafat talked only about the need for Israeli withdrawals and the implementation of previous agreements, mainly Wye.

But what could Arafat do? He had no choice but to go along with his new partner Barak for there was no point in rocking the boat at such an early stage, during his first meeting with the new Israeli Prime Minister. But he did not like it – not one bit.

'I'M EAGER AS A KID WITH A NEW TOY'

Barak's eyes were now fixed on Washington. America, the one remaining superpower, was the only country with enough clout to bang heads together and move things along. And the White House was occupied by a good friend of Israel, William Jefferson ('Bill') Clinton.

Clinton had invested hugely in the Middle East peace process and he knew the ins and outs of it perhaps better than any previous American president. However, this was his final term, and he would leave the White House in January 2001. Thus, if the US President was to help pull the peace process out of the doldrums, things had to move fast.

For Clinton, Barak was a welcome relief from the frustration of having to deal with Netanyahu, who had been regarded in Washington as an obstacle to peace. In fact, Clinton was so thrilled with Barak's election victory that during a Democratic fundraiser in Florida on 13 July 1999, he said, 'I'm eager as a kid with a new toy for the meeting I'm going to have with the new Israeli Prime Minister.'[18] These words hit the headlines in Israel, where commentators complained that the President was patronizing Barak.

Just before Barak's first official visit to Washington, Secretary of State Madeleine Albright sent a confidential memo to President Clinton, advising him that Barak was acting alone, and was a secretive man. A one-to-one relationship with him, wrote Albright, would be 'extremely important'.[19] She was right. Business à la Barak, as it soon became apparent, meant dealing principally with the President and avoiding lesser US officials, particularly Albright, whom Barak held in low esteem.

On Thursday, 15 July 1999, at 2 p.m., Barak launched his first official visit to the US with a press conference with Clinton in the White House Rose Garden. 'Mr President,' asked Shimon Shiffer, an Israeli journalist who had travelled with Barak to Washington. 'You say that you are waiting for Mr Barak as a kid waiting for a new toy ... What kind of game do you want to play with Mr Barak?' Baffled, Clinton first gave a vague answer. American journalist Wolf Blitzer helped him out: 'I don't think the President necessarily understood the question', Blitzer said, and then went on to remind Clinton of his 'kid with a new toy' comment made a few days before in Florida. Now, the usually smooth and eloquent Clinton was evidently thrown:

No, no ... I see, yes ... yes, let me say, though ... I didn't understand. You're right. Thank you, Wolf. That is ... in English, what that means is that you are very excited. It has no reference to the Prime Minister. For example ... I would never do that. For example, if I ... no, no, if I were taking a trip to Hawaii, I might say, I'm as excited as a kid with a new toy ... doesn't mean I think Hawaii's a new toy, if you see what I mean.[20]

Nobody really saw what Clinton meant but with the press conference over, and taking on board Albright's advice to build a one-to-one relationship with the new Prime Minister, Clinton led Barak to the Yellow Oval Room for a two-and-a-half-hour meeting, with not even the usual note-taker present. When Barak emerged from their talk, he said he was 'very satisfied'. He told aides that the President was 'very, very intelligent and knew his stuff'. Clinton had told him: 'There are only two people in the world who I know are capable of thinking of the third, fourth and fifth steps, it's you, Ehud, and myself. But you do it better than I do!'[21] Clinton told his aides that the Prime Minister was a leader who would 'be scrupulous in terms of living up to his obligation'.[22]

That evening, the Clintons took the Baraks by helicopter to Camp David, the presidential retreat in Maryland's Catoctin Mountains. After a fish dinner the two leaders stayed up talking 'until nearly three in the morning'.[23] In an interview for *Elusive Peace* Bill Clinton recalls his night meeting with Barak: 'That night [as we] were talking, Ehud would get excited and move his hands around a lot and I'd get excited and chomp down on my cigar, and it was a night full of hope.'[24] Like their earlier talks at the White House, no note-takers were present, which gave the President's aides some concern. 'It's a rare thing for the President to meet alone without a note-taker', Robert Malley from the National Security Council (NSC)[25] explains. 'You never know if the President's going to remember what he said ... you never know if the other side has said what the President thinks he said.'[26] Clinton's aides also feared that the President's pleasant style might be mistaken by Barak for agreement on specific issues. Malley's boss, National Security Advisor Samuel (Sandy) Berger, dispatched him and his colleague Bruce Riedel up to Camp David, 'to corner the President while he still had some fresh memory of what had happened'.[27]

Malley says Clinton was a 'bit surprised' to find his aides on his doorstep, but he gave them 'as much as he could', reporting that he had had a 'great' meeting with Barak. The good news was that Barak was determined 'to reach two peace agreements in the next fifteen months, one with the Palestinians, one with the Syrians'. But the bad news was that 'to do that, Barak felt he had to renegotiate past agreements [a reference to Wye] with [the] Palestinians'. Barak told Clinton, as he had told Yasser Arafat in their Erez meeting ten days earlier, that he wanted to defer implementing the Wye River Memorandum and renegotiate it. Clinton replied that Barak had 'to sort this out with the Palestinians themselves' and should try to 'sweeten' the bitter pill by offering Arafat some gestures.

There was some bad news on the Syrian front as well. Clinton reported to his aides that Barak would not fulfil the Rabin promise of 1993 – the late Prime Minister's pledge to withdraw from the Golan Heights if Israel's security and other concerns were satisfied. This, in particular, disappointed Clinton. As a Syria-First devotee, he felt that peace with President Assad was within reach. Now, with Barak's reluctance to embrace the Rabin 'pocket', it was clear to Clinton that it would take some time to move Assad. Barak also attached an enormous price tag to his peace package.[28] If peace was to be signed, Barak explained to Clinton, Israel alone would need $23 billion to meet its security and resettlement needs; some $10 billion would be needed as loan guarantees to the Palestinians, in addition to $5 billion which would have to be given to the Syrians. This enormous bill did not deter Clinton, for he believed that if peace was in the offing, the necessary funds could easily be assembled.

On 19 July, Clinton and Barak held a concluding press conference. Barak praised his host and said that he 'would suggest a kind of framework of about fifteen months', within which it would be possible to assess whether there could be a breakthrough or whether 'we are stuck once again'.[29] The fifteen-month timeframe, it is worth noting, was closely related to the time Clinton had left in office. Barak told the President that a breakthrough could only happen while Clinton was still in the White House, as the new president would not be able to devote enough time and energy to Middle East peace during his first months in office.

From Barak's point of view, his first official visit to the United States was a great success. He had managed to convince the Americans that he was determined to propel the peace process forwards, and to let Washington play a leading role. For that, Barak was not only praised by his hosts but was also paid in cash, in the form of a Memorandum of Understanding on US military aid to Israel. It boosted American military aid by a third, from $1.9 billion to $2.4 billion a year, and, among other things, envisaged Washington's financing of Israel's development of a third battery of Arrow anti-missile missiles to the tune of $200 million.

'WE'RE NOT ASKING FOR THE MOON'

Clinton had promised Barak that he would phone Arafat and soften him up, so that the Palestinian leader would be more receptive to the Prime Minister's new ideas.

True to his word, Clinton phoned Arafat and advised him 'to listen carefully' to what Barak had to say and not to reject out of hand the Prime Minister's ideas. According to Arafat's chief negotiator, Saeb Erekat, who usually took part in these conversations to help Arafat with his English, President Clinton said, 'Trust me, this man is serious, this man will be your partner, he will deliver peace.'

As for Barak, he had promised Clinton he would see Arafat immediately on his return to Israel. He planned to do so, but the death of King Hassan II of Morocco on 23 July 1999 delayed things as both Barak and Arafat went to the funeral. Clinton was also at the funeral on the 26th, and it gave him the opportunity to corner Arafat and talk to him again about Barak's plans. The President, red in the face after walking the length of the three-mile funeral procession behind the king's horse-drawn casket in searing heat, reported to Arafat on his Washington talks with Barak. As Robert Malley (Clinton's note-taker) recalls, the President said to Arafat,

Barak wants to renegotiate past agreements. I know you might not like that. Just do me a favour. I'm not asking you to accept this. I'm asking you to listen to him, give him a chance. But don't go in there with the predetermined decision that you're going to reject any amendment to what has already been concluded.

Arafat, who was rarely confrontational with the President, promised Clinton that he 'would not let the President down' and that he 'would listen carefully to Barak's ideas and consider them'.[30] But Arafat also insisted – and this had become a mantra, which he now repeated to the President – that 'We're not asking for the moon, only for what was signed.'

2

From Wye to Sharm

'THIS MAN WILL DO NOTHING'

On 27 July 1999, Barak and Arafat again met at the Erez border crossing, and the Prime Minister again tried to persuade the Palestinian leader to agree to his plan to renegotiate the Wye River Memorandum. Barak had failed to heed President Clinton's advice to offer Arafat some 'sweeteners', but he still hoped that Clinton's two talks with Arafat would have made him more receptive to the idea. They had not. Although he had promised Clinton to 'keep an open mind' and listen to Barak's new ideas, Arafat lashed out at Barak. 'You claim to be the true follower of Rabin [with whom Arafat had signed the Oslo Agreement] . . . but you're not . . . You don't want to implement [Wye] . . .' Arafat then repeated his demand that negotiations on a permanent peace agreement, including the final status of the West Bank and Gaza, should take place *simultaneously* with the implementation of Wye.[1] 'Look,' Barak said, still sticking to his guns, 'let the people meet up and discuss the best ideas for both sides.'[2]

When the two leaders emerged to face the press and others waiting for them in a crowded and sweltering hall, they announced they would start renegotiating Wye. Negotiating for the Israelis would be Gilead Sher, a 46-year-old lawyer and a colonel in the reserves with a long personal relationship with Barak. For the Palestinians it would be the veteran negotiator Saeb Erekat. 'I could sense', Gilead Sher recalls of the press conference, 'that Arafat was very dissatisfied . . . he was forced into this framework.' Saeb Erekat remembers Arafat telling him, after meeting Barak, 'This man will do nothing . . . he will not implement anything ... he will just blame us for the failure of everything.'

Negotiations to revise the Wye River Memorandum started on 29 July, at the Larom Hotel in Jerusalem. The Palestinians played ball, but most reluctantly. 'It was not easy', the Palestinian Mohammed Dahlan, who joined Saeb Erekat, recalls. 'We Palestinians wanted to keep the Wye agreement as it was but Barak wanted to change it.' Acting on Barak's instructions, Gilead Sher offered his Palestinian counterparts very little – he was even reluctant to agree to the safe passage for Palestinians to commute between the West Bank and the Gaza Strip, which had been agreed at Wye. He suggested instead that Israel provide shuttle buses between the two sectors, an idea the Palestinians had rejected in previous negotiations. Meanwhile, in the background, the Israeli press, quoting 'sources close to Barak', kept hammering home the message that there would be 'serious consequences' if the Palestinians failed to accept Barak's new proposals.

With both sides digging in their heels, negotiations were getting nowhere and external involvement became unavoidable. The experienced US special Middle East envoy Dennis Ross intervened, and on 28 August, after weeks of detailed and often acrimonious negotiations, a deal was finally clinched in a session between Sher and Erekat at the King David Hotel in Jerusalem. Then, on Saturday, 4 September 1999, at the Red Sea resort of Sharm el-Sheikh and joined by the Egyptian President Hosni Mubarak, King Abdullah of Jordan and US Secretary of State Madeleine Albright, Barak and Arafat got together to sign the new deal.

However, on the eve of the signing ceremony, the usual pre-arranged agenda for summit gatherings unravelled as Arafat caused trouble at the last minute, refusing to accept various points. Secretary of State Albright scurried between him and Barak in the corridors of the Jolie Ville Hotel in Sharm, seeking agreement on the fine details, particularly on the number of prisoners Israel would release. But late in the day, and after much fuss, Barak and Arafat finally signed the Memorandum on Implementation Timeline of Outstanding Commitments of Agreements Signed and the Resumption of Permanent Status Negotiations, which came to be known as the Sharm el-Sheikh Memorandum.

While generally this reaffirmed what the Palestinians had already been promised by Benjamin Netanyahu back in 1998, it also provided Barak with what *he* wanted, namely a delay of transfer of land until progress was made in the negotiations. His method was ingenious. Under the new Sharm agreement permanent status negotiations would begin soon, no later than 13 September 1999; a framework agreement on permanent status would be reached within five months and a fully fledged peace treaty, namely a comprehensive permanent status agreement, would be reached within a year. At Wye, Netanyahu had agreed to give the Palestinians 13 per cent of West Bank territory, to be transferred in three stages, with the largest portion of 5 per cent of land to go in the final transfer. Now, in the revised Sharm agreement, Barak demanded, and got, a deferral of this transfer, which gave him five months. As it would also take five months, according to the new Sharm agreement, to reach the Framework Agreement on Permanent Status (FAPS), more West Bank land would remain in Barak's hands during the critical talks leading to the FAPS, thus giving him leverage to exert concessions from Arafat.

'I'VE NEVER HUMILIATED ARAFAT'

Renegotiating Wye had put an enormous strain on the already bumpy relationship between Barak and Arafat. Although Barak insisted that 'I've never humiliated Arafat', he did actually often hurt the easy-to-be-offended Palestinian leader. This was nothing particularly to do with Arafat, but more with the sort of arrogant behaviour typical of Barak. He was equally ready to humiliate and hector his own colleagues and friends. The fact that he was poor at managing other people's sensitivities in a part of the world where honour, dignity and respect form an important component of the diplomatic game was a major problem.

With the Sharm agreement giving Barak what he wanted, his aides now pressed him to try to improve his poor relationship with Yasser Arafat. So he agreed to organize a dinner for Arafat and a few of his colleagues.

On 11 September 1999, Barak dispatched a helicopter to collect the Palestinians and bring them over to the house of a close associate of his, Jean Frydman, in Savyon, a wealthy suburb of Tel Aviv. The evening began with good-humoured small talk. Barak teased Yasser Abed Rabbo, Arafat's Minister of Information, when Abed Rabbo requested vodka. 'Aha,' said Barak, 'this is because you were a Communist.' Abed Rabbo remembers something else: 'We had goose liver steaks. Very nice, but one shouldn't eat more than one steak, it's very rich. And the table was full of these steaks. I took one . . . Arafat hardly touched his because he's concerned about cholesterol levels. And Barak comes and devours one after the other . . . Unbelievable.'[3] Barak describes how Arafat kissed the forehead of his daughter. 'She was so deeply moved', he recalls. 'She was so delighted. She's the daughter of a general who spent all his life fighting terrorism. Arafat was a target . . . for many years when she was young. Now to meet over dishes of Moroccan food, to be kissed by the Chairman of the PLO . . .'[4]

However, the gesture did little to improve the long-term relationship between Barak and Arafat. The Prime Minister remained as tough and as uncompromising as ever, with a tendency to stall that irritated the Palestinians. According to the Sharm el-Sheikh agreement, Israeli–Palestinian talks had to resume right away. But the Prime Minister failed to name his delegation, although this timetable had been his own demand. This proved to the Palestinians that what Barak had really wanted was to put negotiations with them on the back burner while waiting for a breakthrough on the 'other mistress' – the Syrian front. They were right. In an interview for *Elusive Peace*, Barak openly admits that 'I wanted to reschedule the implementation of Wye in a way that would delay it . . . I thought it would give us several months . . . it would give us the opportunity to try with the Syrians first.'

3

Talking to 'the mistress'

Attempts at reviving talks with Syria had started even before Israel's 1999 general election. In May of that year, President Clinton had sent Martin Indyk, then Assistant Secretary of State for Near Eastern Affairs, to Damascus with a letter addressed to President Assad. Predicting that Barak would win the election, Clinton wrote, 'I am ready to make an effort to finish the Syrian deal, but this time you are going to have to be more flexible.'[1] After handing Clinton's letter over to Assad, Indyk asked him, 'What shall I tell the President?', whereupon Assad replied, 'You can tell the President that I will be flexible, but I will not be like [Anwar] Sadat [of Egypt], and I will not be like King Hussein [of Jordan], and I will not be like Yasser Arafat.' By which Assad meant he would not settle for less than the return of all the land Israel took from him in the 1967 war. He was not going to risk being shot down in the street by his own people as President Sadat of Egypt was in 1981; nor would he swap the captured territory for other land as King Hussein of Jordan had done in his peace treaty with Israel in 1994; and he would not be like Arafat, who made a partial deal in Oslo in 1993, in which the core issues like Jerusalem, the fate of Palestinian refugees and the borders of the future Palestinian state were left to be worked out later. It would happen only according to Assad's way of making peace. Hence, among the US diplomats involved, Assad's approach earned him the nickname 'the Frank Sinatra of the peace process . . . My Way'.[2]

Soon after Barak was elected Prime Minister, a British journalist

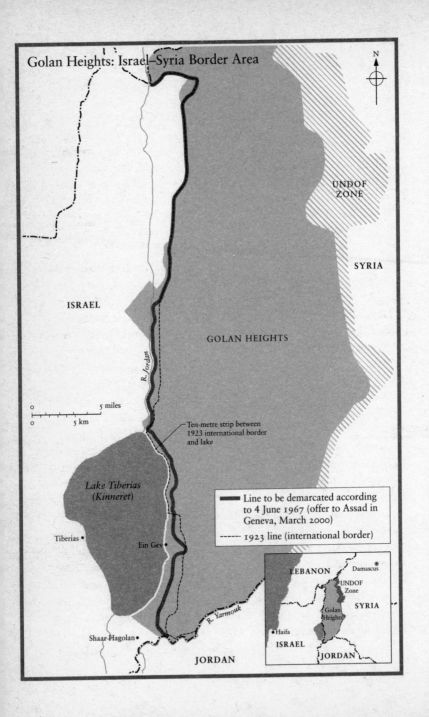

Golan Heights: Israel–Syria Border Area

N

UNDOF
ZONE

SYRIA

ISRAEL

GOLAN HEIGHTS

R. Jordan

0   5 miles
0   5 km

Ten-metre strip between
1923 international border
and lake

Lake Tiberias
(Kinneret)

Tiberias •

Ein Gev •

━━━ Line to be demarcated according
to 4 June 1967 (offer to Assad in
Geneva, March 2000)

------ 1923 line (international border)

R. Yarmouk

Shaar Hagolan •

JORDAN

LEBANON   Damascus ⊙
                      UNDOF
                      Zone
                 Golan
                 Heights   SYRIA

• Haifa

ISRAEL   JORDAN

named Patrick Seale, who was Assad's biographer, enjoying good access to him, made an attempt to revive Israeli–Syrian relations. Seale organized for Barak and President Assad both to publish statements, on 23 June 1999 in the Arab daily *Al-Hayat* in London. Barak praised Assad for having created a 'strong, independent, self-confident Syria', and Assad reciprocated by hailing Barak as a 'strong and sincere man' who 'wants to make peace with Syria and who operates according to a well planned strategy'. It was an unprecedented exchange of public compliments.

After his summit meeting with Barak, Clinton told President Assad that the Israeli Premier was anxious to move quickly to an agreement with Syria. Acknowledging, however, that it was difficult for Assad to have direct contact with the Israelis, Clinton proposed Assad should send his representatives to a secret trilateral meeting with Israelis and Americans. All negotiators would have an open line to their leaders. This would pave the way for a Barak–Assad summit meeting, and, eventually, to a full peace treaty.

'WOULD GENERAL SAGUIE AGREE TO PUT HIS ACCEPTANCE . . . IN WRITING?'

President Assad agreed and dispatched the Ministry of Foreign Affairs' legal adviser, Riad Daoudi, to represent him in talks with Barak's trusted colleague Uri Saguie, former head of Military Intelligence. The meeting would be supervised by Clinton's special Middle East envoy, Dennis Ross.

President Assad instructed Daoudi to negotiate a formula for a resumption of formal negotiations with Israel, a formula that *must* – as Assad made clear to Daoudi – acknowledge Rabin's 1993 commitment to withdraw fully from the Golan Heights to the 4 June 1967 lines. However, Saguie's mandate from Barak was the opposite: to prepare for a summit *without* making a firm commitment on the 4 June 1967 lines.

On 27 August 1999 in Berne, at the residence of the US ambassador to Switzerland, the two negotiators had an amicable and informal breakfast with Dennis Ross. Retired General Saguie spoke of his experience of the pain of war, and his belief in peace. He said frankly that for Barak, the security of Israel's borders and securing the water supply of the Sea of Galilee were the most important issues. He acknowledged he knew what mattered for Assad was the Golan Heights, the land Syria lost in 1967 when Assad had been Syria's Minister of Defence. Daoudi, also, expressed his belief in peace and talked of the need for both sides to have a better future, and he acknowledged that indeed Saguie was right – what *really* mattered for President Assad was the return of the Golan Heights to Syrian hands and a full Israeli withdrawal to the 4 June 1967 lines.

Their talks continued after breakfast until the unavoidable question was raised. 'Do you accept the principle of withdrawal to the 4 June 1967 lines?' asked Daoudi. Saguie replied with a 'yes but'. Yes, Israel did accept the principle of full withdrawal from the occupied Golan Heights, but there were still, as Saguie put it, 'technical questions' about the exact location of the future border between the two countries.[3] Saguie also mentioned Israel's concerns about the exact relationship between the Sea of Galilee's water and the border, by which he meant that Israel wished to see the Syrians deployed *away* from the water. 'Would General Saguie agree to put his acceptance of Israel's withdrawal to the 4 June 1967 lines in writing?' Daoudi asked. Saguie refused. He recalls, 'We discussed water issues, security, normalization [of relations between the two states], but we did not get into details.'[4] For Daoudi, however, this was a disappointment; his instructions were to get Saguie to reaffirm Rabin's commitment to a full Israeli withdrawal to the 4 June lines, and to get it in writing.

The imaginative Ross made a brave attempt to save the day. He drafted a formula that he hoped would please them both. The formula went, 'The Rabin deposit given to President Clinton on full withdrawal stands, should not be withdrawn, and should guide the outcome of negotiations if there is to be an agreement.'[5] When Saguie phoned Barak with this, Barak agreed to accept the formula as a basis for talks – but said he would agree to nothing that went beyond it. But when Daoudi presented Ross's formula to Syria's Foreign Minister, Farouk Shara, supervising the talks from Damascus, Shara refused it. He insisted on a formula that explicitly referred to the 4 June 1967 lines. The negotiators returned home empty-handed.

'YOU WANT SYRIAN LAND'

Secretary of State Albright then visited the region, and Barak pressed her to revive the Israeli–Syrian peace talks. The failure at Berne had not deterred Barak, who remained confident a deal could be made. He even talked in terms of signing an agreement by October 1999. This was typical Barak. He always had a schedule, meticulously planned, and he would expect the Americans, and others, to adhere to it – and they often would. But, he would not remove the main obstacle for a deal, reaffirming Rabin's promise of a full Israeli withdrawal from the Golan Heights. In fact, not only would Barak not reaffirm the 'deposit', but he went on to explain to Albright that he wanted to set a border with Syria which did not touch either the northeast quarter of the Sea of Galilee or the Jordan River just above it, and that border, as Barak put it, must run 'a few hundred metres east of the lake' so that the Syrians had no access to the precious water (see map, p. 20). Such a border, he must have known, could not fulfil Assad's condition, for it meant that Israel would not withdraw to the 4 June lines.

Thanks to pressure from the Secretary of State and her team the talks resumed, this time in America. On 24 September in Bethesda, Maryland, Syrian General Mohammad Omar, head of Syria's Military Intelligence, joined the lawyer Daoudi in talks with Barak's representative Uri Saguie, joined this time by Yoel Singer, a US-based Israeli lawyer who had played a key role under Rabin in peace talks with the Palestinians in Oslo in 1993.

Now, however, the Syrians came up with new demands. They claimed a border extending 200 metres *into* the lake. Saguie surprised them all by suggesting they study a map. The Israelis had always refused to discuss the location of the border on maps before having other issues such as security, the normalization of relations between the two states and water sorted out. But Saguie was confident that this was the right approach and, back in Israel, Barak agreed that if Assad's definition of the 4 June 1967 border was indeed based on where the forces were deployed on the eve of the 1967 war, then Israel could get what it wanted, namely a border to the east of the Sea of Galilee and the Jordan River above it. The Syrian Daoudi agreed to Saguie's new approach and the delegates began poring over maps in the suite of the American team. Saguie recalls, 'The Syrians said, "We are looking for you Israelis to give up the entire Golan Heights down to the 4 June lines." I said to them, "Could you show me the 4 June line on the map? Can you explain to me what do you mean when you refer to the 4 June line?"' This was a legitimate question. The 4 June 1967 line had never actually been drawn on any map. It was not a line but a *concept* – Assad's notion of the deployment on the ground as it existed prior to the 1967 war. According to Saguie, the Syrians replied, 'We mean the positions where you Israelis were deployed before the war.' Saguie:

I brought with me a map. A Syrian map! They looked at it. The [1923] international border was there. But there was no 4 June line. So they changed tactics. They said 'If you show us our [military] positions before the war then . . .' So I did and I showed them that sixty per cent of their positions were in fact east of the 1923 line . . . Then they told me, 'But we controlled this area by fire . . . from a distance . . . even if we were not there physically.' So I told them: 'I control Damascus by my aeroplanes, so is it mine?'

After this exchange the Syrians said, according to Saguie, 'We have to check with our boss Shara.' When they returned they said, 'We agree that there is no 4 June line. But what was taken by you by force should be given back.' They added, 'If you agree to withdraw from the Golan Heights then we'll agree to demarcate the line . . . from scratch. Let's do a new line according to our mutual interest.'

Saguie and General Omar then started going over the map in a detailed examination of the future border in an exercise which went on for two hours or so. The American Martin Indyk, who was present, told *Elusive Peace*, 'They had Saguie's map, and they went down the line, point by point, saying "Where were you exactly? And here . . . And here . . ."' Saguie pointed out that there were no Syrian forces on

the Jordan River north of the Sea of Galilee, but General Omar disagreed, pointing to a bridge where the Syrians had been. Saguie then
said that Syrian forces had left their positions on the northernmost
part of the Sea of Galilee prior to the 1967 war and again Omar
disagreed. It was hopeless and eventually they decided to abandon the
futile exercise. When Daoudi then asked again whether Saguie would
accept the principle of a withdrawal to the 4 June 1967 lines, Saguie said
that he would, but that Israel needed land east of the northernmost Sea
of Galilee and east of the Jordan River just above it. General Omar lost
his temper. 'You want Syrian land', he said angrily to Saguie in Arabic.
Daoudi then rose and stormed out, followed by General Omar.[6]

When tempers subsided and talks were resumed Saguie came up
with a new idea. Why not have a strip of land around the northeast
quarter of the lake which would be, as he put it, a 'Peace Park', with
right of entry to the area for Israelis and nominal sovereignty for
Syria? This idea was to be checked with the respective leaders. While
both sides returned home to report, President Clinton tried other
avenues.

He received Syrian Foreign Minister Shara at the White House on
29 September 1999. Ahead of this visit, Barak phoned Clinton to ask
him to press Shara to accommodate Israel's requirements. Shara must
agree to an Israeli early warning station on the Golan Heights even
after Israel withdrew from the area, to warn Israel if Syria mobilized
to attack her. Shara must also agree that the future border between
the two countries would leave the Sea of Galilee and the Jordan River
just above the lake in Israeli hands.

Clinton did as he was asked – with some success. Shara agreed –
and this was unprecedented – to accept an early warning station on
the Golan after Israel's withdrawal, but insisted that it should be
manned by Americans rather than Israelis, ideally under a UN flag.
Shara also said that Syria would consider some kind of co-operative
arrangement around the Sea of Galilee's water line. Clinton then raised
General Saguie's idea of a Peace Park to be built on the disputed area
with access to both sides (Clinton had been informed about this idea
by Ross who had supervised at the Bethesda talks the previous week).
Shara said he would be willing to consider the idea, provided that

Syrian sovereignty over the land was not questioned.[7] But when Clinton later reported back to Barak, the Prime Minister replied that he would welcome the idea of a Peace Park, provided that sovereignty remained in *Israel*'s hands.

Just days after his meeting with Clinton, Shara was taken to hospital with an aortic aneurysm, a serious heart condition. For Barak this was a major setback, as both leading Syrian authorities on peace with Israel – the President and his Foreign Minister – were now seriously ill. Barak knew if the two were to disappear from the stage it would kill any chance of an Israeli–Syrian deal in the foreseeable future.

At Barak's request, Clinton wrote a letter to Assad on 12 October, explaining that he had reviewed reports on the secret Israeli–Syrian discussions, which, combined with his own talks with Shara, meant he knew that the gaps between Israel and Syria were manageable and could be overcome. They needed to decide only on the location of the border between the two countries and the corresponding issue of control of the water, and the early warning stations on the Golan.[8] The President went on to say that he was convinced Barak was prepared to take account of Syria's needs but that Assad should co-operate and reciprocate. And if Assad played ball, went the letter, there would be an extra reward, namely new bilateral relations between the US and Syria; this last idea was Barak's personal contribution to Clinton's letter. But there was no quick reply from Damascus.

'WHY ARE YOU DOING SYRIA?'

In Israel, meanwhile, there was growing opposition to any deal with Syria, particularly among members of the influential security establishment. When Ami Ayalon, the head of Shin Bet, found out that Barak was secretly trying to strike a deal with Syria, he went straight to see him. 'Why are you doing Syria?' Ayalon asked the Prime Minister. 'There is time . . . you have years for that while with the Palestinians if we don't have something within twelve months from now we shall surely have a disaster. We are losing them as a partner.' Ayalon was not the only one in Israel's security establishment to object to Barak's

Syria-First approach. In an interview Ayalon recalls, '[There was] a big meeting and not a very pleasant [one]. Me, the head of Mossad Ephraim Halevi, [deputy Chief of Staff] Boogie Yaalon, Director of Military Intelligence ... all of us came to Barak to say that to put Syria ahead of the Palestinians was a disastrous mistake. But he wouldn't have it.'

The same debate was also raging within the American Administration. The President himself, Martin Indyk and others were in favour of a Syria-First strategy, while officials such as Robert Malley, the NSC Middle East specialist, and Aaron Miller, a State Department expert, felt it was unwise and an unwelcome distraction from the more pressing Israeli–Palestinian conflict. Syria-First, in the view of those who opposed the strategy, meant that if Assad was offered 100 per cent of land taken from him, Arafat would also insist on 100 per cent, something the Israelis would find it impossible to offer. 'No Palestinian leader', Aaron Miller explains, 'would be able to demonstrate any flexibility after the Israelis were prepared to give Assad 100 per cent of the Golan.' Also, those in the American Administration who objected to a Syria-First strategy felt that it could poison the already suspicious atmosphere between the Palestinians and the Israelis, as the Palestinians would feel left behind. And in any case, should negotiations with Syria fail there would then be too little time left for Clinton to find a solution to the Palestinian–Israeli problem before he left office in January 2001.

But then, as Martin Indyk puts it, 'With all due respect to my colleagues who thought [Syria-First] was a mistake, it didn't really matter what they thought, because the President of the United States and the Prime Minister of Israel had decided that they were going to go for the Syrian deal.'

'I DON'T WANT TO DECEIVE YOU . . .'

Clinton, being careful not to alienate Arafat, insisted that Barak link his efforts on the Syrian track to doing something, even if only symbolic, on the Palestinian front. Barak finally agreed to a summit with

Arafat and Clinton in Oslo, on 3 November 1999. This was officially a tribute to the late Prime Minister Rabin on the fourth anniversary of his assassination, but it was also intended to renew Israeli–Palestinian talks.

It was there in Norway, the birthplace of the 1993 Oslo Agreement, that after weeks of delays and stalling tactics, Barak at last agreed to nominate his delegation for talks with the Palestinians to work towards a Framework Agreement on Permanent Status (FAPS). But the truth was that for Barak this was no more than window dressing, as became clear when he appointed a colourless diplomat, Oded Eran, who had served as Israel's ambassador in Jordan, as the lead negotiator with the Palestinians.[9] Indeed, when the negotiations opened on 8 November in Ramallah, Eran was frank with his Palestinian counterparts. 'I don't want to deceive you,' he said. 'My man prefers to negotiate with Syria [first].' He added, though, 'If we make some progress and show seriousness, we might draw [Barak's] attention and show him that we can do it, even if he prefers the Syrians.'[10] The veteran Palestinian negotiator Saeb Erekat told *Elusive Peace*, '[It was] obvious that it was just a question of wasting time with us ... brainstorming, while [Barak] pushed on with the Syrian track.' This was a fair assessment.

'A CRAZY IDEA'

In November 1999, President Assad at last answered Clinton's October letter; the reply was disappointing. He appeared to retreat from previously agreed concessions, insisting, for instance, that not only must Israel accept Syria's definition of the border, namely the 4 June 1967 line as Syria regarded it, but that she must do so *before* talks proceed. Assad also made it clear that he would not accept what had been previously agreed by his Foreign Minister Shara, namely to have an early warning station on the Golan Heights manned by Americans after the Israeli withdrawal. As for the 'Lake', Syria, Assad wrote, had claims to it too.[11]

When the content of Assad's letter was reported to Prime Minister

Barak, rather than discouraging him, it, in fact, spurred him to make an outrageous suggestion. He now insisted that President Clinton should personally travel to Damascus to 'stun' Assad and impress upon him that he must move, otherwise the opportunity for peace with Israel would be lost. Should Clinton be willing to undertake this mission, promised the Prime Minister, then Barak would reaffirm Rabin's 1993 'deposit' – a full withdrawal from the Golan Heights if all Israel's concerns were met.

Clinton was attracted by this bold diplomacy. However, his aides, particularly National Security Advisor Sandy Berger, were horrified. Berger immediately held a late-night telephone conference with Secretary of State Albright, Dennis Ross and Robert Malley, saying, 'Over my dead body.' He added, 'We're not going to let this happen. We're not going to expose the President to such a high-risk endeavour.'[12] In an interview for *Elusive Peace*, Berger says he thought Barak's idea to have the President travel to Damascus to 'stun' Assad 'a crazy idea'. Berger then had to explain to the inexperienced Barak that the President of the United States could not simply drop into Damascus, particularly not after he had just received a fairly blunt letter from Assad. Martin Indyk recalls going on to explain to Barak that 'the President of the United States is not going to be your messenger boy'.

It was suggested that rather than the President, it should be Secretary of State Albright who would visit Damascus. This, however, so much infuriated Barak – he did not trust her to do the job properly – that, in a telephone conversation with Clinton on 3 December, he insisted that the mission to Damascus must be undertaken by Clinton himself and not by Albright, and should the President insist on sending her then Barak would withdraw his offer to reaffirm the 'pocket'. Upon hearing of that telephone conversation, Albright was deeply offended. Dennis Ross says she felt that she was being treated by Barak like 'chopped liver'.

'MR PRESIDENT, MAY I ASK THE INTERPRETER JUST TO REPEAT THAT AGAIN?'

Other developments on the Syrian front at this time seemed to indicate that, in spite of Assad's off-putting letter to Clinton, a trip to Damascus was perhaps still worthwhile. Lord Levy, a personal friend of British Prime Minister Tony Blair and his roving Middle East special ambassador, visited Damascus on 30 November and paid the usual courtesy call on President Assad. The meeting, as Assad's translator Bouthaina Shaaban recalls, started casually, with Lord Levy 'talking about Prime Minister Tony Blair and how they played tennis together yesterday and how they talk to each other informally about things . . . and that because of this important position he would be able to help in making peace'.[13] After the meeting, which lasted two hours, Levy was having a late meal with the British ambassador when, at around 10.15, a call came through from Syrian Foreign Minister Shara, asking if Lord Levy would be able to stay another day as the President would like to see him again. So, as Levy recalls, 'I didn't have much option. I contacted my wife to say I was safe, changed my schedule and stayed another day.'[14]

The next day Levy went again to the Presidential Palace. The President dropped a bombshell, saying to him, 'Now is the time for us to talk to the Israelis *without any pre-conditions*.' Not entirely sure whether he had understood Assad correctly, Lord Levy asked, 'Mr President, may I ask the interpreter just to repeat that again?', and when the translator Shaaban went over it again, Levy 'realized this was a very significant moment'. Assad then added, 'I want this message passed back by you to Prime Minister Tony Blair . . . but then this must be passed on to the President in Washington, because the Americans will then take the primary role.'[15] The message was clear – Assad was keen to talk peace with no strings attached, not even his traditional demand that the Israelis first reaffirm the Rabin 'pocket'.

On his return to England on 2 December Lord Levy reported to the Prime Minister, and was then grilled by officials at the Foreign Office before the remarkable information was passed on to Washington.

President Clinton immediately dispatched Albright to Damascus, despite Barak's reluctance to reaffirm the Rabin 'deposit', which meant she effectively went empty-handed.

In consultations just before departing for Syria, Albright and her team decided that should Assad be as positive and as forthcoming as he had been in his talks with Lord Levy, she would tell him she would be willing to say the US had 'misunderstood' his letter to Clinton.

'HAVE I REALLY HEARD SOMETHING NEW?'

In Damascus, on 7 December, Albright met President Assad in his Palace. As usual they started with small talk. Assad's translator Bouthaina Shaaban recalls that Albright was wearing a lion brooch – 'Assad' means 'lion' in Arabic – and she went on to tell the President that 'she has a collection of lion brooches back at home'. From there, knowing that she had effectively nothing tangible to offer Assad, Albright went on to explain how 'she doesn't really believe in letters and telephone calls and she prefers to see eye to eye, that's why she made a big effort and came to Damascus, in order to see him'. The President, as Shaaban recalls, 'concurred that it's always better to see the person and talk to them than to phone them or send them letters'. With pleasantries and empty words done, Assad got straight down to business.

He flatly denied that his November letter to the President was in any way negative, and he went on to surprise Albright by suggesting the resumption of talks with Israel – and he even came up with a formula which he thought could make it possible. Peace negotiations, Assad proposed, should be resumed where they had 'left off'. This was a clever idea as it was ambiguous enough for him and Barak to proceed on the basis of their own – presumably different – interpretations of precisely what 'left off' meant. When Foreign Minister Shara, who was also present at the meeting, intervened to say, 'But what about the basis? ... What about the line of 4 June 1967?', Assad flatly replied, in front of Albright and her small delegation, 'We can talk about that when we get to the negotiations ... what we need to do

[now] is to start the negotiations, and we need to finish it quickly.'[16] And then, looking at a baffled Shara, Assad dropped another bombshell. He said that he would upgrade the talks by having the Foreign Minister himself do the negotiating. Assad added that he believed Prime Minister Barak was serious, that Barak wanted to reach an agreement quickly, 'and so do I'.[17] Flabbergasted, Albright requested a brief time-out. Assad said she could go into the adjacent room. Instead, she walked to the rear of the big meeting room, assembled her small delegation and whispered, 'Have I really heard something new?' The veteran Middle East envoy Ross said unequivocally, 'Yes.'[18]

It was a dramatic development and totally out of character for Assad. For years he had made it clear that he was in no hurry whatsoever to make peace. Now, he was in a rush, willing to resume negotiations with no strings attached, and even upgrading the negotiations to a top political level. Was it his realization of his own mortality and his wish to see the Golan returned to Syria before he died? After all, he was gravely ill. Maybe he wished to clinch a quick deal with Israel and leave a clean slate for his son as successor? Whatever the explanation, 'it was a completely different kind of Assad', as Martin Indyk recalls, and it was clear that 'Assad had blinked'.

For Albright, this was a great personal victory. She returned from Damascus, as Martin Indyk recalls, 'triumphant!' and, as she notes in her memoirs, 'no one was more surprised than Barak when I succeeded in persuading Assad to agree to negotiate'.[19] Indeed, when Albright phoned the Prime Minister to say that 'I have wonderful news for you ... Assad has agreed to renew talks and to send Farouk al-Shara ... to Washington', Barak answered in one word: 'Wow!'[20]

It was subsequently announced that Israel and Syria would hold two days of peace talks in Washington at Blair House, a presidential guesthouse, starting on 15 December 1999.

'BARAK SHOULD NEVER TAKE ME FOR GRANTED'

News of the imminent resumption of Israeli–Syrian talks was received with mixed feelings among Palestinians. Some thought that this development would in fact strengthen Arafat's position against the growing influence of extremist groups such as Hamas and Islamic Jihad. This was because President Assad might curb such groups – many of whose leaders were in Damascus – in order to make his own negotiations with Israel easier. It was also thought that the Syrian position on the 4 June 1967 borders, namely a full Israeli withdrawal from the Golan Heights, would also boost Palestinian claims for a full Israeli withdrawal from land claimed by them and also lost in the 1967 war. Aaron Miller of the State Department had evidence that Arafat did not share this view. He happened to be visiting Arafat's headquarters in Ramallah when CNN announced that there would be Israeli–Syrian talks at Blair House. As he sat next to Arafat, who was passively watching the announcement, Miller turned to him. 'Mr Chairman,' he said, 'what do you think of this development?' Whereupon, as Miller recalls, 'Arafat squeezed my hand with great strength and replied, "Barak should never take me for granted." '[21] It reflected Arafat's concern that he was being sidelined while the Israelis went off trying to do the Syrian deal. Arafat also felt humiliated. After all, Syria had done nothing over the years to warm its relationship with Israel, whereas Arafat had officially recognized Israel and negotiated with her at length – yet Barak preferred to court Syria first. Arafat put a brave face on it, however, and announced: 'This is news that brings joy for all the Palestinian people and the Arab world that the peace moves on all tracks in the Arab world, especially the Palestinian, Lebanese and Syrian tracks.'[22] Was it a coincidence that Arafat named the Palestinian track first while, in reality, it was the last on Barak's list?

'A TYRANT AND A CRUEL DICTATOR'

Prime Minister Barak had been the driving force behind the attempts to resume peace talks with Syria, but now he began to slow the whole process down, and for good reason.

In the Knesset, on 13 December 1999, Barak asked for support for his plan to open peace talks with Syria in Washington. Ariel Sharon, leader of Israel's opposition Likud Party, reacted strongly. He called President Assad of Syria 'a tyrant and a cruel dictator'. And he accused Barak of being 'ready to give up the Golan without demanding anything in return' and, what's more, of doing so 'just to distract attention from the economic failures of his government'.[23] When the matter was put to the vote only 47 out of 120 Knesset members backed Barak's Syrian peace initiative – a humiliating defeat.

The picture was similar among the general public, but this was not surprising. Israelis resented the cold disdain with which Syria treated Israel – tourists whose passports were stamped at a border crossing into Israel, for example, were not allowed entry to Syria. Also, a whole generation of Israelis had grown up believing that the Golan, particularly the strategic Mount Hermon from where it was possible to see deep into Syria, was essential for Israel's security and thus should remain in her hands. And the recently arrived Russian community in Israel, immigrants who came from a vast country, failed to grasp why they should support a deal which would probably result in giving up land and make a small Israel even smaller. An opinion poll conducted just a day after the announcement of the resumption of Israeli–Syrian talks showed that only 44 per cent of Israelis regarded the announcement as a victory for Barak, while 38 per cent felt he had given in to Syrian pressure. Other polls showed that only 13 per cent of Israelis were in favour of a full withdrawal from the Golan Heights.[24] Against this backdrop, Barak felt he needed more time to prepare a sceptical nation for a deal with Syria, and so he decided to try to slow the process down.

Just a day before the talks were due to open in Washington, Barak picked up the phone and let the Americans know of his domestic difficulties. He told Dennis Ross that because of his troubles at home he wished the coming summit at Blair House to focus only on 'procedural' matters and to avoid 'substantial' ones. He also said he did not want to meet the Syrian Foreign Minister face to face lest Shara demand that Barak reaffirm the Rabin 'deposit' and promise to withdraw fully from the Golan Heights down to the 4 June 1967 lines. 'Prime Minister,' said a stunned Ross, 'you are the one who insisted that we must move quickly ... We have high-level discussions for the first time and you don't want to discuss [matters of] substance or meet privately with Shara?'[25]

On the evening of 14 December, Syrian Foreign Minister Shara landed in Washington. In the car taking him to his hotel he told Albright and Ross that he could not possibly return to Damascus from the two-day summit without a clear commitment from Barak on the 'pocket'. By then, of course, Ross and Albright knew that they had a problem on their hands with a reluctant Barak, but they failed to mention the matter to Shara, as they were still hopeful that Barak would somehow come round and play ball.

'I CAN'T DO IT'

As Assistant Secretary of State, Martin Indyk had the protocol responsibility of going out and greeting heads of government or heads of state from the Middle East when they landed at Andrews Air Force Base for official meetings with the President. Thus, when Barak landed, it was Indyk who was waiting on the tarmac to meet his plane. However, as the Israelis, who never care much about protocol, came off the plane, the Prime Minister failed to appear. Eventually, as Indyk recalls, somebody came down and said, 'The Prime Minister wants to see you.' Here is Indyk's recollection of what happened next:

I went up the stairs on to the plane ... Barak was sitting there on his chair with a bench in front and he asked me to sit down. I sat down on the edge of the chair and said, 'You know, Mr Prime Minister, everybody is waiting for you', and he looked at me and he said, 'I can't do it' and I said, 'What do you mean?' and he said 'Because my people will regard me as a sucker, they have to see that I'm negotiating, that I'm a tough negotiator. If they don't see that, they won't support the deal. I cannot enter the negotiations and give up all of my cards in the first instance, and that will leak in Israel, and I will be seen as a sucker, and my polls indicate that I can't get majority support from the Israeli people [for a full withdrawal from the Golan Heights to the lines of 4 June 1967].'

Eventually they left the plane together and Barak was driven to his hotel. Indyk went off to meet Dennis Ross and Secretary Albright, who were dining at the Daily Grill in downtown Washington. He went straight to their table and said, 'Houston, we've got a problem.'

'SHARA HAD SCREWED US'

In a ceremony in the chilly White House Rose Garden, President Clinton, flanked by Barak and Shara, launched the summit. Perhaps already aware of Barak's cold feet, Clinton spoke with measured optimism of the prospect of the millennium ending with a comprehensive settlement between Israel and all its Arab neighbours. Clinton warned of the difficulties ahead. 'What we are witnessing today is not yet peace,' he said, 'and getting there will require bold thinking and hard choices . . . the road to peace is no easier, and in many ways it is harder than the road to war . . . there will be challenges along the way.'[26]

Originally, only the President was to speak. First, because it was very cold outside and second, as the American diplomat Robert Malley explains, 'We had no idea what the visiting leaders would say and we didn't want to set it off on the wrong tone.' Those who knew the Syrian Foreign Minister also acknowledged that 'Shara is uniquely capable of saying the exact wrong things . . . he's brilliant at it', and they were reluctant to take any chances by allowing speeches.[27]

However, shortly before the ceremony Barak, wanting a positive message for Israel's evening news, suggested to Clinton that he and Shara should also give speeches.[28] The President, aware of Barak's difficulties at home, agreed. In the Oval Office, just before emerging to face the press, Clinton warned them, 'OK, you can say a few words, but it has to be really short, no more than two minutes, and keep it positive.'[29] Barak, in a short, unprepared and terse statement said,

We came here to put behind us the horrors of war and to step forward towards peace. We are fully aware of the opportunity, of the burden of responsibility, and of the seriousness, determination and devotion that will be needed in order to begin this march together with our Syrian partners, to make a different Middle East where nations are living side by side in peaceful relationship and in mutual respect and good neighbourliness.

Then, it was Shara's turn and, as Bouthaina Shaaban who joined him at the summit recalls, 'Before the summit we got conflicting reports whether there were going to be speeches or not and Minister Shara said "Let us prepare a speech just in case." And so a speech was prepared, and I kept it with me.' Now, Shaaban walked towards the podium where the three leaders were standing and handed the speech over to Shara to read out.

It was a long and winding speech; large chunks of it were historically correct and it had some very positive elements, most notably Shara's statement that the conflict between Israel and Syria was no longer a conflict of existence but one over borders. But the passage that grabbed all the attention was this:

The image formulated in the minds of Western people and which formulated in public opinion was that Syria was the aggressor, and Syria was the one who shelled [Israeli] settlements from the Golan prior to the 1967 war. These claims carry no grain of truth in them ... it was the other side who insisted on provoking the Syrians until they clashed together and then claimed that the Syrians are the aggressors.

It was the negative tone, rather than the actual contents, which was dissonant with the spirit of reconciliation that Clinton wished to attach to this opening ceremony. What made things even worse was that, despite calls from photographers, Shara refused to shake Barak's hand. Bouthaina Shaaban explains:

We decided not to shake hands with the Israelis ... because we believed that the Israelis would use the handshake to dilute the issues and to make it appear to the world that there's no problem, there's no occupation of territory, and for us this would be harmful. And that's why we said that we shake hands after making a deal, not before.

Clinton glossed over the awkward moment, saying 'We're going to work', but actually he was fuming with rage at Shara, snapping at him while walking away, 'We talked about a short statement!' Later, when Dennis Ross went to see Clinton in the Oval Office, he found him 'pacing and muttering that Shara had screwed us'.[30]

Thus, Barak's attempt to get a nice sound bite for the news in Israel backfired, but the episode actually played straight into his hands. The Prime Minister was looking for any excuse to slow things down and now took advantage of Shara's behaviour and complained to Clinton,

I've just been embarrassed in front of my people ... the ceremony's being transmitted throughout Israel and throughout the world. It looks as if I'm just there as a potted plant as the Syrians attack Israel ... You can't expect me now to move as fast as you want me to in terms of saying what kind of territorial compromises I'm gonna do; I'm in a corner now and public opinion in Israel is moving against the Syrian deal.[31]

Shara tried to explain to Albright afterwards that he was, in fact, positive in his speech, but she was in no mood to listen. 'Farouk,' she said, 'don't insult my intelligence. You blew it and we have a big problem.'[32]

'ARE YOU INTERESTED IN INVESTING?'

The delegates then crossed Pennsylvania Avenue to Blair House for face-to-face negotiations. Albright, as the Syrian delegate Shaaban recalls, 'tried to calm the atmosphere down and just before going into the room she started talking about her daughters and asking them how many children they had, and Barak told her he had three daughters, Shara a daughter and a son'. Indeed, the private talks,

across a long, highly polished table, went far better than the Rose
Garden ceremony. The Prime Minister's Chief of Staff Danny Yatom,
who was sitting next to Barak, recalls how Shara said to them, 'Look,
I did not mean to hurt you [in my speech] ... nor to snub you ...
I just wanted to express what we, the Syrians, feel and I wanted it
to be heard.'[33] Attorney General Elyakim Rubinstein recalls Shara
joked with Barak: 'I hear that your stock market went up because of
the announcement of the resumption of talks.' 'Are you interested
in investing?' Barak shot back: 'No, I will make do with investing
in the peace.'[34] But for Bouthaina Shaaban, sitting with Israelis for
the first time, 'it was a little bit odd really ... to sit at the table and
look the Israelis in the eye ... and they were just ... you know ...
opposite us'.

<h2 style="text-align:center">'WE DON'T ERASE HISTORY'</h2>

It was perhaps no surprise that Shara insisted on going back to the
heart of the matter – the demand that Barak reaffirm Rabin's 1993
'deposit' that Israel would withdraw to the 4 June 1967 lines. 'Shara',
as Shaaban recalls, 'looked at Secretary Albright and Dennis [Ross]
and said, "Could you take that deposit out of your pocket and put it
on the table?"' A silence settled in the room and it was in fact Barak
who responded. He said, 'While my government has made no commitment on territory ... we don't erase history ... we don't erase
history ...'[35] He repeated the last phrase twice. He meant that, while
he was not yet ready to spell it out, he nonetheless recognized that
promises had been made in the past and he took note of them. This
was significant and Secretary Albright tried to make the most of it,
saying to Shara after the meeting: 'What you accomplished today was
historic ... You got what you need, you can go back to Assad and
say Barak stands by the "pocket", even if indirectly.'[36]

Indeed, Shara was so impressed with Barak's reaction that he rushed
to make an urgent phone call to the Saudi ambassador to Washington,
Prince Bandar bin Sultan bin Abdulaziz al-Saud.[37] He told him to call
an urgent meeting of the Arab ambassadors in Washington. Bandar

said it was the period of Ramadan so perhaps the meeting could be postponed. But Shara insisted, and a meeting was gathered at Bandar's. There, Shara told the ambassadors that he had met Barak, from whom he learned that Syria's conditions would be met, and that Shara was going to tell President Assad that 'within a few weeks we are going to sign a peace agreement with Israel'.

Unfortunately Shara's optimism was premature, as the rest of the summit saw direct confrontations. Barak, trying to stall, said that the purpose of the talks was merely 'to shape the next meeting', while Shara insisted on talking substance. He said, 'I came to Washington in order to get back the Golan Heights. So let's talk content, not technicalities.' Barak's approach also disappointed his American hosts. Although they sympathized with his domestic difficulties, they also felt that Barak was going back on his promises.

On 16 December 1999, in a five-minute statement outside the West Wing entrance of the White House, with Barak standing tight-lipped on his right and Shara standing in impassive silence on his left, President Clinton announced the close of the summit. 'Over the past forty-eight hours,' Clinton said, 'Israel and Syria have taken critical steps in the journey toward peace. That journey will be a difficult one. But with courage and perseverance on both sides, the result will be deeply rewarding to the people of Israel and the people of Syria.'[38] After these remarks, the three men returned to the White House with Clinton guiding them. The Americans had learnt the lesson of the disastrous opening ceremony. Barak and Shara were not allowed to open their mouths this time.

Although he was the one to stall, Barak now insisted that talks should be resumed 'as quickly as possible' in order 'not to lose momentum'. But, as Robert Malley put it, ' "As quickly as possible" meant Christmas and for a few of us Christmas was something that we really didn't want to sacrifice. We hadn't had a family vacation in a long time and even though many of us were not Christians [but Jews] . . . we did our best to salvage that period.' They succeeded. The next round of talks was fixed to start on 3 January 2000 at a location yet to be chosen.

'PEACE SHACKLES'

Barak now had a really serious attack of cold feet. It dawned on him that in coming meetings with the Syrians he *would* have to discuss the border between the two countries, and he knew precisely what Assad was after: a clear reaffirmation of Rabin's 1993 pledge that Israel would withdraw *fully* from the Golan Heights – something Barak felt he could not yet do. What also concerned Barak was that he, a Prime Minister with the authority to make decisions, was negotiating a critical deal with a Foreign Minister who had to consult his boss. Where was Assad? If he was serious about making peace with Israel then why was he not taking a direct part in the talks? What would happen if Barak revealed his bottom lines to Shara and back in Damascus Assad did not approve the deal but instead pocketed Barak's proposals, as he did Rabin's in 1993?

In long telephone conversations with US special envoy Dennis Ross, Barak vented these concerns, making it clear that in the coming talks he would insist on retaining a strip of land along the northernmost part of the Sea of Galilee and along the eastern bank of the Jordan River just above it. Barak said to Ross that he would also insist on Israelis – not just Americans – being present in the Mount Hermon early warning station; on an exchange of ambassadors in the first phase of implementation; and on a two-year grace period to relocate Jewish settlements from the Golan Heights. To these demands Barak also added a long 'shopping list', which, as he said to Dennis Ross, would help him to sell a Syrian deal to a sceptical Israeli public and enable him to determine how serious President Assad was about making peace.

Barak's key demand was that Assad should instruct Lebanon to renew peace talks with Israel, something which Assad could do as he called the shots in Lebanon. Barak reasoned that if talks with Syria could also lead to peace talks with Lebanon and perhaps put an end to attacks on Israel by Hezbollah, the radical Islamic movement operating from south Lebanon, then it 'would help to encourage the Israeli public to accept concessions in the Golan Heights'.[39] Next on the Prime Minister's list was a request for 'at least' one Arab state – preferably Tunisia – to upgrade its diplomatic relations with Israel. The logic behind this request, as Barak explained to Ross, was that Israelis wanted to know that they were not giving up tangible assets such as the strategic Golan just for pieces of paper but that they would get in return a genuine change in the entire region. Barak's list continued: there should be a Free Trade Zone on the Golan Heights after Israel withdrew, forming 'Peace Shackles', as Barak called it, since it would not then be economically viable for Syria to initiate war as it would harm business on the Golan.[40] Syria should also help Israel to recover bodies of her soldiers missing in action since the 1982 war in Lebanon. And Barak insisted that the US should provide Israel with state-of-the-art military equipment to demonstrate to Israelis that giving up such a strategic asset as the Golan would not weaken Israel militarily.[41]

This was a tough list, but, eager to have Barak fully on board, and acknowledging that he needed a hand in selling a deal to the Israeli public, President Clinton and his peace team set out to get it for him. The President personally phoned President Assad on 19 December, asking him to instruct Lebanon to resume peace talks with Israel and to help retrieve the remains of Israeli soldiers missing in action. Assad agreed to help but he would not instruct Lebanon to resume peace talks before some progress had been made in Syrian–Israeli talks.[42] Meanwhile, Clinton dispatched high-level envoys to Morocco, Tunisia, Qatar and Oman in an effort to get them to upgrade their diplomatic relations with Israel. But while Arab countries showed some willingness to be helpful they all remained noncommittal. On the Free Trade Zone, the Americans opened negotiations with businessmen but with few results. As for US military support for Israel, Barak himself seemed not to be in any hurry to send a military delegation to Washington to present specific requests on Israel's military needs. But preparations to resume Syrian–Israeli talks went ahead.

'WHY ARE YOU STAYING? WHY DON'T YOU
COME HOME?'

Barak insisted that the January peace talks should take place in an isolated setting, to minimize leaks that could expose him politically. 'I can't believe', Barak said in one of his long phone calls to Clinton, that 'the only remaining superpower can't find an isolated place . . . take an island . . . a cruiser . . . have the talks there.'[43] The Americans decided on the semi-secluded Clarion Hotel and Conference Center just outside the little sleepy town of Shepherdstown in West Virginia. There was only one road leading into it, so it was possible to isolate the place and stop press intrusions, thus ensuring a total media blackout. Shepherdstown also suited Assad. He would not agree to have the talks at Wye River, as he did not wish to be seen to be following in the footsteps of Yasser Arafat, who had negotiated there with Benjamin Netanyahu in 1998, nor at Camp David where, back in 1978, President Sadat negotiated a separate peace deal with Israel, which Assad had vehemently opposed.

At Ben-Gurion Airport, just before embarking for the US, Barak announced, 'I am leaving on a mission of the entire nation to bring peace.' Polls clearly indicated, however, that the 'entire nation' was not at all behind its Prime Minister, and Barak's departing speech, in which he said that he expected the negotiations to be 'difficult' and marked by 'ups and downs', was to reassure his sceptical public that he would not sell Israel's interests cheap. In Damascus, meanwhile, the government newspaper *Tishrin* said Syria was heading into the talks 'with an open heart'. And in the US, President Clinton, who had promised President Assad that he would be 'an active participant' in the talks, cleared his schedule to preside over the first day of talks. Clinton would then hand over the reins to Secretary Albright and her team.

Clinton arrived in Shepherdstown on Monday, 3 January 2000, by helicopter to launch the conference. Just before talks were due to start he strolled with the principals through the grounds of the hotel. The Syrian delegate Bouthaina Shaaban recalls how, 'Barak, Clinton and

Shara walked together [in front of us] . . . and I walked with Madeleine [Albright] and she was telling me again about her lion brooch and she said she had a huge collection at home.' In what was clearly a moment made for television, they all then stepped on to a 200-foot-long pedestrian bridge over a 25-foot-deep gully, pausing about two-thirds of the way over to gaze out over the Potomac River. They then walked silently into the stone Commons Building.

Clinton now had a tête-à-tête with Barak, whom he found uncompromising and unwilling to reaffirm the Rabin 'pocket' about withdrawal to the 4 June 1967 lines. Barak said to Clinton that the President, should he wish to talk to Shara in Barak's name, was only permitted to go as far as saying that 'the endgame would be determined by the "pocket"' and, added Barak, even that should only be said if Shara first agreed to the resumption of the Lebanese peace talks.[44] This demand really annoyed the President as he knew from Assad that he was reluctant to instruct the resumption of the Lebanese peace talks at such an early stage in these talks, and Clinton suspected that Barak was raising the issue in order to stall, knowing that Assad was unlikely to agree to this condition.

While the President talked to Barak, Secretary Albright sat with Shara, who was also uncompromising, insisting that he must have Barak reaffirm the Rabin promise that Israel would withdraw to the 4 June lines, and further insisting that the demarcation group – as the Syrians called the border group – where the location of the future border between Israel and Syria was to be discussed, must start its work immediately, which he knew Barak was reluctant to do. When Shara saw the President later he was, as usual, more conciliatory – he was no doubt instructed by Assad to behave himself in the presence of the President – but he did repeat that Barak's reaffirmation of full withdrawal was the key to progress.

On the second day of the conference Clinton departed, leaving the talks in Albright's hands. But the parties remained stuck in a war over the order in which the various issues should be negotiated, and which of the four groups – normalization (of relations between Israel and Syria), security, water or borders – should start first. 'Barak wanted', as Robert Malley of the NSC recalls, 'to delay the meetings of the border committee. He did not want to start talking about delineation of the borders until he felt that everything else was in place. So he was taking the position that the border committee should wait a few days until the other few [committees] had settled and shown enough progress, enough Syrian compromise and flexibility so that he could feel like he could move into the territorial issues which are the most difficult for Israel.'

Barak's demand put Foreign Minister Shara under enormous pressure, as President Assad phoned him in the morning to say, 'If the demarcation committee does not meet then what are you doing there? Why are you staying? Why don't you come home?'[45] And with the procedural war continuing there was, as the Israeli negotiator Uri Saguie recalls, 'a lot of confusion. Many people were walking around . . . aimlessly . . . moving around without really doing anything. A very confusing scene . . . a lack of determination.' Finally, Dennis Ross came up with a solution which was accepted by both Barak and Shara. Two groups, security and normalization, would start talks that evening, and the border and water groups would meet separately with the Americans, who would assess their needs.

However, there was still no progress on substance. The feeling among the Syrians, and indeed Americans, was that Prime Minister Barak was the main obstacle. He was not helpful, not allowing his negotiators any leeway and not compromising at all.

'GUYS, WE'VE GOT A PROBLEM . . .'

Clinton returned and decided it was time to shake the parties up. On the morning of Friday, 7 January, he presented an eight-page American draft for an Israeli–Syrian peace treaty, where gaps in positions on various issues were identified with brackets. Clinton urged Barak and Shara to do their best to bridge these gaps. The Israelis and Syrians then left to study the document.

For the Syrians the paper was disappointing, as on the most critical issue for them – the need for Israel to withdraw fully from the Golan – there was little on offer. And while their bracketed language said that the border between the two countries was to be based on 'with-drawal to the June 4 line', the Israeli bracket said only that the border would be 'mutually agreed'.[46] As neither party sent back comments, the Americans decided to reconvene the group meetings.

In the discussions on security that followed – by now Barak had agreed for all groups to meet up and negotiate – the Syrian General Omar was forthcoming, bold and imaginative. But he also tied his offers to the Israeli delegate, General Shlomo Yanai, accepting 4 June 1967 as the basis for border demarcation, which Yanai could not do as he had no mandate from Barak. General Omar also demonstrated flexibility in the border group, suggesting that the 1967 line could be adjusted by as much as fifty metres to meet mutual needs and concerns. This was unprecedented. General Omar implied that this principle could apply throughout the length of the border, provided Israel was prepared to agree that the 4 June 1967 line was the basis for any discussion on the border.[47] But, like his colleague General Yanai, the Israeli representative Uri Saguie had no mandate from Barak to negotiate the 4 June 1967 line – he only had permission to discuss such general issues as the kind of border there should be between Israel and Syria, namely whether it should be an open border, customs arrangements, whether there would be a fence along the border, etc. The Syrian said he would deal with these issues if his Israeli counterpart would agree on the basis, namely that they were dealing with the 4 June line as the basis for discussion. But Saguie could not even refer to this. Thus, another deadlock.

Syria was also co-operative in the meetings on water and the normalization of relations between the two countries. Here, the Syrian lawyer Daoudi and his colleague, former US ambassador Walid Moualem, went out of their way to accommodate the Israelis. Daoudi accepted the Israeli demand for a water management board to monitor the quality and quantity of water flowing from Syria into the Sea of Galilee. Moualem also proposed a number of confidence-building measures to improve Syrian–Israeli relations. But Syria's flexibility was not reciprocated by Barak's negotiators. It was apparent that the Prime Minister was holding back and he would not even hide it any more, pegging it to information on polls held in Israel, brought to him in Shepherdstown, which showed he had no support for a deal. After a meeting with Barak, Robert Malley recalls Clinton's brief:

Clinton gathered us around a table with his head a little bit down and he said, 'Guys, we've got a problem. I just met with Barak and he's telling me that he can't move forward here, this can't be the decisive summit because he's facing problems at home and if he reaches a deal too quickly, the Israeli people are gonna think that he gave in too soon and that he didn't put up a fight. He needs the appearance of a fight, he needs to have this dragged out longer, he needs to slow walk it.

In an interview for *Elusive Peace*, US National Security Advisor Sandy Berger recalls how 'Barak told us that he didn't intend to make any movement . . . that he couldn't seem to appear to be moving too quickly. That didn't please the President very much.' Indeed, it was all becoming an embarrassing and depressing situation. A summit that Barak himself had called for, and been the driving force behind, had now been scuttled by him.

'AS THOUGH I WAS A TRANSPARENT FIGURE'

The atmosphere at Shepherdstown was sour, which did little to help break the ice or bridge the gaps. Barak's Chief of Staff Danny Yatom, who knew some of the Syrian negotiators from previous rounds of talks, was hurt when the Syrians continued to 'refuse to shake hands . . . They looked through me as though I was a transparent figure.' While Barak was unwilling to move ahead and give any ground, he still tried to improve the atmosphere. After being tipped off by the Americans that Shara was in the hotel gym, Barak rushed down and invited the Syrian Foreign Minister to try out the various bits of kit. Shara agreed and the two found themselves comparing gym equipment. Noticing that one of the Syrian delegation's members was on a treadmill, Barak joked, 'Look how she's moving towards peace but all the time staying in the same place.' Shara laughed.[48] But there was no real social interaction between the teams and as the Israeli delegate

Amnon Lipkin-Shahak recalls, 'The atmosphere was frozen . . . It was like North Koreans and South Koreans.'[49]

'YOU BROKE YOUR PROMISE'

On 9 January 2000, six days after the opening of the summit at Shepherdstown, a dinner was arranged to end the conference. It started with some small talk in which Israelis and Americans joked about a picture on the wall of some piece of land in the US and about how this could be the land Israelis handed over to the Syrians. Then, three of each delegation gathered around the table and there were speeches by the heads of the delegations. Israeli negotiator Saguie was there:

The last dinner was very sad. I call it 'the last supper'. [Shara] gave a speech. He expressed himself very clearly . . . Explicitly. He told Barak, 'You broke your promise . . . I failed my president. I was fooled or cheated by you. I told my president [after the previous Blair House summit, in which Barak hinted he would withdraw to 4 June 1967 lines] that there is a chance for peace . . . You say that you need to consult your advisers [at home]. What kind of advisers do you need? You have the best advisers here in Shepherdstown. I don't believe you. You've simply got cold feet.'[50]

Shara then added, 'I came here determined to move. I had a mandate to reach an agreement. Now I'll have to go back and report that we got nothing . . . Nothing. This was an opportunity!'[51] Shara's speech, according to the Israeli Lipkin-Shahak, was 'spontaneous . . . from the heart . . . very emotional and . . . impressive'. Shara said, looking at Barak, 'You're a great general in front of the Israeli public, but not in front of us. You've misled me and I misled my president by letting me present things we agreed between the two of us a few weeks ago . . . and now that's not the way.' Israeli negotiator Uri Saguie recalls, 'It was terrible to watch and listen. After all, Shara was right . . . Clinton . . . blushed . . . It was a very difficult dinner.' And that was not all: at the climax of his speech Shara turned to Barak again, asking if he would reaffirm the Rabin commitment to withdraw to the 1967 lines. Barak's response was a smirk. Later, when Barak gave his speech, he talked about how great a man President Assad was, but, as Ambassador Martin Indyk recalls, 'it didn't cut any ice this time around'.

After the dinner Clinton went up to Shara and said, 'You did well. That was very good. I know you are going to go back and talk to Assad. I'd like to speak to him first.' Clinton thought it important he speak to Assad first, to give him a more positive picture of what went on in the summit than he feared Shara would give. This would also protect Shara, who, according to an American, 'was reporting back to Assad quite positively, more than it actually was'. While the Americans praised Shara, they criticized Barak sharply, with Secretary of State Albright telling the Prime Minister that he had misled them all, including President Clinton, and in doing so had 'risked the credit of Clinton'.

Before the delegates dispersed, they decided to convene again in ten days' time to continue the talks. But this was not to be. Even before Shepherdstown had adjourned, a piece appeared in the *Al-Hayat* Arabic daily in London with details of the issues discussed there. It was quite general but what was there clearly reflected Syria's priorities and it appeared to have been leaked by sources in Syria. Barak was furious and claimed again, in American ears, that he could not possibly trust the Syrians. They always break the rules, he said, and it was further evidence of the danger of saying anything new to them, particularly on the border question. Then, on 13 January, the actual bracketed draft presented by Clinton at Shepherdstown was published in the *Haaretz* newspaper in Israel. This time it was Assad who was furious, as it appeared from the document and an attached report listing concessions Syria had made, as if Barak had held fast and the Syrians had given up.[52] With the publication of the draft, Foreign Minister Shara came under severe criticism in Damascus. This set off alarm bells for President Assad at a time when he was concerned about his son's succession. Two days later, Assad phoned Clinton and said he would not send representatives to the next round of talks with the Israelis.

'A GOOD DAY'

The failure of Shepherdstown did not in any way deter Barak, however. On the contrary – it was a good demonstration to his unsupportive public that he was fighting hard and not giving up on Israel's vital interests. Making peace with Syria remained his goal, but events now brought the Palestinian front centre stage.

The roots of these events lay back in a meeting between Barak and Arafat in early January 2000, in the course of which Arafat made a discreet personal plea to Barak to include the three villages of Abu Dis, Azariyya and Ram, all bordering on the municipal boundaries of East Jerusalem, in the land transfer that was due to take place the following month according to the Sharm el-Sheikh agreement. Barak promised nothing, but he did let the Palestinian leader believe that he would take this request on board. This encouraged Arafat enormously, as he urgently needed some tangible achievements to show to his desperate people. In the end, however, Barak thought that the villages were too close to Jerusalem for him to turn them over to Arafat, as his political opponents at home could then accuse him of 'dividing Jerusalem'. But instead of letting Arafat know discreetly of his decision not to transfer the villages, Barak went public, telling the Israeli press of his decision not to include the three villages. Hurt and deeply humiliated, Arafat hit back by going public himself. He announced that he would not accept the February land transfer at all unless it included the villages. The three villages had turned from a side issue into a matter of prestige for both leaders.

The Americans intervened. When Barak turned to them again to help him on the Syrian front, US special Middle East envoy Ross took advantage and said that the President would help Barak only if the villages' crisis was quickly resolved. The ploy succeeded; Barak agreed to a deal in which two of the three villages would be transferred to Arafat on 23 April, and the third on 23 May.

On 5 March 2000, Barak and Arafat met in Ramallah to put the finishing touches on the transfer package, deciding to get together again the next day at the California Hotel to announce the deal publicly. Excited, the Palestinians organized a large ceremony, and decorated the hotel and the route leading to it with Palestinian flags. But, concerned that this was too big a demonstration of Palestinian joy, which could be interpreted in Israel as his failure to insist on Israel's interests, Barak let Arafat know that he would not show up in Ramallah unless all the Palestinian flags were removed. Only after the Palestinian flags came down – including one tiny flag at the reception desk of the hotel – did Barak show up. Nevertheless, a beaming Arafat described it as 'a good day'.[53]

4

The Lion Comes to Geneva

Barak now felt he was in a good position to demand American help on the Syrian track. And, being Barak, he already had a ready-made plan, which went as follows: as the Syrian President would not meet him face to face to negotiate, President Clinton would act as Barak's mouthpiece and represent him in a make-or-break summit with President Assad, in which Clinton would present Assad with the Prime Minister's bottom lines. When the Syrian President agreed to a deal, Clinton would then bring Barak and Assad together to sign a peace treaty between their two countries.

It was an interesting plan, but with Barak's dismal track record in dealing with Syria so far – raising expectations sky high only to retreat at the last moment – the Americans were wary. To shield their President from what might well be a very public failure, Clinton's aides proposed that rather than Clinton it should be Secretary of State Albright who should travel to Syria and preview with Assad some of Barak's ideas, testing the water to judge whether it was safe for the President to jump in.

Despite Albright's considerable success in Syria in the past, Barak hit the roof. Albright 'must absolutely not go to Damascus', he said.[1] Only Clinton, Barak insisted, had the authority and charisma to play the endgame, which needed to be carried out with panache. Clinton eventually relented, as he was still strongly convinced that a deal with Syria was possible, and with time running out for him – it was now less than a year to January 2001 when he would have to pack up and leave the White House – he decided to take on this mission.

Robert Malley explains that what actually persuaded the Americans that there was a good chance for peace was something that came up at Shepherdstown. Then, Clinton's aides now informed him, there had been a meeting between Albright, Ross and the Syrian Foreign Minister in which Shara seemed to say that, from the Syrian perspective, there was no difference between the 1923 international border and the 4 June 1967 border when it came to the northeast quadrant of the Sea of Galilee, and that 'sovereignty on the lake would be Israel's'.[2] This was significant for, as the 1923 international border runs ten metres inland from the water's edge, it meant that Shara effectively agreed to Barak's demand that the Syrians would have no access to the Sea of Galilee's water.[3] When Clinton heard what Shara had said, he leapt on it and concluded that 'Once you have established she is a prostitute you are just talking about the price.'[4] In other words, with the Syrians apparently having agreed not to have access to the water of the Sea of Galilee, the issue at stake was to determine the distance they would be kept from the water, and the price Israel would pay for that.

'THEY COULD CREATE A POND AND SAY "WE HAVE DIRECT ACCESS TO THE WATER"'

It was now time for Barak to come up with his bottom lines and to spell them out with precision, so that Clinton could assess whether there were sufficient grounds for going to a summit, and, if so, he could know what *exactly* he could offer Assad in Barak's name. So far, even with the Americans, Barak had remained vague, stating his requirements only in a very general way. On the future border between Israel and Syria he would say he needed 'a few hundred metres off the lake', and 'several dozen metres off the Jordan River' just above the Sea of Galilee. On early-warning stations on the Golan Heights he would say he needed a few Israelis to stay on the strategic Mount Hermon for a number of years. On security arrangements, Barak would ask for a monitoring and verification regime that would show changes in military installations and arms depots beyond Damascus. He would also ask to have ambassadors exchanged during the first phase of implementation.[5] Now it was time to pronounce the real, rock-bottom lines.

On 26 February 2000, at his home in Kochav Yair, Barak went over the maps with US special Middle East envoy Dennis Ross. While agreeing to return the Golan Heights to Syria, Barak said he would have to keep a 600-metre-wide strip off the northeast quadrant of the Sea of Galilee. This was very problematic as Barak was using a 1967 map to show his line and as a result of subsequent droughts the waterline had receded over the years from where it had been in 1967 and had moved westward – so Barak was effectively asking for a strip of some 1,000 metres from the water's edge. When pressed by Ross to spell out the *real* minimum distance he felt he must have from the lake, Barak said he could live with 500 metres, and he then went down to 400.[6] With regard to early warning stations to warn Israel of impending Syrian attack, Barak said to Ross that he would need one on Mount Hermon manned by approximately nine Israelis for seven or eight years. By that time, so Barak explained, new technology would make the physical presence of troops in the station obsolete. With regard to security zones – areas on the Golan Heights where there would have to be a limited number of Syrian forces after Israel returned them – Barak was flexible. He said that rather than asking to remove Syrian forces all he would require was monitoring by cameras. Barak also said to Ross that he needed a clear signal that signing a peace treaty with Syria meant a new dawn, and that in return for getting back the Golan Heights from Israel, Assad would agree to open borders and embassies in the first phase of implementation within three or four months, return the remains of Eli Cohen, an Israeli spy who was caught in Syria and publicly hanged in 1965, Syrian support in determining the fate of Ron Arad, an Israeli pilot who had been shot down over Lebanon and captured by Hezbollah in 1986, and support in finding the remains of Israeli soldiers missing in Lebanon since 1982.[7]

As the US ambassador in Israel, Martin Indyk was called in to sit down with Barak and script the exact words that the President would read to Assad, namely 'the talking points, six pages ... no more negotiations, go straight to the top and make the deal'.[8] The Prime Minister made it absolutely clear to the Americans that, while 'it would be fine for the President to improvise the opening generalities', the description of Israel's needs 'had to be recited word for word'.[9] Indyk also spent much time with Barak's Chief of Staff, Danny Yatom, working on maps and trying to come up with creative ideas regarding the border between the two countries. According to Yatom,

Martin Indyk and I used air photos from 1967 which showed five [Syrian] fishing villages, and we drew the line so that all these villages remained in Syrian territory and were returned to Syria ... but there was no Syrian access to the water, because the [1923] international border didn't give access to the water. And we came up with creative solutions ... digging a canal ... and this canal would lead water into Syrian territory and they could create a pond and then they could say, 'We have direct access to the water of the Sea of Galilee and we can swim.'[10]

With the Americans generally satisfied and the Prime Minister promising to spell out his *real* rock-bottom lines on the day of the summit itself (Berger: 'Barak said to the President that he was afraid of leaks [and so] he would not be able to actually fill in the number until we got to [the summit]'), Clinton decided to go ahead and see if he could stop over in Damascus for a short summit with President Assad while on his way to a pre-scheduled trip in Asia.

'YOU'RE GOING TO LIKE WHAT I HAVE TO TELL YOU'

On 7 March 2000, Clinton phoned President Assad from Camp David to tell him in very general terms about the 'fantastic' offer that Prime Minister Barak was about to put on the table. He said, 'I have some very good news for you ... I have something to tell you that you're going to like to hear ... You're going to like what I have to tell you.' In the adjacent Situation Room some of Clinton's aides were listening in to the conversation and, as Robert Malley recalls, 'We all rolled our eyes a little bit at how far the President got describing what was on offer.'[11]

Assad was quite lukewarm in his response. He was formulating a new Cabinet and the timing of Clinton's proposed summit was not ideal for him. 'I'm sorry,' he said. 'We can't do it on your way to Asia . . . perhaps on your way back . . . you can stop over in Damascus or we can meet up in Geneva.'[12] Assad, we should recall, had already been very disappointed by Barak. That he now agreed to resume indirect talks with the Prime Minister was largely thanks to a meeting he had had with a good friend of his, Prince Bandar, the legendary Saudi ambassador to Washington.

Prince Bandar had visited Damascus in January 2000, just after the failed Shepherdstown summit, carrying a message from President Clinton that he still believed a peace deal could be done with Israel and that Clinton would contact President Assad when he knew that he had got from Barak what Assad required. But Bandar got it wrong. The message he was supposed to convey to Assad was different. It was that the Americans would try to find out Barak's bottom lines and they would then present them to Assad so that he could decide for himself whether he was interested in striking a deal on that basis. Now, presumably, when Clinton phoned Assad to propose a summit, Assad concluded that this was the phone call Bandar referred to, and that Clinton had got from Barak what Assad was after. Even so, with Barak's track record Assad was still hesitant, as his translator Bouthaina Shaaban, who was the interpreter on the phone call, recalls:

President Assad was really not comfortable with the fact that he didn't know what President Clinton had. And he pressed hard to know, and kept saying 'Could you just give me an indication of what you have for me?' And Clinton said to President Assad, 'I think I have what you need', and of course, it was obvious . . . that what Assad insisted on having was the line of 4 June 1967. And therefore, he assumed that President Clinton in pressing so hard for this meeting certainly had the line of 4 June 1967. But the nagging feeling of President Assad was that that was not the case. After finishing the phone call he would say, 'I don't think they will have that for me. But then why do they want the meeting if they don't have that for me?'

However, Assad put aside his doubts for the time being and agreed to meet the President on 26 March in Geneva, where Clinton would stop over on his way back from his trip to south Asia.

In Syria, the *Al-Baath* newspaper, the mouthpiece of the Syrian ruling party, noted that Assad would go to Geneva with a 'positive attitude', but added that 'if this golden opportunity, which is perhaps the last one, fails, Syria and President Clinton will not be to blame'. In that case, went the Syrian announcement, 'the Israeli side and the Barak government, which is playing for time and dreams of imposing its will on everyone, will bear full responsibility for the failure'.[13]

The day before the summit, Barak phoned US special Middle East envoy Ross to tell him of his concern that Assad would pocket his offer without offering anything in return. Barak also said to Ross, as he had said to President Clinton before, that he wished to come personally to Geneva. This, Barak explained, could enable Clinton to shuttle between him and Assad and then bring them together for the endgame to clinch a deal. The offer was politely rejected by Ross, as it had been by Clinton, and the Prime Minister was told that 'if things are going well, then we'll call you and you can come'.[14]

President Assad, meanwhile, had mixed feelings about the coming summit. On the one hand he was confident that a deal was at hand, given that Prince Bandar had told him that Clinton would phone him only if he had received from Barak a commitment to a full withdrawal from the Golan Heights. Assad's optimism can be seen in the fact that he gathered a delegation of more than 100 officials to take to Geneva and hired 135 rooms in the Intercontinental Hotel where the summit was due to take place.[15] On the other hand, Assad had a nagging feeling that something was wrong, saying to aides on the plane taking him to Geneva that he 'does not think anything's going to come out of the meeting'.[16]

Assad's doubts were not unfounded. On the day of the summit things did not unfold according to plan in Geneva. As Robert Malley recalls,

Barak was supposed to call the President and give him his bottom, bottom line. This phone call did not happen until an hour before the meeting with

Assad! And the President had a stomach upset. And the legend was that Assad would not pee during an eight-hour meeting. So the President had the runs . . . we are meeting in a room waiting for Barak's call. The President is going to the bathroom every five minutes.[17]

Eventually Barak phoned to relay his bottom, bottom line. Israel, Barak explained, after withdrawing from the Golan Heights, would keep along the northeast shore of the Sea of Galilee a strip of 400 metres (using a 1967 photomap); on the early warning station on Mount Hermon, Barak now said he would accept a presence of only seven Israelis, instead of the nine he had insisted on before, and for only five years instead of seven; and regarding the timetable for Israeli withdrawal from the Golan Heights, Barak now said this could be over two and a half years instead of the previous demand of three. On the secure line on which the offer was made, Barak said to Clinton, according to his Chief of Staff Yatom, 'That's it. There's no way that I, Barak, can go further and there's no way I can persuade the Israeli people to accept more than that.'

This offer was a massive disappointment for Clinton and his team. As Robert Malley later put it, 'Barak's red-line was so close to what he had already told us, that we were pretty aghast.' National Security Advisor Berger recalls: 'The President [was] quite upset that we had gotten Assad to this meeting based upon the impression that we were going to make a serious new offer.' Indeed, it now dawned on Clinton that he had not much to offer Assad and that, yet again, he had been let down by Barak, who had raised expectations so high before the summit only then to come up with such a meagre offer. But with Assad already in town, in fact in the very same hotel, the show had to go on. After amending his notes Clinton went out to meet Assad.

On his way down in the lift, Assad repeated to Bouthaina Shaaban, 'I don't think anything will come of this meeting . . . I don't think they have what they say they have for me.'[18]

'THIS IS A HISTORIC TRAGEDY'

When Assad emerged from the lift Clinton went over to meet him and, stretching out his hand, said, 'I wish I had your vitality, Mr President. I am simply finished after my exhausting trip to Asia. It is amazing how much energy you have.'[19] They walked together into the ballroom of the Intercontinental Hotel, where a circle of chairs had been laid out in the middle. Present were, from the US: President Clinton, Madeleine Albright, Dennis Ross and Gamal Helal, President Clinton's official Arabic translator and a top Middle East expert, and from Syria: President Assad, Foreign Minister Shara and Shaaban. They all sat in armchairs, with the two Presidents next to each other at the centre. At the far end of the room, behind a screen, the rest of the American delegation – National Security Advisor Sandy Berger and his note-taker, Robert Malley (Albright: 'Our delegation . . . was very curious about what was going on, so they were hidden in another part of the room behind a wooden screen and . . . they had agreed that they would not cough, or move, or speak, if they would be allowed to listen.').

Although Assad looked frail and pale – the rumour was that the Syrian leader had had a massive blood transfusion before the meeting – he still seemed as sharp as ever. Albright was wearing her lion brooch, and Clinton began by proffering a gift to show that he too knew Assad was Arabic for lion – a tie with a lion on it. Bouthaina Shaaban recalls that 'President Assad was quite entertained and he took the gift gratefully.'

Clinton then pulled out his papers and said that he would read out his points from a prepared note to ensure precision. In an interview for *Elusive Peace* Clinton recalls, 'I opened the meeting and I said that Barak was prepared to withdraw to a commonly agreed border.'[20] Sitting next to Assad, his translator Shaaban simultaneously translated Clinton's words. She recalls, 'President Assad said to me: "Ask him what does this 'commonly agreed border' . . . what is this phrase? Let him say that again!"' When President Clinton repeated that Barak would agree to withdraw to a 'commonly agreed border', Assad turned again to Shaaban: 'Tell him I'm not interested in that offer.' Assad wanted to leave then and there, and, as Shaaban recalls, 'I was almost pushing him down, because I felt, my God . . . not so quickly.'[21] Upon hearing Assad's response to this first point, Dennis Ross leaned over to Secretary of State Albright and whispered, 'We are in trouble. This guy ain't interested.' President Clinton said, 'I have other points', and asked to continue; he then read, 'Israel would have sovereignty over the water of the lake of Galilee and the River Jordan.' This meant, of course, that Syria would have no access to the water of the Sea of Galilee and the Jordan River just above it. Now, an irritated Assad said, 'If he wants sovereignty over the water then he doesn't want peace!' Surprised, Clinton looked at Shara and said to Assad that at Shepherdstown, his Foreign Minister had accepted that from a Syrian perspective there was no difference between the 1923 border and the 1967 line, and that as the 1923 line ran ten metres away from the lake's edge, Syria, by implication, accepted not having access to the water. Turning to his Foreign Minister, Assad said in Arabic, 'Have you said that?' The Secretary of State looked at Shara, who looked, as she recalls, 'actually quite sheepish, began to waffle and be quite ambivalent about it, and you could see that this was an issue where he had gone beyond what his instructions had been . . . it was an uncomfortable moment between a Foreign Minister and his President'. Shara recovered his thoughts and said to his President: 'No, no, no, this is not what I said in Shepherdstown, I must have been misunderstood . . . What I've said is that even the 1923 border [which is ten metres inland from the water's edge] isn't acceptable to us [let alone several hundred metres].'[22] Behind the wooden screen, National Security Advisor Berger took a piece of paper and a pen and scribbled to Robert Malley next to him, 'Shara's trying to redeem himself.'[23] Clinton tried to explain to Assad that 'Barak is in a tough position. Barak doesn't have the support that he needs [among the Israeli public], and he won't get the support if he doesn't have a strip along the lake.' To which Assad said, 'That's Barak's problem. We're here to reach a just peace, and a just peace means we get the land that we had in 1967, and in 1967 I, along with my officers, were swimming in the lake. So don't tell me that Israel wants a strip along the lake.'[24]

Clinton recalls how Assad added with a smile, 'Look, you and I are friends, but there's not gonna be a deal if I don't get to run my feet in the lake.'[25]

When Clinton again asked permission to proceed with his presentation, Assad replied, 'Well, I don't want to waste your time, Mr President, it's clear Barak does not want peace.' Trying to soften Assad, Clinton said Barak was only talking about a narrow strip of land around one part of the lake, and turning to Dennis Ross he asked him to show Assad a map that portrayed the withdrawal line. Reluctantly Assad agreed and Ross then spread a large map on the table in front of them. The map was based on the 1967 photomap of the whole Golan Heights and on it were sketched three lines. One was the 1923 international boundary line, one was an expert's interpretation of what the 4 June line might be, and the last one was 'the line to be demarcated according to June 4 1967', namely the Barak line, which provided for a strip off the Sea of Galilee.[26] Foreign Minister Shara glanced at the map and immediately hastened to say that the strip off the lake was to the *east* of the 1923 line. Dennis Ross replied that, while Shara was right in saying that the line was marginally to the east of the 1923 line in the northeast sector of the lake, in the south it was well to the *west* of the 1923 line, thus Syria was compensated. President Assad intervened to say, 'Well, I know the territory they are going to give me, it is rocky mountain, I have nothing to do with it. I have no business with that. I want the line of 4 June 1967.' Madeleine Albright intervened: 'Mr President, you are being offered ninety or ninety-five per cent of your land which you might never be offered again, and I just can't understand why you are not willing to use this or to consider this.'[27] Assad replied: 'Well, I said many times that the Golan is Syrian, and I want the withdrawal to the line of 4 June 1967.' Turning to Clinton, Assad added, 'The lake has always been our lake . . . it was never theirs . . . There were no Jews to the east of the lake',[28] and he said there was no point in continuing the meeting. Clinton asked Assad to listen to the rest of the presentation but Assad wanted to hear no more. He said to his translator, 'Ask him to give us a copy of the points he has so that we can look at them and see what they are.' Barak had given Clinton clear instructions *not* to leave anything in writing with Assad, so Clinton said, 'No, I can't because I wrote things with my handwriting on these, and I can't give them to you.' Behind the screen, where the rest of the American team was hiding and listening to the conversation, National Security Advisor Berger scribbled on a piece of paper which he gave to Malley, 'This is a historic tragedy.'[29] Then another scribble: 'Fifty years of hostility towards Israel doesn't go away easily. No compromises, no willingness to see others' needs.' Another American, who prefers to remain anonymous, recalls how 'The maps got rolled out . . . and Assad was stunned. And it wasn't for show, it was real. It was no act . . . He was shocked and Clinton was shocked in response.'

There was a short break in which Foreign Minister Shara listened to the rest of the presentation, which was read to him by Dennis Ross and Madeleine Albright. He requested to have it in writing, but was turned down by Albright in order not to let the Syrians formalize and pocket Barak's positions. After the break, when they all got together again, Clinton said to Assad that he was not in a position where he could go back to Barak to ask for more and that, if there was to be any progress, then Assad must give him something to take to Barak.[30] But Assad would not budge, saying 'the lake is too dear to us'. Still hoping to get Assad to agree to the offer, Clinton said, 'I just wanted you to know that if we don't reach peace between Israel and Syria in this generation, it might be that it would be necessary to wait for many generations.' Assad replied, 'Syria can wait.' As they prepared to leave, the Syrians asked Clinton not to lay the blame for the failure of the summit on them, to which Clinton said, 'The world will judge.'[31]

As Clinton boarded Air Force One to return to Washington, Joe Lockhart, the White House spokesman, was sent to brief the press. The sight of Lockhart rather than a higher-ranking official was a clear sign to the world press waiting that the summit had not gone well. 'We don't believe', Lockhart said, '[that] it would be productive for Syrian–Israeli talks to resume at this point.' Meanwhile Clinton phoned Barak at his office in Jerusalem. His Chief of Staff Danny Yatom was listening in and recalls how 'Clinton said, "Listen, we have tried to bridge the gaps . . . but we failed . . . Assad insisted on the fourth of June boundaries . . . [and] access to the water [of the Sea of Galilee]." '

Even before the Americans had time to digest the embarrassing failure at Geneva, 'a high-visibility failure' as Dennis Ross put it,[32] Barak – always ready with a plan – was phoning to talk to National Security Advisor Sandy Berger. He said, 'I'm going to move quickly now on the Palestinian track', and he wanted to come over and see the President to present his plan, which included a summit meeting with Arafat. But Sandy Berger told him, 'We can't move too quickly . . . we can't expose the President. We don't want to go through a blind alley and then fail . . . we can't afford another failure.' But Barak, totally oblivious to how badly Geneva had gone and how he had humiliated President Clinton, replied, 'History will not record Geneva as a failure. We crystallized the issue . . . we exposed what Assad really wants.' Robert Malley, who was in the room with Berger when Barak said these words, recalls how 'Berger's eyes and face just showed utter disbelief that a summit where the President goes to Geneva, has a private meeting with Assad and it ends not only in failure but complete collapse . . . and that there's nowhere else to go after that, that that could somehow be viewed as a success.' In an interview for *Elusive Peace*, Berger recalls how 'I said to Barak, "If you think Geneva was a success, you're wrong. Geneva was a failure. We ought to acknowledge that." '

Next day, when Clinton and his aides gathered to discuss the failure at Geneva, Sandy Berger self-deprecatingly said, 'Mr President, from the team that brought you Geneva, we bring you the Palestinian track!' Berger recalls: 'The President smiled in a somewhat ambivalent way.'

5

Stockholm Calling

Low-level talks between Israelis and Palestinians had continued all the while in various locations including Bolling Air Force Base near Washington, where, one morning soon after the failure at Geneva, the ubiquitous US special envoy Dennis Ross arrived. He entered the room and announced to the delegates that 'the second mistress' was dead. Now, with no more talks with Syria, said Ross, all attention would be focused on the Palestinian track.[1]

These public and open talks had been meeting since November 1999, in an attempt to reach a framework agreement between Israel and the Palestinians. The Israeli team was led by the diplomat Oded Eran, and the Palestinians by Yasser Abed Rabbo and Saeb Erekat. However, the talks had got nowhere because Barak's eyes were too firmly fixed on Syria and, in any case, he had not allowed Eran much leeway. There were other reasons why nothing came of the talks. Palestinian negotiators would often let Eran sweat by keeping silent, taking notes and waiting for him to come up with all the ideas, only to pocket them. Barak also – rightly or wrongly – regarded the two Palestinian negotiators as compulsive leakers. None of this was constructive.

However, with Syria out of the way, at least for the time being, and Barak shifting his attention to the Palestinians, Abu Mazen, a very senior Palestinian politician, suggested establishing a secret channel for talks. The idea was that in this channel Israelis and Palestinians could discuss their differences without fear of leaks, away from the press. They could talk openly and discuss the compromises needed to reach agreement. Arafat agreed with this but Barak was reluctant. Secret channels were at odds with his belief in make-or-break summits. He had poured scorn on the architects of the 1993 Oslo Agreement, who, as he put it, came up with a deal full of holes like a 'Swiss cheese', made while strolling through the Norwegian woods. Eventually, however, Barak conceded and agreed to two parallel channels. The existing Eran–Abed Rabbo open channel would deal only with 'softer issues', like water, economics, regional co-operation, law enforcement and bilateral relationships. This front channel, it was envisaged, would attract attention and insulate a secret back channel, which would discuss the core political issues of borders, settlements and refugees – though Barak forbade any discussion of the most political of all: Jerusalem. The aim of the back channel would be to close gaps and prepare for a summit where, it was hoped, Barak and Arafat could clinch a final deal.

After agreeing to establish this secret channel Barak immediately informed his representative Eran. But Arafat failed to notify his negotiators in the old open channel that they would now deal only with peripheral issues. This was Arafat's style, the way he operated: he preferred to foster competition among his people, the principle of divide and rule, so that no one could ever be in a position to challenge him.

The secret channel started meeting, mainly around Jerusalem. But it soon became apparent that it needed more focus. Abu Mazen, in consultation with the Swedish Prime Minister Goran Persson and his Chief of Staff Par Nuder, arranged for the talks to move to Sweden.

The first meeting of what came to be known as the Swedish channel or the Stockholm talks took place on 8 May 2000, when Barak met Arafat in Ramallah at Abu Mazen's house. It was, according to Shlomo Ben-Ami, one of Barak's Cabinet ministers who was to lead the Israeli delegation, 'a bizarre encounter . . . [where] there was no conversation at all. Arafat and Barak did not talk to each other. They just sat side by side.'[2] By then relations between the two leaders had become strained. Arafat was deeply hurt by Barak's attempts to negotiate first with Syria, and his failure to honour his previous pledge to transfer the three Arab villages near Jerusalem, which had been scheduled to take place on 23 April.

The embarrassing silence was finally broken by Barak, who suggested to Arafat that they retire for a tête-à-tête. When they were alone, Barak tried to make the Palestinian leader understand the domestic political pressure on him not to transfer the three villages. The Sephardic religious party Shas, which had seventeen seats in the Knesset and was part of the ruling coalition, Barak explained, was blackmailing him, demanding money for its educational system in return for support for the transfer of the villages, while the National Religious Party (NRP) was also threatening to abandon the coalition should Barak return Abu Dis, one of these villages. Should he lose these coalition partners, Barak tried to explain, he would either have to consider a national unity government with the enemy – the right-wing Likud Party – or an early election. In either case this would mean the end of the peace process. But Arafat could not care less. He had his own troubles at home and he desperately needed to show his people that he had obtained concessions from the Israelis. Still, the two agreed that their representatives should go to Sweden to continue with the secret talks and lay the ground for a summit.

In the car on the way back to Tel Aviv after the meeting, the Prime Minister revealed his true feelings about Arafat and the people around him. Barak, a former commando who had been involved in assassinations of leading Palestinians in the past, now said to his colleagues, 'I used to shoot these guys', and he added, pointing at his forehead, 'Here . . . just between the eyes.'[3]

'HE WAS SMOKING WITH BOTH HANDS'

Just two days later, Israeli and Palestinian teams travelled together on board the Swedish Prime Minister's private plane to Stockholm. Barak dispatched Shlomo Ben-Ami, and loyal aide Gilead Sher and a few others, including the team's secretary Gidi Grinstein and a representative of the security service Shin Bet. Arafat sent Abu Ala (also known as Ahmed Qurei) – perhaps the most creative negotiator on the Palestinian side – and Hassan Asfour. These two were close to Arafat but not to Abu Mazen – Asfour was, in fact, his sworn enemy. Arafat refused Abu Mazen's pleas to send one of his lieutenants, either Hussein Agha or Ahmed Khalidi. This angered Abu Mazen and led to growing tensions within the Palestinian leadership. But again, this was Arafat all over – fostering division among his own people so they would not challenge him.

Upon landing in Sweden, the teams were taken to the Swedish Prime Minister's official country residence at Harpsund, some ninety minutes outside Stockholm, where they were put up in two simple cabins. After a short nap they met early in the morning in the main building, and Par Nuder opened the conference. 'We, the Government of Sweden, and its representatives here,' he said, 'are committed to the future of the Middle East and to efforts to resolve its conflict. From this point on, we will be here, at hand, at your service.'[4]

There was a good atmosphere and solid determination to get some results. 'We must do all we can so that we will not regret missing the opportunity', said Ben-Ami. His counterpart Abu Ala reciprocated: 'I am delighted that we are meeting here. We had better start putting something in writing: borders, refugees, Jerusalem . . .' Jerusalem, as Abu Ala knew quite well, was off the agenda for the Israelis, but it was just the sort of thing he liked to say.

They negotiated around a table with the participants sitting together, rather than in teams facing each other, and some discussions were held while walking in the woods. Serious discussions took place on the borders of the future Palestinian state, on settlements and what to do with Palestinian refugees. A very delicate set of understandings started to emerge on these issues.

Before Ben-Ami left for Sweden Barak had authorized him to put on the table an increased withdrawal from the occupied territories – 20 per cent more than his diplomat Eran was allowed to put forward in the official front channel. What Ben-Ami now put to Abu Ala was an offer to give the Palestinians 87 per cent of the occupied territories – 77 per cent up front and an additional 10 per cent of 'grey areas', which would largely become Palestinian over a period of five to ten years. Abu Ala replied: 'No grey areas . . . two colours . . . make it simple ... Yours and ours ... No grey areas.'[5] Instead, Abu Ala wanted a clear timeline of specific dates on which Israel would withdraw from the territories and transfer them to Palestinian control.

In spite of the good atmosphere, these were tough negotiations, because the parties came to the table holding very different perceptions. The Palestinians felt that they should compromise with the Israelis as little as possible. In their view, as they repeated time and again in Sweden, they had already compromised in Oslo in 1993, when they effectively agreed that 78 per cent of historic Palestine would be Israel's. Now, in Sweden, they insisted that what remained of old Palestine should go to them. 'I told them directly', the Palestinian negotiator Hassan Asfour recalls, 'the historical compromise had already happened, and we agreed our land to be twenty-two per cent of historical Palestine ... this is the historical compromise and we can't continue every time in talks saying we need to compromise inside the compromise. We have already compromised.'[6]

However, the Palestinians did understand that compromises would have to be made, and the informal, private conversations in Sweden helped to clarify what they were. According to Ben-Ami, Abu Ala would come to him and say, 'Tell me, Shlomo, exactly how much [of the occupied territories] do you *really* need [to annex in order to keep big settlement blocs as part of Israel proper]?' Ben-Ami would be quite open with Abu Ala in these small side talks, saying to him that eventually Israel could live with 'eight per cent [of the occupied land to remain in Israel's hands, leaving] ninety-two per cent for the Palestinians [on which to build their future state]'.[7]

Barak took the Stockholm talks very seriously and closely monitored their progress from Israel. 'I would phone Barak from Sweden', Ben-Ami recalls:

We had long conversations ... for hours on the phone ... using the special [secure] line [called 'the carpet']. He would go with us almost sentence by sentence through the papers that Gilead [Sher] was producing. [It would usually be] late at night. Very, very meticulous ... as if these were the final peace agreements. Every letter ... Every word ... Every sentence ... Endless revisions ... He was very keen on seeing everything.[8]

The imaginative Barak would often offer technological solutions to particular problems, such as building tunnels and flyovers to reduce friction between Israelis and Palestinians. But the Palestinians hated Barak's sophisticated solutions. 'Stop making peace of tunnels and bridges', Abu Ala would tell the Israelis.[9] Some progress was made and gaps started to close. But an 'innocent' piece in the Associated Press, citing 'Palestinian sources' and saying that there were secret negotiations in a European capital, meant that the secret channel in Sweden was exposed. The leak was a devastating blow, particularly to the senior Palestinian negotiator Abu Ala, as it pulled the rug out from under his feet and he now felt exposed to accusations in the occupied territories that he was selling out Palestinian interests to the Israelis in Sweden. The Israeli negotiator Ben-Ami recalls that

The effect of the leak on Abu Ala was devastating. [It] meant that he was being criticized. He couldn't bear it. He started to speak to the gallery. Now he needed to go back to the fundamental positions ... Basically that was the end of it. He was a different man. I said to Abu Ala, 'you're a different man'. But he would never admit that this was linked to the leak.

Another Israeli negotiator who witnessed the effect the exposure of the secret talks had on Abu Ala was Gidi Grinstein, who recalls how 'Abu Ala started to get all these phone calls, he was walking out to the balcony, he was chain-smoking cigars ... it was over.' And Gilead Sher recalls Abu Ala 'on the phone for hours ... he was pale ... he was smoking with both hands ... one cigar here ... one cigarette in the other hand. He was angry and upset.'

Why the leak and who was responsible for it? It is hard to say. Perhaps it was leaked by Israelis opposed to Barak and the peace process. There is a theory that the story was leaked by the Palestinian Abu Mazen. Deeply hurt that his political rivals Abu Ala and Hassan Asfour had now taken over the secret channel he himself had established, and realizing that success at the Stockholm talks might diminish his own chances of succeeding Arafat in the future, he decided to kill the talks by leaking them.[10] There is no firm evidence for either theory.

'I'LL SEE WHAT I CAN DO'

In the meantime, a hunger strike had been started by Palestinian prisoners in Israeli jails, and Israeli intelligence had found out that riots were planned in the occupied territories, in sympathy with the prisoners. It would all reach its peak, so intelligence reports said, on 15 May, the anniversary of Israel's War of Independence in 1948, or, as the Palestinians knew it, 'al Nakba', 'the catastrophe'.

On 14 May, when US special Middle East envoy Dennis Ross visited the Israeli and Palestinian negotiators in Sweden, he received a phone call from Prime Minister Barak's Chief of Staff Danny Yatom, who told him of the expected riots. Yatom hoped that the Americans would press Arafat to put a stop to the violence. Ross got President Clinton to write Arafat a letter, calling on him to restore calm. 'I'll see what I can do', was Arafat's reply, which 'in Arafatspeak', as Ross puts it, meant 'he would not take any serious steps to stop the violence'.[11]

To persuade Arafat to curb the violence, Barak dispatched his personal special emissary and go-between with Arafat, Yossi Ginossar, to explain that, with the Knesset back in session, Barak was going to present the promised transfer of the three villages for a vote on that very day. Should violence break out, went Barak's message, it would make the Prime Minister look a fool and jeopardize the transfer.

Back in Sweden, on 15 May, Israeli and Palestinian delegates heard of the outbreak of riots in the occupied territories. It was indeed a major embarrassment for Barak. For while he was fighting in the Knesset to win approval for transferring the three Arab villages to Arafat, Israeli TV was showing Palestinians using weapons – given to them by Israel as part of the Oslo Agreement – to attack Israeli security forces.

In 1996, during the 'Tunnel Riots' (which erupted following Israel's decision to open a passageway along Jerusalem's Western Wall), the Israelis learnt that the immediate use of massive force could stop the escalation of Palestinian violence. Now, this lesson was put into effect. Just north of Ramallah at al-Bireh the army reacted with just such force, using both rubber-coated bullets and live ammunition to quickly quell Palestinian riots – ten Palestinians were killed and hundreds more injured in these clashes. 'We were prepared', the head of Shin Bet, Ami Ayalon, recalls, 'and so we could contain it . . . We saw their plans, we knew what would happen and where.' The military's head of Planning Division, General Giora Eiland, recalls how 'the Palestinians planned violence north of Ramallah, in which masses would march, but they were also going to use fire. We knew about this before, we could prepare with snipers and Special Forces at the location and when the violence had broke out we immediately hit those who were leading it.'[12]

The Knesset did eventually vote to approve the transfer of the three Arab villages to Arafat, but, apprehensive that this gesture might be interpreted by Palestinians as a reward for violence, Barak stopped short of actually making the transfer. Nor did he go ahead with another promise to provide at least a down payment on purchase tax money that Israel owed the Palestinians. Most important of all, he failed to release the Palestinian prisoners whose captivity was the official reason why the violence had erupted in the first place.

On the day of the riots Barak phoned his delegates in Sweden to instruct them to return home. Four days later, on 19 May, the Israeli and Palestinian teams were back in Sweden to continue their talks. They made progress on a draft agreement listing 'I's', Israeli positions, put side by side with 'P's', Palestinian positions. But again, back in the occupied territories, the Palestinians declared two 'Days of Rage' to take place on 19–20 May. With violence erupting, the Prime Minister yet again instructed his team of negotiators to return home. On 21 May the Swedish channel was dead and attention shifted to another front – Lebanon.

6

Farewell Lebanon

Israel had invaded Lebanon in 1982 and had remained in the so-called 'security zone' in southern Lebanon since 1985. This area, which was patrolled by Israeli troops and the 6,500-strong, Israeli-backed South Lebanon Army (SLA), constituted a buffer zone, protecting northern Israel from attacks. But over the years this buffer zone had become a trap, an Israeli-style Vietnam quagmire, where Israeli troops came under daily attack from the militant Shiite guerrilla movement Hezbollah.

During his election campaign Barak pledged that he would get Israeli troops home from Lebanon by July 2000. He had hoped a withdrawal from Lebanon would form part of an Israeli–Syrian deal, from which both would benefit. Israel could withdraw from Lebanon peacefully trusting that Syria would curb Hezbollah attacks on Israel from southern Lebanon, while Syria could keep her 35,000 troops there, apparently in order to rein in Hezbollah, but effectively to impose her will on Lebanon, which she regarded as her backyard. But now, with his Syrian peace initiative on the rocks, Barak decided that he would leave Lebanon anyway. Here, he was less dependent on the good-will of Arabs and he could unilaterally fulfil a pledge to the Israeli electorate.

Just two weeks after Shepherdstown, Barak first instructed the military to prepare plans for a unilateral withdrawal from Lebanon. This immediately led to a fierce debate in his government and the military establishment between those in favour of a unilateral pull-out and those against. Those who opposed this idea had two reasons why it should be avoided. First, the unilateral withdrawal in response to

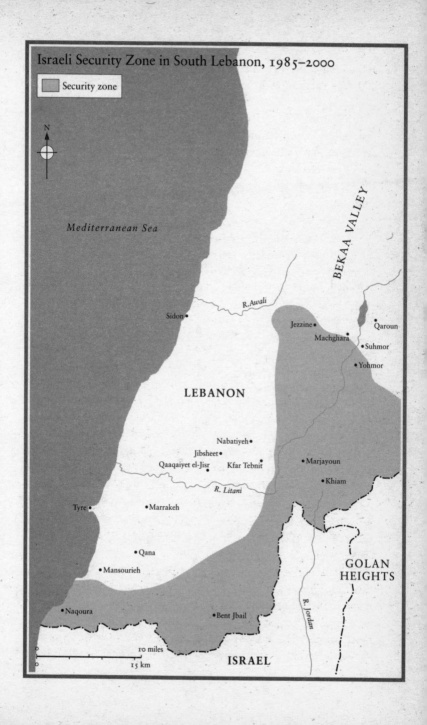

Israeli Security Zone in South Lebanon, 1985–2000

Security zone

N

Mediterranean Sea

BEKAA VALLEY

R. Awali

Sidon

Jezzine
Machghara
Qaroun
Suhmor
Yohmor

LEBANON

Nabatiyeh
Jibsheet
Qaaqaiyet el-Jisr
Kfar Tebnit
Marjayoun
Khiam

R. Litani

Tyre
Marrakeh

Qana

Mansourieh

GOLAN
HEIGHTS

R. Jordan

Naqoura
Bent Jbail

10 miles
15 km

ISRAEL

Hezbollah's pressure might inspire the Palestinians. General Giora Eiland explains: 'The main concern was [that] this was what the Palestinians would try to emulate if they thought Israel withdrew under pressure of terror. They would adopt the same strategy [as Hezbollah].' And second, pulling out from the self-declared security zone in southern Lebanon would expose Israeli civilians, villages and towns to Hezbollah attacks. But Barak was immovable and he left his instructions to the army in place: prepare to leave Lebanon unilaterally.

'THE IDF WOULD NEVER DO THAT'

Throughout April 2000, Barak worked closely with both the US and, particularly, with UN Secretary-General Kofi Annan and his Middle East envoy Terje Roed-Larsen on the plan for Israel to pull out of Lebanon and deploy behind a newly demarcated Blue Line, in accordance with UN resolution 425 of 1978, which called on Israel to 'withdraw all forces from Lebanon and respect its sovereignty'.[1] For Barak it was critical to wrap an Israeli withdrawal in legitimacy, so that if Hezbollah continued attacking and Israel retaliated, it would be regarded as justified. Barak gave clear and precise instructions to the military to co-operate fully with UN experts in redrawing the Blue Line. He said, 'I am not playing with one hill here and one hill there . . . in order to get this international support it's important for me to do *exactly* what these UN experts demand.' This, to be sure, was more easily said than done because, in order to get the process under way, the military had already started to erect the new fence according to their estimates of where the right line would probably go. But then, as Israeli General Giora Eiland recalls,

The UN experts came with very accurate GPS and made investigations and several times we had to move the fence, sometimes because the fence was a few dozen metres from the right place, sometimes a few metres, and in one case – forty centimetres! We had to move ten kilometres of fence . . . because it was a forty-centimetre violation inside Lebanon![2]

However, the Israelis also played a few tricks. On one disputed hill, they claimed that a rabbi was buried in the tomb at the top of the hill, while the Lebanese insisted that it was in fact a sheikh who was buried there. In consultation with the UN it was decided that the Blue Line would bisect the hill. But then the UN envoy Terje Roed-Larsen was phoned up by the Lebanese, who said, 'The Israelis have demolished half the hill. They've cut us off from the tomb.' Larsen phoned Barak's Chief of Staff Danny Yatom and said, 'Is this true?', to which Yatom replied, 'No, the IDF [Israeli Defence Force] would never do that.' The UN envoy then flew out there by helicopter to discover it was indeed true – half the hill had disappeared and the Lebanese could not get to the tomb. Larsen organized a meeting with the Israelis, into which he walked and said, 'Fuck you. Rebuild the hill . . . if you don't, I will make sure that the UN doesn't say Israel has complied with UN resolution 425 when you withdraw.' The Israelis complied. They put the hill back up.[3]

'INTERNATIONAL LEGITIMACY IS THE KEY'

Even with demarcation of the new border well under way, the debate in Israel over the merits of a unilateral withdrawal from Lebanon continued. On 27 April 2000, the Prime Minister clashed with his military chiefs, who argued that tactical considerations indicated that it would be too risky to leave Lebanon unilaterally. Chief of Staff Shaul Mofaz, in particular, thought it would be a better idea not to withdraw right down to the international border but to stay and control a few hills north of it, in order to give more tactical security.[4] But Barak was insistent, telling Mofaz, 'We are going to withdraw . . . [and] exactly to the international line . . . international legitimacy is the key point, not tactical advantages.'[5] However, it was not as simple as that. With preparations to leave Lebanon accelerating, events on the ground started to dictate the agenda – and eventually the decision on exactly when the Israelis would pull out.

'WITHDRAW!'

On 21–22 May 2000 the Lebanese took matters into their own hands. Here is the testimony of Israeli General Giora Eiland:

The decision to withdraw from Lebanon was made neither by the Prime Minister nor the General Staff. It was decided by Hezbollah and the Lebanese people ... they began it. Hundreds of Lebanese, some civilians and some Hezbollah activists, began to march from their villages towards our positions and those of the [Israeli-backed] South Lebanon Army [SLA]. In some places the SLA forces evacuated their positions. So a momentum began to emerge.

This was a public relations coup – it looked like the Lebanese were literally pushing the best army in the Middle East out of Lebanon. At first, when the march began, the Israelis attempted to stop the marchers by firing over their heads and into the crowd, killing more than ten. This stopped the march, but upset international opinion. The dilemma before Prime Minister Barak, as explained to him by the military, was as follows: 'Either we start a big military operation to reverse the situation and capture the southern Lebanese army outposts ... or we understand that this is the new reality ... and [we] carry out the withdrawal quicker than we had planned.'[6] Realizing that the game was up, Barak picked up the phone to tell American and UN officials that he would be out of Lebanon 'within twenty hours'. To the military he said: 'Withdraw!' By 24 May 2000, there were no more Israeli troops in Lebanon.

'WHAT HAVE YOU DONE TO US WITH THIS CRAZY WITHDRAWAL?'

The withdrawal itself was efficient, but it was regarded in the Arab world as a Hezbollah victory over the Israelis. And while Israel was praised by the international community for complying with UN resolution 425, the example it gave to the Palestinians was devastating. They had negotiated with Israel since 1993 and all they had achieved was a tiny slice of land. Hezbollah, on the other hand, had chosen the path of armed struggle against Israel and had succeeded in forcing a total withdrawal. The Palestinian head of Preventive Security forces, Mohammed Dahlan, said the Israeli withdrawal 'gave our people the message that violence wins ... the message from Barak was that he would move under pressure ... that he would withdraw only if forced to'.[7] And on 1 June 2000, at a meeting of the Swedish channel in a hotel in Tel Aviv, the Palestinian negotiator Abu Ala complained to Barak's man Gilead Sher, 'What have you done to us with this crazy withdrawal from Lebanon? What have you done to us?'[8]

7

Dragging Arafat to Camp David

'WE'VE REACHED OUR RED LINES'

Talks continued in the Swedish channel, which retained its name despite the fact it was now meeting in Israel and elsewhere. The aim remained the same: to close the gaps between Israeli and Palestinian positions, and prepare the ground for a summit at which Barak and Arafat, helped by US President Clinton, could clinch a final deal to end the conflict. However, by mid-2000 Prime Minister Barak wanted to put an end to this channel. 'Barak's position', as his representative in these talks, Shlomo Ben-Ami, recalls, 'was that it was time to go to a summit.' Barak said that in the Stockholm talks and elsewhere, 'We've reached our red lines and I'm aware that we'll need to make more concessions but if I continue to make them now what will I have to [offer] in the summit? That's the moment to go there.'[1] There was another reason: a sense among Israeli negotiators that the Palestinian camp was too divided to negotiate usefully. There were rivalries between 'old guard' and 'young guard', West Bankers and Gazans, local leaders and those who had returned from Tunis in 1994, all pulling in different directions. 'We had times', the Israeli negotiator Gidi Grinstein recalls, 'when we had more than one person claiming to be the authorized negotiator tracing himself back to Arafat.'[2] The only way out of this mess, thought Barak, was to cut the Gordian knot and talk to the top man himself – Arafat.

On 31 May 2000, Barak travelled to Lisbon to talk in person to President Clinton, who was meeting with EU leaders, to plead with him that now was the time for a summit. Clinton, however, insisted that Barak must first take measures to remove Arafat's grievances, particularly with regard to the three Arab villages near Jerusalem which the Prime Minister still had not transferred to Arafat, even though he now had the Knesset's approval. Barak would also have to transfer money Israel owed the Palestinians and release Palestinian prisoners held in Israeli jails. Dealing with these issues, Clinton said to Barak, would put Arafat in a better position to accept a summit, and deny him any excuse for not taking part. Barak particularly resisted the transfer of the three Arab villages to Arafat. He said to Clinton that, by not stopping the violence earlier that month – the Nakba riots and the two Days of Rage – Arafat had made it politically impossible for Barak to turn the villages over. 'Think it over', advised Clinton, and said he would dispatch Secretary of State Madeleine Albright to the region to assess the situation and report back to him if the time was right for a summit.

On 5 June 2000, Albright visited the parties on their home ground, and found Arafat very reluctant to go to a summit. He told her that the gulf between the parties was too wide and that it would be wiser first to try to narrow the gaps by continuing talks at a lower level. Should a summit be convened and fail, Arafat told Albright, desperation among Palestinians would increase rapidly and might even lead to violence.[3]

Ten days later, Arafat was received in the White House – during the Clinton days he was a frequent visitor. This time he was fuming, and with good reason. He complained that Barak had still not transferred the three Arab villages, nor released Palestinian prisoners – at least not the hundreds Arafat had demanded but an insulting meagre three. The Clinton–Arafat meeting went badly and Arafat strongly resisted Clinton's advice to attend a summit. Barak, Arafat said to Clinton, was attempting to lead the Palestinians into a trap whereby they would be blamed for the failure of the summit. Clinton responded categorically that, 'irrespective of the outcome of this summit, Mr Chairman, there will not be any finger pointing at any side'.[4] But Arafat was adamant that a summit was not a good idea and the fact that it was Barak's brainchild was enough to set a red light flashing in his head.

After the meeting Clinton phoned Barak to tell him how badly it had gone – he said it was the worst meeting he had ever had with Arafat – and that the Prime Minister should try to engage Arafat directly. This Barak would not do, as he feared Arafat would pocket whatever he heard from him and use it later as a departure point for further demands. Instead, the Prime Minister sent his minister Shlomo Ben-Ami and his right-hand man Gilead Sher, both of whom had represented him in the Stockholm talks, to meet Arafat. They were joined by Yossi Ginossar, Barak's emissary to Arafat and a close friend of many Palestinians.

'A SUMMIT IS OUR LAST CARD'

They met on 25 June 2000 in the Palestinian town of Nablus, in the residence of Mayor Ghassan Shakar. They all sat in a big square room, with drinks, nibbles and crystal ashtrays in front of them. Shlomo Ben-Ami sat next to Arafat, his notes ready. His plan was to update Arafat on progress in the Stockholm talks and then try to persuade him to agree to join a summit with Barak.

Ben-Ami opened. 'You know, Mr Chairman,' he said, 'I would like to share with you some of our negotiations in the back channel, which you call the "bad channel". I would like to tell you what we have achieved.'[5] Arafat cut him short. 'They tell me', he lashed out at Ben-Ami, 'that the Hezbollah are better than us.' Arafat was referring to Israel's unilateral withdrawal from Lebanon, which had hurt him as the Arab world ridiculed him for negotiating with the Israelis when Hezbollah had, as they saw it, kicked the Israelis out of Lebanon by force. Then, referring to the proposed summit, Arafat said, 'We have to prepare well for the summit. That is your mission, together with our people.' Ben-Ami responded: 'Because of [the failed summit with Assad at] Geneva the US will not allow us to fail.' Ginossar intervened: 'It is only with you that Barak can reach a historical agreement, Abu Ammar.'[6]

Ben-Ami then turned to the issue of Jerusalem, the most important issue of all as far as Arafat was concerned. 'You are aware of the extent to which you, as Muslims, have autonomy on the Temple Mount. [Moshe] Dayan gave you this in 1967.' This was a reference to the fact that although Israel occupied the Temple Mount, or the Haram, when it took control of the Old City of Jerusalem during the Six-Day War, Muslims still effectively ran the place. Ben-Ami added, 'No agreement can violate this status quo. You will have full and secure autonomy for all worshippers.' Arafat, unhappy with 'autonomy', said, 'Is there an Arab, a Muslim, who would accept your offer [to settle for less than full Palestinian *sovereignty*]? With the issue of [Haram] al-Sharif unresolved? Forget it. I will be kicked out.' Ben-Ami replied: 'Mr Chairman . . . this is an issue we need to discuss at the summit.'[7] Then, according to Gilead Sher, 'Arafat burst into a long story about when he was five, living near the Wailing Wall, with his aunt, and how he played with the Jews, everyone was friends.'[8] When Arafat eventually paused in his story, Ben-Ami managed to get a word in, saying, 'Listen, Barak's character is such that he holds the cards to the last minute, and if you want an agreement, then it's in your best interests to bring Barak to a summit.'[9] While they were talking, a phone call came through from the Egyptian President, Hosni Mubarak, who advised Arafat to accept a summit. This was no coincidence. Barak had sent an emissary, Yossi Beilin, to Mubarak to ask him to help persuade Arafat to attend.

Three days after the Nablus meeting, on 28 June, Secretary of State Madeleine Albright visited Arafat in the *muqata*, his residence and headquarters in Ramallah,[10] to press him to attend a summit with Barak. She said to him,

We need to move quickly because otherwise the President's time is elapsing. He's soon going to be out of office. We have an opportunity to close this deal . . . Trust the President. He's not going to trap you. Let's have a summit very quickly in the United States to try to wrap this up. You've said to us in the past that this is the President with whom you're going to reach a final deal. The President only has a few more months left in office. Now is the time.

But Arafat was unconvinced. 'A summit is our last card,' he said to Albright. 'If it fails, everything will explode in our faces. We're not ready. We need more preparation.' He went on, 'Madam Secretary, if you issue an invitation to a summit, and if it is held and fails, then this will weaken the hope of the [Palestinian] people in the possibility of achieving peace. Let us not weaken this hope.'[11] As Arafat walked Albright back to the lift he said to her, 'We can't afford a Geneva. We can't make the same mistake twice.'

'SHOULD WE GO TO THE SUMMIT?'

Back in Washington, Albright and her team reported to Clinton in the Oval Office, to help him decide whether to call a summit. Clinton, as diplomat Robert Malley recalls, 'seemed more hesitant than we expected him to be . . . we thought he would jump on this and in fact we would have to hold him back. But he was hesitant.' The President asked to hear personally from everyone who attended the meeting and, going around the room one by one, he asked, 'Should we go to the summit? . . . Should we go to a summit?' Clinton's National Security Advisor Sandy Berger recalls his answer: 'I cannot, Mr President, with good conscience, tell you that I know we will succeed . . . I know, however, that if we fail to have this meeting, there will be an explosion in the West Bank.' Indeed, the unanimous opinion, despite the risks acknowledged by all, was: 'Yes. If we don't do it now, we will never do it because this is our only window of opportunity.' It was the 'only window of opportunity' because the President was due to leave the White House in January 2001, just a few months away. Also, the Republican Party convention was due to take place in August, and it could be called dirty politics if a Democratic President held such an attention-stealing summit during a rival convention. The death of President Assad of Syria on 10 June 2000 had also made it clear to those at this critical meeting that peace with Syria would not happen for a long time as the young Bashar Assad needed time to stabilize his regime, and therefore the only peace initiative that could now proceed was the Israeli–Palestinian track. Finally persuaded, the President, as he recalls in an interview with *Elusive Peace*, said, 'Look, one of two things gonna happen at Camp David. We'll either make peace or we'll get caught trying – I'd rather get caught trying than say, Oh, I avoided failure by not trying. I think that's a silly thing for a president to do.'[12] And that was that.

On 1 July, Clinton phoned Barak and, knowing just how desperate the Prime Minister was to have a summit, again attempted to extract some concessions from him. He said he would not convene a summit until the Prime Minister had given Arafat some real sweeteners. Three days later, Clinton and his peace team gathered at the formal meeting room in Laurel Cabin at Camp David, and Clinton talked to Barak on a secure line. He wanted to hear what concessions the Prime Minister had, to tempt Arafat to come to a summit. Barak said he would free thirty-two Palestinian prisoners once the summit began, and he also said to the President, asking Clinton to keep this in his pocket, that if pushed in a summit he would be willing to consider limited compromises on East Jerusalem neighbourhoods; he would also act on the three villages, transferring them to Arafat.

So certain was the President that Barak would agree to concessions that a call had already been arranged to Arafat. The day before, a technician from the US Consulate had installed a secure telephone line so the two could talk privately. At 1 a.m. in his office in Gaza Arafat received the call from Clinton, who told him, 'Here are the commitments I've just heard from Barak, and you have my word [that] the three villages and a few other things will be done.'[13] Clinton then went on to invite Arafat officially to a summit at Camp David, to take place on 9 July. After Clinton had repeated his pledge that he would not blame the Palestinians in the event of failure, Arafat reluctantly agreed, though he insisted the date be delayed for two days, as he had a pre-scheduled African summit to attend. The die was cast; Barak had persuaded Clinton, who in turn persuaded Arafat. There would be a summit at Camp David.

That afternoon, Arafat called an emergency meeting of the eleven members of his negotiations team in Ramallah. He told them: 'We're going to face a disaster. We are being set up. They want to take us for a summit. Barak has convinced Clinton . . . Clinton went along with Barak all the way . . . they want to take us to Camp David so they can blame us [for the failure of the peace process].'[14]

'BARAK IS TAKING ALL OF US FOR A RIDE'

When Clinton invited Arafat to a summit at Camp David, the two agreed that Israeli and Palestinian negotiators would meet in the US several days before to try to narrow gaps. However, when Clinton later raised this with Barak, the Prime Minister was reluctant. Why not preserve all his assets for the moment of truth? After all, he was going to have a summit with Arafat in which he would *have* to compromise and make serious concessions. Barak finally persuaded Clinton to agree to the two teams coming to Washington for just two days before the official opening of the summit at Camp David, and the President had to call Arafat back. Reluctantly, the Palestinian leader agreed.

On Sunday, 9 July, the delegates met at the Madison Hotel in Washington for pre-summit talks, but the discussion focused on technicalities and ground rules rather than on content. Secretary of State Albright explained that each delegation would have only twelve members at Camp David; support personnel must stay outside the camp and would be allowed in with special permission only; no delegates would be allowed to leave the camp without American permission, and there would be only two outside phone lines – one for Arafat and one for Barak. It was at this pre-summit meeting that the Palestinian chief negotiator Saeb Erekat begged Albright: 'Madam Secretary, you know we're not ready, you're not ready, they're not ready . . . Barak is taking all of us for a ride . . . if we fail in Camp David it's going to be disastrous, it's going to explode, it's going to explode.'[15] But there was no way back. They would all meet in two days' time at Camp David.

8

Showdown at Camp David

DAY I OF THE SUMMIT: *TUESDAY, II JULY*

The Palestinian delegates got lost on their way to Camp David from Washington. 'We went up, we went down', the Palestinian chief negotiator Saeb Erekat recalls, 'we went in, we went to the trees . . . we were lost.' They were not the only ones confounded by the backroads of the Catoctin Mountains of Maryland, as the van carrying the American peace team also got lost. As US special Middle East envoy Dennis Ross joked, 'here is the peace team, lost on the way to Camp David, and praying we are not going to be lost once we get there'.[1] Rescued by Maryland state troopers, they got to Camp David just two hours before Arafat, who arrived by helicopter from Andrews Air Force Base where his plane from Togo had landed. He was in a black mood. 'Arafat arrives on the helicopter', Secretary of State Albright recalls, 'and I went to greet him, and I took him to his cabin, and he said, "Where is Barak?" and so the mood immediately was wrong.'

Prime Minister Barak had had to delay his departure from Israel, as he narrowly lost a vote of no confidence in the Knesset on 10 July, 52–54. As only a two-thirds' majority could remove a serving prime minister, Barak was still in office, but this humiliating defeat weakened him on the eve of a historic mission. The US ambassador to Israel, Martin Indyk, flew to Camp David on Barak's plane:

It was an old 707 Israeli Air Force Jet . . . and there was a little cabin there for the Prime Minister's use, with a double bed, that took up all of the space of the cabin. He called me in there to have a talk, and we sat on the bed together, and it was clear that he was completely exhausted . . . he told me that he hadn't slept in three days. And he told me that he felt like a trapeze artist who was about to let go of the pole and do his jump, without any safety net, and without any knowledge that his partner on the other side, Yasser Arafat, would be there to catch him.

With Barak late to arrive at Camp David, the Americans thought they ought to talk to Arafat first, as an aloof and unengaged Arafat could be a serious obstacle to progress. Clinton, master of the one-on-one charm offensive who could sell anything to anybody, took it upon himself to try to shift Arafat's mood, and sat with him, talking of his wish to be there with Arafat 'when the flag was raised on the new state of Palestine'.[2] This seemed to work, as Arafat's spirits appeared to rise.

Meanwhile, the delegates moved into their quarters, the wooden cabins scattered around the woods of Camp David. Aspen, the most spacious cabin, was reserved for the President. Dogwood – rapidly to be renamed 'Doghouse' by the Israelis – was given to Prime Minister Barak, while Birch, a two-room cabin with a sitting room and a small balcony, was assigned to Arafat. Other delegates shared cabins.

Just before 2.30 in the afternoon, delegates gathered at the Laurel conference room for the official launch of the summit, and watched Barak and Arafat sparring over who would cross the threshold of the conference room first. It was Arafat, pushed gently but firmly by Barak under the eyes of a laughing Clinton. A few minutes later, the delegations were seated at a table, each with a notebook and a Parker pen with the signature and portrait of President Clinton. Clinton opened: 'This summit is a historic opportunity to reach an agreement . . . We want to reach a just solution for the benefit of both parties. If we fail, the parties will lose . . . I'll stay here for as long as it takes to reach an agreement.' Arafat was the next to speak: 'I would like the Russian Federation and the European Union to be associated with this process. Likewise Morocco and Jordan . . .' Barak then talked, saying, 'We have come to Camp David in a spirit of responsibility . . . The time has come to live side by side, to make an honourable peace, to work for a better future . . . I have great respect for the Russian

Federation and the European Union, but no one can take the place of the United States and President Clinton.' Arafat responded, 'What the Prime Minister is saying is very important. The contribution of the President of the United States . . . is crucial.'[3] After the speeches, the formal opening of the conference was over, and they all left the Laurel conference room and got down to work.

Joined by his National Security Council note-taker, Bruce Riedel, for meetings with Barak, President Clinton went to see the Prime Minister, who had already devised a complete script for the summit *à la* Barak. He told Clinton that nothing substantial should happen during the first two days of the summit in order to demonstrate to sceptical Israelis and Palestinians back home that things were not easy, that tough negotiations were under way and that their respective leaders were working hard and not giving up on vital interests.[4] Was Barak so naïve as to think that, even without wasting two days, the negotiations would not be tough enough? Clinton politely brushed aside Barak's artificial concept and went on to present his own plan, which he believed should guide the summit.

Clinton's ideas were, in fact, the reverse of Barak's. He thought that rather than stalling, as Barak wished, the parties should give the talks a push-start by abandoning old, outdated arguments and begin, instead, with a few parameters concerning the stumbling points already acknowledged. These ideas, prepared in advance by the American peace team, were a careful balancing act between Israeli and Palestinian needs regarding the main issues which made reaching a deal so difficult: borders, settlements, refugees and Jerusalem.

The American plan that Clinton now presented to Barak suggested the discussion of the borders of the future Palestinian state should be based on the boundaries that separated the West Bank and Israel proper before Israel occupied the territory in the 1967 war (the so-called Green Line). Talking in terms of the '1967 lines', explained Clinton, was critical for Arafat. But in order to accommodate Barak's concerns, the future western border of the Palestinian state would be modified sufficiently to enable Israel to annex West Bank land on which the main blocs of Jewish settlements, with some 80 per cent of settlers, were built. On the eastern border of the future Palestinian state, along the Jordan Valley, the Palestinians would have sovereignty. Again, explained Clinton, it was critical for Arafat to be able to show that his state had borders with neighbouring states – in this case Jordan. But to take on board Barak's concerns, Israel's security needs would be met with arrangements on the ground to deal with Israel's traditional fear of an Eastern Front – a potential combined Iraqi-Syrian-Jordanian invasion coming from the east across the Jordan River.

The Palestinian refugee problem, Clinton went on, would be dealt with on the basis of a very limited return of Palestinian refugees to Israel proper, and an international mechanism which would be established to deal with the remaining refugees by helping them to rehabilitate and resettle in the future Palestinian state. As far as Jerusalem was concerned, the American ideas were very vague, as Clinton did not wish to touch too early on this, the most sensitive issue of all.

Barak resisted the American plan. For him, to start from such an advanced point would be to surrender vital assets at too early a stage, and Barak now insisted, and so he told Clinton, on an 'I' and 'P' document, a paper with Israeli and Palestinian views on the core issues presented side by side. This, to be sure, meant returning to a struggle over former positions – something which the Americans had wanted to avoid – but Clinton reluctantly agreed. First, he did not want to rock the boat at such an early stage, and second, Clinton sympathized with Barak, feeling that he was the one who was taking the big leaps and putting himself in the firing line by attempting to tackle, for the first time in his nation's history, such difficult issues. Clinton instructed his aides to work on a new paper which would be given to the parties two days later, by Thursday night.

This was a bad start to the summit and a devastating blow to the key element of the American strategy, which was to have the parties accept relatively advanced ideas at an early stage, then to discuss and crystallize their differences regarding these ideas, and then to deliver an American bridging paper to overcome these gaps. It also gave the wrong signal to the parties: that the Americans would back away at any sign of resistance. What made Clinton's acceptance of Barak's position even more questionable was that the American ideas, just rejected by Barak, had also been presented to the Palestinians and they had, in fact, quite liked them.

DAY 2: *WEDNESDAY, 12 JULY*

With both sides anticipating a new American draft to be delivered on the next day, they saw no reason to negotiate at all. So, while the American team, led by Madeleine Albright and Dennis Ross, was hard at work on a framework agreement for peace, still trying to avoid the 'I' and 'P' document requested by Barak, which they regarded as a recipe for endless arguments, Israelis and Palestinians took advantage of Camp David's recreation and relaxation facilities – watching films and playing billiards in the large games room.

DAY 3: *THURSDAY, 13 JULY*

The President had promised Barak 'no surprises'; this was the non-written, American commitment to share all their ideas with Barak first, so the Israelis were the first to see the American paper. Foreign Minister Shlomo Ben-Ami, Barak's loyal aide Gilead Sher and others from the Israeli team sat with Dennis Ross while he read out the paper. They did not like what they heard. They objected because the Americans still based the borders of the future Palestinian state on the 1967 lines, with modifications taking into account Israel's demographic and strategic needs. The Israelis also opposed the section on the refugees, which, as they saw it, implied that Israel bore some responsibility for the birth of the Palestinian refugee problem. In fact, almost every section in the new American paper evoked opposition, and the Israelis again – as Barak did in his Tuesday meeting with the President – insisted on an 'I' and 'P' paper. Shortly after his team had reported to him on the new American paper, as Madeleine Albright recalls, 'Barak's thumb pointed down.'[5]

A disappointed Ross then went to see the Palestinians, to whom he presented his paper in very general terms. They were more open to it, although Abu Ala insisted that the Jerusalem clause should be more specific.

When Ross reported to the President the negative Israeli reaction, Clinton immediately instructed him to take on board their concerns and produce a new paper with 'I' and 'P' positions written side by side, as demanded by Barak and his team. Clinton suggested that, in addition to the 'I' and 'P' positions, Ross should add 'alternative possible solutions' to the paper – namely, an American view of how the different positions could be bridged. Ross, always obliging, sat down with his team to prepare the new document. Again, it was the same pattern – the Americans backed off when facing objection. This did not escape either party.

The new paper was ready late at night, and Clinton took it first to Barak, in accordance with the 'no-surprise' rule. This time the President was quite firm with the Prime Minister, telling him that he had no intention to negotiate it with him and that now it was time to present the paper as it was to Arafat, which is what Clinton then did.

When the President explained to Arafat what was in the paper he was at first satisfied, but not for long. After seeing the President, Arafat immediately summoned his advisers, who reluctantly left the cinema where they had been watching *What Planet Are You From?*, about an alien, Harold Anderson, whose mission was to impregnate an earthwoman. As Arafat started to read from the draft document the mood among the Palestinians changed dramatically. Saeb Erekat recalls, 'When I translated to [Arafat] what it said about Jerusalem . . . he was extremely upset. President Arafat took the paper out of my hand, threw it in the air and said, "This is a non-starter." I told you it was a set-up for us.' What so upset Arafat was the fact that the new American paper made reference to Israel's plan to expand Jerusalem so that Arafat could establish the Palestinian capital in an outlying neighbourhood instead of within the city's traditional boundaries. Furious, Arafat instructed Erekat to phone Clinton at once, to reject the paper. 'I can't phone the President of the United States at two o'clock in the morning', protested Erekat. But then, as he recalls, 'Arafat started shouting and screaming' and it was Gamal Helal of the American peace team, who was there to deliver extra copies of the paper, who suggested waking up Albright instead. From Birch Cabin, Helal then phoned to warn Albright. Albright recalls:

I had gone to bed, and I got a call from Gamal, and he said, 'Madam Secretary, you are not going to believe this, or maybe you will believe it . . . the Palestinians . . . they are in uproar, they have to come and see you', and I said: 'You've got to be kidding', and he said, 'No', and I said: 'What time is it?' and he said, 'It's two-thirty.' And I thought, well, this is what I get paid for, so I got up and I got dressed.

Accompanied by Abu Ala, Saeb Erekat walked to Albright's living room (Erekat recalls: 'I was so ashamed . . . to go out to a lady's compound'), where he protested about the paper, saying he could clearly see Barak's 'fingertips' on it, and that instead of this 'I' and 'P' document the Americans should go back to the original paper which was presented on the summit's first day. Dennis Ross, who had rushed round to help Albright, shot back, 'If you don't like our paper, fine. Just negotiate directly with the Israelis.' He had said this sarcastically, without really meaning it, but Erekat leapt on it, saying, 'You mean we can ignore the paper?' and Ross then said, 'Yes.'[6] It was now the Palestinian turn to throw the American machine into turmoil. Saeb Erekat and Abu Ala left, satisfied that as far as they were concerned the American paper was dead.

'So after three days', as Secretary of State Madeleine Albright puts it in her memoirs, 'we had drafted one paper rejected by Barak and a second rejected by the Palestinians . . . we were left with no paper and no progress.'[7] This failure to steer the summit firmly during its first three days led to growing tensions within the American delegation, with National Security Advisor Sandy Berger and his team often at loggerheads with Secretary Albright and her State Department team.

DAY 4: *FRIDAY, 14 JULY*

Clinton set up four groups to tackle the core issues: borders (and settlements), refugees, security and Jerusalem. The President himself then moved between the groups to offer ideas – he was very imaginative and had mastered the details of the conflict as well as those negotiators who had been dealing with it for years. On his tour, Clinton joined the refugees group, where Israelis Eli Rubinstein and Oded Eran were negotiating with Abu Mazen and Nabil Shaath.

They were discussing a deeply emotional subject. By 2000, there were about 4 million Palestinians who had been made homeless or who were descended from those who had been made homeless, mainly by the 1948 creation of Israel and the 1967 war. Now, at Camp David, the Palestinians, particularly Abu Mazen, insisted that these refugees should have a 'right of return' to Israel proper. But if Israel, a Jewish state with 4.5 million Jews, allowed a return of some 4 million Palestinians, the majority of them Muslims, the state would lose its Jewish character. Abu Mazen insisted on Israel accepting the principle of the right of return, and argued that few Palestinians would actually exercise it.

President Clinton intervened to explain the Israeli position. He said that a bungee-jumper cannot accept the 'principle' that he could leap off a cliff without knowing whether the gorge he was leaping into was deeper than the length of the bungee cord. The Israelis, Clinton went on, could not be expected to permit a return of Palestinian refugees into their Jewish state without guarantees that this was somehow limited.[8]

Leaving the refugees group, Clinton then joined the Jerusalem group, where Saeb Erekat and Yasser Abed Rabbo were negotiating for Arafat, with Gilead Sher representing Barak. Jerusalem was more complicated than the refugee issue, or any other issue on the negotiating table. In 1967, immediately after seizing Arab East Jerusalem from Jordan, the Israelis took down the wall which until then had separated the two parts of the city, expanded Jerusalem's municipal boundaries to include more distant suburbs and declared it the 'eternal and undivided capital' of Israel. Barak, like prime ministers before him, vowed not to divide the city ever again. The Palestinians, on the other hand, demanded that Arab East Jerusalem should become the capital of *their* future state.

The heart of the problem focused on the ancient walled city of Old Jerusalem, situated in the Arab part of the city with its Jewish,

Armenian, Christian and Muslim Quarters. Deep in Old Jerusalem, there is a thirty-five-acre area that Jews refer to as the Temple Mount and the Muslims as Al-Haram al-Sharif (Arabic for Noble Sanctuary). For the Jews this area is where the First and Second Temples stood.[9] For Muslims, this same land encloses the Dome of the Rock, the third holiest site in Islam after Mecca and Medina, and the historic Al-Aqsa Mosque. Muslims believe that their prophet Muhammad ascended up to heaven from this place, following his night journey from Mecca to Jerusalem. How to deal with this 'hot potato' – a Muslim compound built on the remains of a Jewish site so that both the Israelis and the Palestinians wanted sovereignty over it – was a problem that would require a great deal of imagination, sensitivity and bravery to solve.

Now, sitting with the Jerusalem group's negotiators, Clinton said, 'Do me a favour. Each of you is to assume that you get the sovereignty outcome you want', and with this in mind Clinton asked the negotiators to try to concentrate on the aspect of living side by side in Jerusalem – on what life would look like in a future Jerusalem, on how things would actually operate and, generally, on how Israelis and Palestinians would run the city. His hope was that a deal could come out of such day-to-day realities, rather than the age-old arguments that had been repeated so often before.[10]

It was Friday night and the Israelis invited the US and Palestinian teams to share the Sabbath dinner with them. They gathered at 9 p.m. at Laurel, where Eli Rubinstein, flanked by Clinton and Yasser Arafat – the latter, in a gracious mood, blessed everyone and even spoke a few words of Hebrew – sang Friday songs, and then Rubinstein prayed over wine and bread. It was a pleasant moment but, after four days of non-progress, the US team was really worried.

DAY 5: *SATURDAY, 15 JULY*

That morning, the increasingly frustrated President met the borders group. Soon after he came in, General Shlomo Yanai offered a map showing the West Bank as Israel envisioned it in a future Palestinian state. But Abu Ala rejected the map out of hand, refusing even to look at it until Israel first accepted the 'principle' that any territorial agreement had to be based on the lines of 4 June 1967. Clinton lost his patience. The Palestinian Mohammed Rashid recalls how 'the President was losing his temper and when he loses his temper his nose turns red', and how Clinton then blew up at Abu Ala:

OK, we know that you think that your position is that you should get the 1967 line. We agree that's your position. And let's assume that the Israelis accept it. Now draw me a line [on the map] of the kind of things you could accept, what percentage of land could you accept [to be annexed by Israel so that large Jewish settlements could be included in Israel proper]?[11]

But Abu Ala still would not look at the map. Robert Malley, with the President, describes how 'You could see the President's face getting redder and redder and redder' until Dennis Ross went over and whispered to the President that 'it might make sense to take a break'. But Clinton burst out again at Abu Ala: 'OK you don't like the map, but it's an Israeli proposal and either you get specific about what you need to change or offer your own map.'[12] Still Abu Ala was insistent; Clinton then lashed out at him again: 'You know, this is not a UN Security Council meeting. You're not here to posture. I invited you here for a summit. I'm doing this for your sake, and all you can do is come back with posturing. This is not a negotiation. This is a joke.' The Israeli negotiator Shlomo Ben-Ami recalls how 'Clinton really yelled at him, he screamed at him, he said "you are not coming to this negotiation in good faith, contrary to what Arafat promised me".' Then, as Albright confided in her memoirs, 'Having made his point, Clinton motioned to me and we strode dramatically out – at precisely the moment a downpour began. It was either get wet or forfeit the drama of our exit, so we went and got drenched.'[13]

Recalling the event Abu Ala told Elusive Peace, 'It was a shock when Clinton was angry and he was pointing at me . . . he was very angry.' To the American peace team Abu Ala later bitterly complained that 'it's one thing to get mad at me, but to get mad at me in front of the Israelis . . . to take sides with the Israelis in a meeting with us, you've undermined my position as a negotiator for my side'.[14] Israeli and Palestinian rivals rejoiced. 'We liked to see Abu Ala sweating',

Dan Meridor recalls, and that evening in the dining hall one of Abu Ala's colleagues (but certainly no friend) Mohammed Dahlan was very happily cracking jokes about the event. Abu Ala himself was saved from this public humiliation for, as he recalls, 'the same night I didn't go to the dinner'. Later that evening President Clinton bumped into the Israeli negotiator Shlomo Ben-Ami; 'I screwed up your meeting, didn't I?' Ben-Ami replied, 'You're the President of the United States.' However, the US President's outburst had effectively cost the Palestinian team one of their most experienced and respected negotiators as from that moment, as Ben-Ami recalls, 'almost the only thing Abu Ala did at Camp David was drive around the lawns in a golf cart'.

Was it all one big show aimed at putting pressure on the negotiators, to try to move them from their entrenched positions? To make it clear to them that they were not doing enough, not compromising? According to Rashid, the Palestinians suspected that Clinton's 'outburst' was pre-planned, and that 'the President's arrival to that meeting was a set-up or a trap'.[15] Trap or not, with the topic of the day at Camp David being Clinton's explosion, the President felt he could play it tough on the Israelis as well. Later, in a conversation with the Prime Minister, Clinton said that he 'had beaten up on the Palestinians', but in truth Barak was doing nothing in a summit on which he had insisted.

To break the stalemate, Clinton proposed a secret channel of two Israeli and two Palestinian negotiators locked in a room. They would be given whatever they needed but would not be allowed to leave. The channel would be unknown to anyone but the two leaders, and there would be no limits on the discussion. Clinton hoped blue-skies thinking, thinking outside the box, in one marathon discussion, would lead to a breakthrough. This small group of negotiators, proposed Clinton, would try to forge the contours of an agreement and would have total deniability. Anything agreed in this secret channel, Clinton promised Barak and Arafat, could be denied and would be non-binding should the two leaders feel it went too far.

Realizing that they were now dealing with an impatient President, both Barak and Arafat agreed. The Prime Minister dispatched Shlomo Ben-Ami and Gilead Sher to represent him. Arafat, summoning Saeb

Erekat and Mohammed Dahlan from the cinema, said to them, 'President Clinton asked me to choose two, I choose you ... use your brains.' Then, as Erekat recalls, 'Arafat grabbed me and said, "Saeb, the most important thing for me is Jerusalem – the Haram [al-Sharif]." '

DAY 6: *SUNDAY, 16 JULY*

Just after midnight the four negotiators came to Aspen to see Clinton, who tried to encourage and motivate them for the task ahead. It was all quite dramatic; rain was pouring down, and just before leaving for the talks they all stood outside Clinton's cabin under umbrellas and the President hugged the negotiators, saying, 'You're probably setting out on the most important mission in the world ... God bless you.'[16] Dennis Ross, who was present, recalls how, 'as the four came out of Aspen I saw very different looks on their faces: Shlomo [Ben-Ami] and Gilead [Sher] clearly saw this as an opportunity. But Saeb [Erekat] and [Mohammed] Dahlan had a look of dread on their faces – suggesting they did not know whether Arafat would truly back them if they compromised on any of the core issues.'[17]

The four then walked into Laurel where they were sequestered with guards to ensure they did not leave, as per Clinton's clear instructions. Shortly afterwards, with Clinton's consent, Gidi Grinstein and Israel Hasson joined the Israeli team and Akram Hanieh, Hassan Asfour and Ghaith Omari the Palestinian. 'It was surreal,' Grinstein recalls. 'We were in Clinton's big meeting room, next to his personal office. We sat on his desk, working. All around were his personal souvenirs, photos ... his whole life, at school, at college, as a state politician, as a very young governor ...'[18]

They tried to tackle the most difficult of all problems – Jerusalem. They talked about the relationship between East and West Jerusalem, between Arab and Jewish neighbourhoods, and about the holy sites. Erekat insisted that Jerusalem should be divided in such a way that ensured all Arab neighbourhoods came under Palestinian sovereignty and all Jewish neighbourhoods remained in Israeli hands. The Israelis, for the first time, moved on Jerusalem by agreeing to Palestinian sovereignty over some outer Arab neighbourhoods. Erekat, for his part, moved on Jerusalem as well. 'I said,' he recalls, 'you want the Wailing Wall [which is part of the Western Wall just below the Temple Mount/Haram al-Sharif, and is the holiest site in Judaism] and the Jewish Quarter. I believe we can accommodate your needs and concerns ... you can have sovereignty over the Wailing Wall and the Jewish Quarter in Jerusalem.' He also agreed to Israeli sovereignty over Jewish neighbourhoods of East Jerusalem, areas that were not part of Israel before the 1967 war. But that was all he was willing to concede, even when Gilead Sher and Shlomo Ben-Ami moved further by agreeing, for the first time, to give most of the border with Jordan to the Palestinians and to cut the amount of land they needed to retain, so that big settlement blocs could remain under Israeli sovereignty, to 10.5 per cent of West Bank land.[19]

At about six in the morning, Saeb Erekat fell asleep on a sofa, though not for long as Ben-Ami spotted him and went wild. 'What! You don't want your state? You don't want your independence? What are you doing?', and he shook Erekat, shouting, 'Let's get back to work.' Erekat recalls how 'I told them, "If you repeat only the same old stories then I will go and sleep. I'm tired."' And with tiredness taking hold, tempers continued to flare. At one point the Israelis suggested having a fund that would be used to compensate both Palestinian refugees and the Jewish settlers who would be removed from occupied territories. Saeb Erekat exploded at Sher:

No sir, you are not going to be compensated for your years of occupation. We will demand compensation for every day of your occupation, if you're going to go down this line. Somebody who has occupied me for thirty-five years and then comes to ask me for compensation? You took my childhood. I was twelve years old when your occupation came to my home town Jericho. I was never again the same person. You have denied me the right to live normally for thirty-five years. And now you want compensation for this! I will calculate every hour, and find every legal way to make you pay for every damn hour, killing, bulldozing of homes, confiscating of land, closing schools, deporting, wounding, killing ...

Sher shot back, 'Is this the way you intend to proceed? We are trying to end the conflict – and you come up with this . . . compensation! Now? To introduce this claim? Now?'

There seemed no point in continuing and after almost twelve hours of negotiations both sides called a halt, and each reported to its respective leader. Arafat praised his negotiators for standing firm, but when Gilead Sher and Shlomo Ben-Ami reported to Barak his hair stood on end. 'Barak said', Ben-Ami recalls, 'he didn't like the propositions that I raised regarding Jerusalem . . . that this was far beyond what we could accept.' In an interview for *Elusive Peace* Barak said, 'they went further than I authorized'.[20]

When, at around two in the afternoon, the negotiators returned to Laurel to report to Clinton, it became apparent that the Israelis had moved in a big way both on Jerusalem and on territory.[21] Now Saeb Erekat, in front of the President, suggested that the two sides should carry on with their negotiations from the point where the back-channel talks had left off. But this was precisely what the Israelis had feared – that the Palestinians would pocket their offers and then haggle for more. 'You think you can just take this as a new floor and negotiate from there?' Sher burst out at Erekat. 'We came to make a deal, not to haggle in the *souk*.'[22] In *My Life*, Clinton records that he thought 'Ben-Ami and Sher had, *with Barak's blessing*, gone well beyond previously stated Israeli positions'.[23] He was wrong. In fact, as soon as the negotiators left, a livid Barak sat down to write to the President. 'I took the report of Shlomo Ben-Ami and Gilead Sher of last night's discussion very badly', he wrote:

This is not negotiation. This is a manipulative attempt to pull us to a position we will never be able to accept, without the Palestinians moving one inch. Yasser Arafat would not dare to do it without believing that in the US delegation there is a strong bias among many of the American team for his positions. The President is of course objective but . . . the American team is not objective . . . This is an unusual moment of truth. Only a sharp shaking of Arafat by the President will give a chance to the process . . . Peace will be achieved only if there is a real willingness to negotiate on both sides.[24]

When Barak finished his letter – it was handwritten – he gave it to his Chief of Staff Danny Yatom, who in turn phoned US ambassador Martin Indyk. Indyk recalls how 'suddenly I was called to an urgent meeting with Danny Yatom, the Prime Minister's Chief of Staff, in which he dictated to me a letter from Barak to Clinton, which was apocalyptic in its view'.[25] Yatom asked Indyk to ensure the President read the letter *before* he went to see Arafat, but it was too late, as by that time the President was already sitting with the Palestinian leader.

Clinton said to Arafat: 'All the good things and all the suggestions [in the back channel] came from the Israelis ... your team sat there doing nothing.'[26] Robert Malley, there taking notes, recalls how Clinton told Arafat how disappointed he was that Arafat was not giving anything. With his voice rising, Clinton continued, 'You haven't moved one inch, whereas Barak is moving. And you haven't done a thing ... you're now wasting this opportunity.' At first Arafat was dismissive, playing down what was achieved in the night's discussions. He said that the 89.5 per cent of territory offered by Gilead Sher and Shlomo Ben-Ami in the back channel for a Palestinian state, with sovereignty in several outer neighbourhoods of East Jerusalem and an independent border with Jordan, were, as Arafat put it to Clinton, 'less than Rabin offered', and that 'Rabin promised me ninety per cent [of land].' This was sheer nonsense, as Clinton knew very well, and so he lashed out at Arafat. 'We can all go home and I will say [that Barak] negotiated seriously and you did not.' Arafat now became emotional and, as Malley recalls, 'he took the President's hand and said, "You're my only friend. I can't afford to lose you ... Who else can I talk to? You are the only one I can talk to." '[27] Clinton said: 'You lose me ... our relationship will be over ... Barak came a long way. You're pocketing things ... you'll lose everything, you'll leave empty-handed, everything will be off the table.'[28] Getting down to details, Clinton said to Arafat that he needed answers to three questions. One, what was Arafat's reaction to Barak's requirement to keep 10.5 per cent of the West Bank, as was proposed in the back channel? Two, what was his reaction to Barak's demand for a military presence in the Jordan Valley for some time after Israel's withdrawal? And three, would Arafat accept that whatever agreement was reached, it would mark the end of the conflict? In *My Life* Clinton describes 'a tough meeting'.[29] When Clinton rose to leave, Arafat promised he would come back with his answers.

At around 10 p.m., after getting a partial answer from Arafat, Clinton came to Barak and sat with him on the front balcony of Dogwood, with Danny Yatom, Barak's Chief of Staff. Clinton said that after his tough meeting with Arafat, the Palestinian leader had come back with a concession – he would agree to 8 to 10 per cent of the West Bank being annexed by Israel so that big settlement blocs remained under Israel's sovereignty. True, this was less than the 10.5 per cent requested by Barak, but it was nevertheless a breakthrough.

DAY 7: *MONDAY, 17 JULY*

This was a day of stock-taking for Prime Minister Barak and his team, as they discussed how best to proceed, particularly on Jerusalem, the fate of which, it was now clear, had turned into the make-or-break issue of the summit. And what, after all, *was* the Israeli position on Jerusalem? Thirteen Israelis squashed into Barak's porch – they sat on the porch to avoid any bugs the Americans might have installed inside – for a meeting which, as Barak recalls, 'was one of the most weighty and fateful discussions I had ever participated in'.

After Barak's opening words, the first to speak was Israel Hasson, a straightforward, no-nonsense man, and former number 2 at Shin Bet who had spent much of his career in Jerusalem. He said they had two options. First, the city would remain united under Israeli sovereignty but the Palestinians would be granted 'functional autonomy'. The other option, said Hasson, was a clear-cut 'division' of Jerusalem according to agreed sovereignty. In any case, Hasson urged that the decision be taken now, before Israel found herself having to negotiate with hardline Islamists rather than with Arafat's moderates.[30] Barak's negotiator in previous formal talks with the Palestinians, Oded Eran, said that in the outer neighbourhoods of East Jerusalem, areas with which Jews had no historic connection, there lived some 130,000 Palestinians. Why on earth should Israel want to

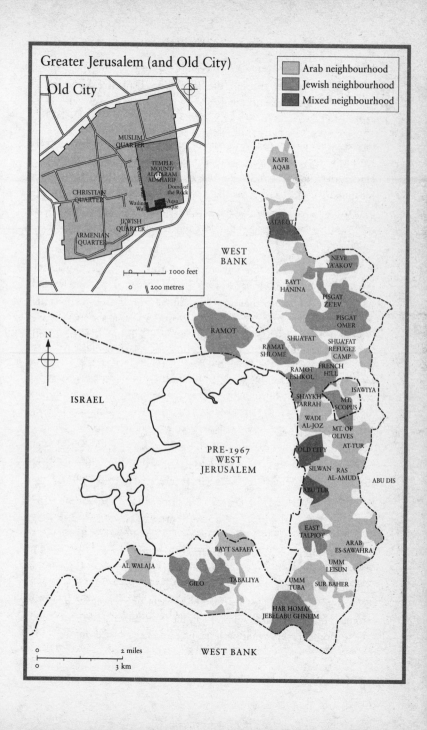

Greater Jerusalem (and Old City)

Arab neighbourhood
Jewish neighbourhood
Mixed neighbourhood

Old City

MUSLIM QUARTER

TEMPLE MOUNT/ AL-HARAM AL-SHARIF
Dome of the Rock

CHRISTIAN QUARTER

Wailing Wall
Aqsa Mosque

JEWISH QUARTER

ARMENIAN QUARTER

0 ————— 1000 feet
0 ——— 200 metres

N

ISRAEL

WEST BANK

KAFR AQAB

ATAROT

NEVE YA'AKOV

BAYT HANINA

PISGAT ZE'EV

PISGAT OMER

RAMOT

SHUA'FAT

SHUA'FAT REFUGEE CAMP

RAMAT SHLOME

RAMOT ESHKOL

FRENCH HILL

ISAWIYA

SHAYKH JARRAH

MT. SCOPUS

WADI AL-JOZ

MT. OF OLIVES

PRE-1967 WEST JERUSALEM

OLD CITY

AT-TUR

SILWAN

RAS AL-AMUD

ABU DIS

ABU TUR

EAST TALPIOT

ARAB ES-SAWAHRA

BAYT SAFAFA

UMM LEISUN

AL WALAJA

GILO

TABALIYA

UMM TUBA

SUR BAHER

HAR HOMA/ JEBELABU GHNEIM

0 ————— 2 miles
0 ——— 3 km

WEST BANK

annex these places? Annexation would be 'like accepting the principle of the right of return through the back door'. Dan Meridor, a former Likud Party member and the most hawkish delegate of Barak's team, said,

I'm against any concession when it comes to Israel's sovereignty [in Jerusalem] . . . any [attempt to] divide Jerusalem . . . is a serious blow not only for Jews in Israel. It also touches on Jews in New York, Moscow and Johannesburg . . . We have to offer Arafat a whole attractive package without however giving up our sovereignty in Jerusalem. Let him decide. Even if this leads to the collapse of the deal still I'm not willing to give up [on Jerusalem].

Barak intervened. 'It's a moment of truth,' he said; 'the Zionist movement has . . . put together two peoples [on one land] and it would be wrong to assume that the Palestinians' aspirations will simply disappear while with us it would continue to be a leading motive.' Amnon Lipkin-Shahak, a close associate of the Prime Minister, said,

What is Jerusalem? Large chunks of today's Jerusalem are not mine . . . The Israeli interest is to transfer as many Palestinians as possible to the Palestinian [Authority] and to remain with as few Arabs as possible under Israeli rule. Of course, we can't give up sovereignty on Temple Mount. We can't give that to Arafat, it's the cradle of Jewish history, but [on the other hand] we mustn't run Al-Aqsa. We have to find a way of giving the Palestinians a compound in the Muslim Quarter . . . if we don't get from them [a declaration of] End of Conflict it would not be wise to sign an agreement.

Barak's Chief of Staff Danny Yatom called for the adoption of a 'realistic' rather than an emotional approach, saying, 'We all know how the boundaries of Jerusalem were drawn [after the 1967 war] . . . they are not sacred . . . it is important to adopt our real red lines.' Eli Rubinstein, the right-wing religious Attorney General, agreed. 'We need to include as few Arabs as possible in Jerusalem . . . We have to get rid of Arab villages in the outer parts of Jerusalem. This is a moment of truth.' Barak, expressing the importance and the difficulty of the moment, said what perhaps reflected the general mood:

We're sitting here for three and a half hours in a discussion which tears each of us from the inside. And we have to decide . . . This decision is similar to that about [whether to accept the 1947] partition plan, or [whether to declare the] establishment of the state of Israel [in 1948], or Menachem Begin's decision to return the entire Sinai for a peace agreement with Egypt [in 1978] . . . We're sitting here, thirteen people, and we have to decide on matters which will affect millions. We can't delay . . . this decision . . . there is no way to avoid it . . . we cannot postpone it . . . and it is painful and tortuous . . . Without a decision . . . we are heading for a catastrophe, we see the iceberg in front of us, and we must make a decision.[31]

It was a long meeting, which started at 2.15 in the afternoon and went on until 6, resuming at 11 in the evening and not ending until well after midnight.

DAY 8: *TUESDAY, 18 JULY*

With Barak and his entire team in discussion the summit came to a virtual halt. The American Martin Indyk recalls how 'we were waiting and we were waiting, the hours rolled on, and dusk turned to darkness and still no sign of Barak'. The President became increasingly frustrated – after all he was supposed to be running the show – and finally sent Indyk to deliver the message that 'the President was waiting'. When Indyk got to Dogwood, Barak's Chief of Staff Danny Yatom told him the Prime Minister was 'indisposed'. Indyk asked: 'What's wrong?' Yatom replied: 'Well, he's just choked on a peanut . . . he is just recovering from that.'[32] Indyk had in fact showed up at Dogwood just at the end of a big drama that had started when one of the Israeli delegates told a joke:

Clinton went to Barak and Arafat and said, 'I've had enough of you here in Camp David. So look, there are three hundred monkeys out there in the nearby woods, and only one is male. I give you three minutes to bring me the male. Whoever brings me the male is the winner.' Barak goes off to the woods and in a very methodical, Barak-sort-of-way, arranges all the monkeys in rows and starts checking them one by one. He misses the target and returns empty-handed. So Arafat sets off. He stands in front of the monkeys and tells them, 'I am the President of Palestine, I am telling you, I will have the fourth of June borders, I will have Jerusalem, I will get the right of return.' From the top of a tree a monkey says, 'Come off it, if you get all of that, I'll cut my dick off.' So Arafat takes this one, and leaves the forest.[33]

Barak, rarely to be seen without a snack of some kind, was eating peanuts as the person telling the joke reached the punchline. He laughed so much that a peanut went down the wrong way and, unable to breathe, he started turning blue in the face. Gidi Grinstein recalls, 'We could see Barak was choking . . . everyone had their head in their hands. And Barak was on his way out. He was walking towards me, rocking from side to side and trying to breathe. Then, one of the team's members yelled, "He's suffocating, help him."' Grinstein remembered performing the Heimlich manoeuvre in his youth, and so tried it on Barak. He recalls, 'I grabbed Barak as he passed and . . . bumph. I had done this with friends and my brothers for years when we were young, playing around. It is very uncomfortable. But now I did it, and for real, for the first time. The peanut shot out.' Grinstein had saved the Prime Minister's life.

As soon as he had recovered, Barak took Shlomo Ben-Ami and Danny Yatom with him to see President Clinton. He brought a paper based on the Israeli team's long discussion, which posed a list of questions aimed at crystallizing the Palestinian positions on various matters, not least Jerusalem. But the paper was a retreat from some of the offers that Ben-Ami and Gilead Sher had made in the back channel. While the two had suggested Israel retained 10.5 per cent of the West Bank to preserve her large settlement blocs, Barak now said Israel must keep 11.3 per cent. And while in the back channel the Israelis had offered the Palestinians at least three Arab suburbs in East Jerusalem, Barak offered only one village. On almost every issue there was a retreat.

Forgetting (on purpose?) his promise that the back-channel negotiations were deniable and non-binding, the President lashed out at Barak: 'This is not real . . . this is not serious. I went to Shepherdstown [the Israeli–Syrian summit in January 2000] and was told nothing by you for four days. I went to Geneva [to meet Assad in March 2000] and felt like a puppet doing your bidding.'[34] With his voice rising even further and his face turning redder and redder, Clinton went on, 'I will not let it happen here. I will simply not do it.'[35] Robert Malley, note-taker at the meeting, recalls how the President 'exploded . . . and in language that I had not heard him use with Barak before, if with anyone . . . he said . . . "You've made me wait here for thirteen hours, and you come back with this? You go sell that to Arafat, if you want to. Don't ask me to do it. I'm not going to do that . . ."' In his memoirs President Clinton confirms this conversation, in less colourful language, when he writes, 'It was after midnight when Barak finally came to me with proposals. They were less than what Ben-Ami and Sher had already presented to the Palestinians. Ehud wanted me to present them to Arafat as US proposals. But I couldn't do that. It would have been a disaster, and I told him so.'[36]

Stunned by the President's outburst, Barak now spoke in a very soft voice. 'I cannot continue to play Arafat's game of manipulation,' he said. 'I find the way the Palestinians negotiate completely outrageous; their behaviour should not be tolerated.'[37] At 2.30 in the morning the meeting was over.

Martin Indyk, who was waiting outside, recalls Barak and his colleagues coming out of the President's lodge 'looking quite per-plexed and quite shocked . . . it was very clear . . . that the meeting had not gone well'. When Indyk walked into the cabin, the President was livid and red-faced. 'You won't believe what your friend Barak did', Clinton said to his ambassador to Israel. Indyk asked what happened. Clinton replied, 'He offered me less than his negotiators had offered the Palestinians already . . . he is just screwing around with me.' Indyk said, 'Look, you're his ally, you're his friend, you have to call him back and sit him down and ask him what's going on, and you have to ask him to level with you. He owes you that, he brought you here.'[38]

So Clinton called Barak back at 3.15 a.m. for a one-to-one meeting, with only a note-taker present, on the back patio of Aspen Cabin. This was now a critical moment and, as Clinton wrote in his memoirs,

'We talked for another hour on the back porch of my cabin. Essentially he gave me the go-ahead to see if I could work out a deal on Jerusalem and the West Bank that he could live with and that was consistent with what Ben-Ami and Sher had discussed in the back channel . . . That was worth staying up for.'[39] This was, indeed, a major break-through.

Optimism, however, was premature. When Clinton went to see Arafat to try to work out a deal based on the Israeli proposals made in the back channel, and a solution to Jerusalem Barak could 'live with', Arafat insisted that he would accept only full Palestinian sovereignty in East Jerusalem. Clinton knew that Barak could not live with that.

So it was deadlock again, and time was running out now because Clinton was scheduled to leave for a G8 summit in Okinawa, Japan on the following day. Originally, Clinton had hoped that by that time the summit would be over and he could go to the G8 triumphant with a settlement and ask them to help foot the bill.

It seemed as if only shock treatment could pull the summit out of the doldrums and it was US special envoy Dennis Ross who delivered it. He went to both the Israelis and the Palestinians to tell them that if Clinton did not hear something new from them in the next two hours, then he would declare the summit over. Ross proposed a package to the Israelis Shlomo Ben-Ami and Amnon Lipkin-Shahak: Jerusalem's outer neighbourhoods would be put under Palestinian sovereignty; the inner neighbourhoods would get 'meaningful' Palestinian self-government, including planning and zoning, security and dispute-resolution responsibility; in the Old City, the Palestinians would get sovereignty over the Muslim and Christian Quarters; on the Haram/Temple Mount, the Palestinians would get only custodianship, that is, they would run the place, but would have no sovereignty over it. Ben-Ami and Lipkin-Shahak were not happy, particularly with the idea of Palestinian sovereignty over the Christian Quarter, but nonetheless, with the two-hour deadline in mind, they took the package to Barak. Ross then took the same proposal to the two Mohammeds – Dahlan and Rashid – and sent them off to talk to Arafat.[40]

There was no word from the Palestinian camp, and the two-hour deadline passed with no response. Barak, on the other hand, responded in a big way – shocking everyone, including the Americans. He met Clinton on the front balcony of Dogwood at 10.30 in the evening and, dismissing their note-takers, the Prime Minister and the President stayed alone.

Barak now produced exactly the sort of package the President was waiting for. He said he would insist on retaining not 10.5 per cent but only 9 per cent of West Bank land for Israeli settlements. The Palestinians would be given a 1 per cent swap in Gaza by way of compensation. The Palestinians would also get sovereignty over 85 per cent of the border with Jordan. In Jerusalem, seven out of the nine outer neighbourhoods would come under Palestinian sovereignty; in the inner neighbourhoods they would be in charge of planning and zoning; and in the Old City the Muslim and Christian Quarters would come under Palestinian sovereignty. Regarding the Temple Mount/ Haram, the UN Security Council would pass a resolution to hand custodianship over it jointly to Palestine and Morocco, the Chair of the Jerusalem Committee (the higher Islamic commission in Jerusalem). On security, went Barak, Israeli needs would be met and Israel would have control of the Jordan Valley for up to twelve years before turning it over to the Palestinians. There would be a 'satisfactory solution' to the refugee question. Barak asked Clinton to present the offer to Arafat as a *US* proposal which the President would try to extract from Barak, *not* as Barak's idea.[41]

This was a generous, even stunning, offer, at the heart of which was something that had never before been proposed by an Israeli prime minister – the partitioning of Jerusalem. What brought Barak to put that offer on the table is a mystery. Perhaps the pressure-cooker atmosphere worked on him. Or perhaps he was gambling that Arafat would reject the offer and reveal his true colours as a fanatic who had come to Camp David only to squeeze concessions from Israel, not to strike a deal. As Barak said to *Elusive Peace*, 'if . . . Arafat would not consider this [generous offer] an opening . . . refuses to move forward, that would mean that indeed . . . he looks like a fanatic . . . walks like a fanatic . . . quacks like a fanatic and he is probably a fanatic'. Be it

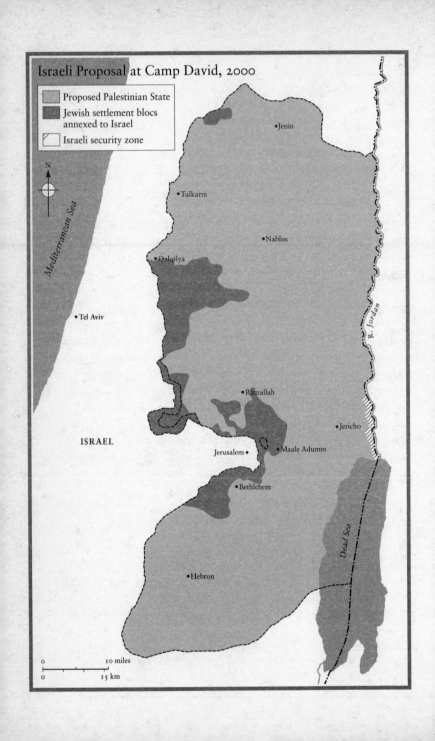

Israeli Proposal at Camp David, 2000

Proposed Palestinian State
Jewish settlement blocs
annexed to Israel
Israeli security zone

N

Mediterranean Sea

•Jenin

•Tulkarm

•Nablus

•Qalqilya

•Tel Aviv

ISRAEL

•Ramallah

•Jericho

Jerusalem • •Maale Adumin

•Bethlehem

R. Jordan

Dead Sea

•Hebron

0   10 miles
0   15 km

such a Machiavellian trick – a finely judged gamble to flush out Arafat's intentions – or a genuine attempt to break the deadlock, either way it was a remarkable offer. After the meeting Barak went straight to one of the cabins shared by his negotiators. He walked in and asked for a whisky.

According to Clinton's National Security Advisor Sandy Berger, 'What Barak presented to the President was extraordinarily dramatic ... And the President came back to Aspen lodge, asked to see just Madeleine [Albright], Dennis [Ross], myself alone, sat down and said, "I think we now have something to work with." ' But Camp David is a small place and the news of Barak's concession-cum-gamble quickly spread. According to the US ambassador Martin Indyk, 'The idea that half of the Old City would be under Arafat's sovereignty was completely unthinkable to any American at Camp David, and any Israeli, other than Ehud Barak himself.' Shlomo Ben-Ami of the Israeli team recalls Martin Indyk saying to him, 'Well, Barak's gone crazy.'

Clinton now asked for a face-to-face meeting with Arafat at Aspen, with only Gamal Helal present to interpret the conversation; all other members of the American team retreated to the kitchen. Here is Clinton's National Security Advisor Sandy Berger on what happened next: 'Madeline [Albright] and Dennis [Ross] and I and Rob [Malley] and Bruce [Riedel], we were all relegated to the kitchen. There was a kitchen door that led to the living room ... one of these swing doors with a little square window ... And we were all huddled behind the door, and alternatively one of us would go to the door and open it just a crack, peek through the window just a little bit so we could see what was going on.'[42]

In the main room, Clinton presented the offer to Arafat. Here is Sandy Berger again:

Clinton was using the full range of the piano board on Arafat. Every key, every note, he was cajoling, he was persuading, he was in some cases intimidating a bit. At one point he's leaning over Arafat. And Arafat listened mostly. I thought he looked like he was overwhelmed by this looming six-foot-four presence who was leaning, getting closer and closer and closer to his face as he was talking about this as being an historic moment.

Arafat listened carefully without responding. He said he wanted to go back and think about it, and he would then come back with an answer on whether or not he accepted the President's ideas as 'the basis to conclude a deal'. At the end of the meeting, the President and Gamal Helal accompanied the Palestinian leader outside, where Arafat kissed them, which left them hopeful. It was one o'clock in the morning and the ball was now squarely in Arafat's court. Would he grab the offer? Would he regard it as an opportunity not to be missed?

DAY 9: *WEDNESDAY, 19 JULY*

It was not, however, as straightforward as the President, his team and perhaps even Barak had thought. During the night Arafat dispatched emissaries to the Americans with a list of queries. What was the meaning of 'custodianship' for the Haram al-Sharif? Who would have sovereignty there? Since the Palestinians would have sovereignty over 85 per cent of the length of their border with Jordan, who would have control or sovereignty over the remaining 15 per cent? What was meant by a 'satisfactory solution' to the refugee problem? Why were only seven of the outer neighbourhoods going to get sovereignty and not all nine?[43] 'Then', as Robert Malley recalls, 'Arafat asked one more thing. He said, "Can I have a period where I will go and consult? Could we take a break? Could I consult with my Arab colleagues, because this goes way beyond my own prerogatives. We're talking about Jerusalem."' But Clinton would not accept this, fearing that if people left the pressure cooker of Camp David the whole deal would be frittered away. The President also feared, as did Barak, that Arafat would simply pocket the offer and use it at a later stage to ask for more concessions. Clinton insisted on a straight yes or no then and there, and that Arafat should spell out whether he regarded the offer as a basis for concluding a final deal.

When this answer came it was a no, which was, as Sandy Berger recalls, 'a very big setback for us'. Clinton thought there was no point in returning to Barak, who had conceded enough, and even if he were prepared to go further there was little chance that Barak could sell any more than was already on the table to his public.

At nine in the morning, Clinton went to see Arafat to press him to agree the deal; Arafat refused to budge. Madeleine Albright then tried, saying to him, 'You are blowing it', whereupon Arafat said, 'Do you want to come to my funeral?' He meant that if he accepted a deal which gave up the claim to Muslim sovereignty over the Haram al-Sharif, he would be finished in the Arab world, perhaps even assassinated.

Clinton started phoning Arab leaders, asking for their support to move Arafat to accept the deal. But it was to no avail. Arab leaders had not been involved before, and therefore they now refused to put pressure on Arafat as they were unsure of the full context of the negotiations. It was particularly difficult for them to press Arafat on the issue of Jerusalem, as Sandy Berger explains:

It was very unsettling for these Arab leaders, who have never been to Jerusalem, to visualize physically, let alone conceptually, what Barak was offering. Crown Prince Abdullah had never seen a map of Jerusalem, we later found out . . . it was too abrupt for them to absorb and deal with politically and otherwise.

When Arab leaders did intervene, it was not in the direction Clinton wanted. According to Arafat's close confidant Mohammed Rashid, the Saudi Foreign Minister, Prince Saud al-Faisal, who was on a visit to the United States, phoned Arafat to ask, 'What's going on there?' Arafat said, 'Well, Your Highness, they are trying to take Jerusalem from me, and to impose solutions about Jerusalem on me.' To which Prince Saud al-Faisal replied, 'Be careful, you can do everything, but nothing concerning Jerusalem. May God help you.' It clearly troubled Arafat. Rashid recalls how

Arafat came to my room and . . . he took me for a walk . . . and after that walk we went to his cabin . . . and he was jerking his legs in all directions [a sure sign of anxiety in Arafat], and he said, 'Listen, if they offered an acceptable solution on Jerusalem I could be flexible on other matters [but] I cannot go back to the Palestinian people and the Islamic and Arab nations without bringing Jerusalem back to Palestinian sovereignty . . . I cannot be flexible in terms of the Islamic and the Arab interests, otherwise this will lead to my assassination.'

When Clinton talked again to Arafat, trying to persuade him to accept the offered deal, Arafat now told Clinton that, in fact, the Jewish Temple was not in Jerusalem but in Nablus, and therefore there was no reason why Israel should have sovereignty over the Haram. Arafat was now challenging the core of the Jewish faith, and it was not the first time he had done this. Barak's right-hand man Danny Yatom recalls a conversation between Clinton and Arafat about Jerusalem:

Arafat said [to Clinton], 'You know, it is not at all a sacred place to the Jewish people. There is an instruction from the Chief Rabbi that no Jewish people should put their feet on Temple Mount.' And Clinton started laughing and said, 'On the contrary. This instruction is because it is so sacred . . . no one knows exactly where the remnants of the Jewish Temple are . . . so to avoid any transgression [Jews are not allowed to put their feet there]. Even I, a Christian, know this . . . How can you claim this is not a sacred place to the Jewish people?' And Arafat said, 'That's not the way I know it.'

As Clinton was preparing to leave for the G8 meeting in Okinawa, the Camp David summit was on the verge of collapse and preparations were under way to take the delegations back home. But then some Israeli and Palestinian negotiators got together. 'How can we leave? We haven't exhausted it yet . . . It's difficult but we must not fail', they said to each other.[44] They hatched a plan to draw Barak to the dining room and there press him to stay longer. By saying to Barak that they had better have one last meal before departing, the Israelis managed to entice their Prime Minister to the dining room. According to Israel Hasson,

When we got there we said, 'Ehud, you must listen to him . . . to him . . . to him.' And it worked. And then we arranged for Barak to talk to a group of our people – Israelis who we thought could convince him to stay on and we talked and said to the Americans, 'Make sure that Clinton is here', and then Ross isolated a Palestinian opposition . . . and Indyk . . . and then Clinton came in . . .

Clinton sat with Barak in the big room adjacent to the dining room and they talked alone for half an hour. Then, at 9.50 p.m., the Prime Minister convened his delegation to hear from them how they thought it best to proceed. Here are extracts from this meeting based on the diary of a member of the Israeli team:

GENERAL SHLOMO YANAI: 'We have to stay to discuss other issues [apart from Jerusalem], for example, security.'

ISRAEL HASSON: 'We have to stay on.'

DAN MERIDOR: 'We should not stay . . . Today it's clear who is responsible for the failure [of the summit].'

DANNY YATOM: 'We have to stay. Ehud [Barak] needs to talk to Arafat about Temple Mount.'

EHUD BARAK: 'I don't have any flexibility when it comes to Temple Mount.'

ELI RUBINSTEIN: 'When it comes to Jerusalem we have already passed the red lines . . . It's problematic if we stay here.'

AMNON LIPKIN-SHAHAK: 'If we leave now, there will be no meetings in the near future . . . Although the chance of reaching an agreement is lower than 50 per cent there is [some new] dynamic there [on the Palestinian side]. It would be right for Ehud [Barak] to meet with Arafat. If within 24 hours there are no results we should return home tomorrow afternoon.'

GILEAD SHER: 'Ehud [Barak] should meet Arafat.'

EHUD BARAK: 'I'm not going to sit with Arafat in order that he documents me in his notebook.'[45]

SHLOMO BEN-AMI: 'Arafat needs respect. You show no respect towards him. He can adopt more comfortable positions when there is respect. It's necessary to meet him.'

After the discussion Barak phoned Clinton and suggested the following arrangement: he would stay on at Camp David while the President went to the G8 summit, but on one condition – Arafat must first accept the deal put to him by Clinton the previous day, except for one issue, Jerusalem. On this, and *only* this issue, further discussions would continue to work out a formula.[46] At 11.40 p.m., Clinton went to see Arafat at Birch Cabin, but what he suggested to him was not quite what he had agreed with Barak. According to Akram Hanieh, who was present in the meeting, Clinton said, 'I have a new deal . . . I suggest that you stay here at Camp David until I return from Okinawa. Let a delegate from each side meet with the other and discuss the issue of Jerusalem and the Haram. The rest of the issues can also be discussed. I have spoken to Prime Minister Barak.'[47] Under the impression that nothing else was required of him other than to carry on negotiating as he had been, Arafat was happy to stay on, saying to Clinton, 'I consider this an order!' Clinton then rose, shook Arafat's hand and left the room. After that, as Robert Malley recalls, 'The President, Sandy [Berger] and I went to see Barak. And the President related his conversation with Arafat . . . making it sound like Arafat had agreed to what Barak wanted.' That is, that Arafat accepted the plan, and was staying to discuss *only* Jerusalem. In his memoirs Clinton wrote: 'Apparently I had not been as clear with Arafat as I thought I had been about what the terms of staying on should be.'[48] Referring to this bizarre episode, an American diplomat explains that 'we didn't wrap ourselves in glory', and that Clinton was so economical with the truth because he 'didn't want to go to Okinawa with a failure'.

DAY 10: *THURSDAY, 20 JULY*

The President departed for Okinawa leaving behind him a tangle of misconceptions, with Barak and Arafat having completely different understandings of the basis on which they had stayed on, and what should happen next. Arafat thought that discussions would continue on *all* subjects, while Barak thought the only stumbling block to be tackled while the President was away was Jerusalem. When Barak discovered the truth soon after Clinton's departure, he was livid with Arafat, thinking he was playing one of his tricks and acting in bad faith.

It was left to Secretary of State Albright to sort out the mess, and she thought a social event might do the trick. She organized a dinner for the delegates, to take place at nine in the evening at Laurel. However, Barak refused to play the polite guest. Gilead Sher recalls, 'He came into the dining room and avoided Arafat, sliding past him without any contact.' During the meal Barak was grumpy, miserable and distant. Then Albright stood up and gave a speech, admitting there was a mistake – it was the Americans' mistake and 'none of the leaders is to be blamed'. She added, 'The President's ideas are off . . . negotiate as if the President's ideas are null and void.'[49]

This, in fact, brightened Barak's mood a bit. The 'President's ideas', we should recall, were in fact Barak's ideas, which he had asked the President to present to Arafat as if they were his own. When Arafat rejected these ideas, Barak felt he had exposed Arafat as not interested in a deal. Now, with the real Arafat unmasked, Barak was satisfied to have the offer declared 'null and void' and returned to him. When Barak left the table and went to help himself to pudding he passed by one of the Israeli negotiators, leaned over and whispered in his ear, 'Have you heard? The President's ideas are off, it's good for us.' According to this delegate, 'This strengthens my feeling that Barak was looking for a way to retreat from things he had probably told the President regarding the Old City – the Muslim and Christian Quarters.'[50] After dinner, Barak instructed his delegation that there should be no discussions on either Jerusalem or any other issue – no talks with the Palestinians at all – until the President was back.

DAY 11: *FRIDAY, 21 JULY*

Barak now isolated himself in his cabin and sent word that he was not to be disturbed. When his loyal aide Gilead Sher cycled over to see that Barak was still OK, he found the Prime Minister 'very upset, unshaved, reading'.[51] Barak recalls: 'I preferred to close myself up in my cabin, and I sat there . . . I took walks around the camp, which looked like a prison, and I read a book about Churchill.' During the day, Albright phoned Barak's Chief of Staff Danny Yatom to say that she was on her way to talk to Barak. Yatom recalls:

I rushed to Barak. I got there before she did, of course, and I said, 'Listen, Albright's on her way to here.' He said, 'Danny, hold her up, I don't want to see her, I'm going for a walk.' He put on his sneakers and his old tracksuit, and when Albright reached the cabin I said, 'I'm sorry, Barak's out on his daily walk.'

Albright then had a new idea to brighten Barak's mood. She knew the Prime Minister was a keen pianist and thought that 'we might arrange for a piano to be moved into his cabin, allowing him to practise'. But realizing she would need to ask him first, and since Barak was not taking phone calls, she decided 'to bump into him during his afternoon walk'. Albright asked the Secret Service to report to her the route which Barak would usually take, and this is what happened next, as she recalls:

In the woods I strode toward him and he toward me. His eyes were on the ground . . . I said, 'Hello.' 'Hello,' he replied. I said, 'How are you doing?' 'Fine.' I said, 'With the President away, we thought you might want a diversion. Would you like us to have a piano moved into your cabin?' He answered, 'No.' I inquired, 'No?' Again, he said, 'No.'[52]

It was the Sabbath, but Barak failed to join the Sabbath meal. An Israeli delegate wrote in his diary: 'Ehud will not join us at the Sabbath dinner. I suppose this is all to do with his feeling that the American president "tricked" him and he can't see how to proceed from here.'[53] At around 10.30 in the evening, delegates joined Albright at Hickory Cabin, where she hosted a 'boy' movie, *U-571*, the story of an American mission during the Second World War to capture an Enigma machine from a German submarine. 'We have seen better', an Israeli delegate confided to his diary.[54]

DAY 12: *SATURDAY*, 22 JULY

George Tenet, the director of the CIA, arrived at Camp David to see if he could help with the talks, particularly on security matters. When told by colleagues about the latest Barak offer, Tenet was surprised how far the Prime Minister was willing to move, and stunned that Arafat had not grabbed it. Knowing how much Barak respected Tenet, Martin Indyk of the American team went to see if the Prime Minister would agree to see the CIA director, but Barak refused.

Barak requested a day trip out of Camp David, and a visit to the Gettysburg battlefield was organized for the next day. Of course,

1. (*Above*) As top-level Israeli–Syrian talks take place in Shepherdstown, West Virginia, in January 2000, more than 100,000 Israelis gather in Tel Aviv to protest against withdrawal from the Golan Heights. The demonstration does not go unnoticed – President Clinton and his team (*below*) have just learnt that Prime Minister Barak would not offer any concessions to the Syrians, because of the pressure he was under at home.

2. (*Above*) Clinton watches Yasser Arafat shake hands with Ehud Barak at Camp David on the first day of a summit aimed at sorting out the Israeli–Palestinian conflict. (*Below*) Clinton meets Arafat and Barak on the last day of the summit, as it collapses after fifteen days of intense negotiations.

3. Surrounded by bodyguards, the leader of the right-wing Likud Party, Ariel Sharon, smiles as he departs the Temple Mount/Haram al-Sharif in Jerusalem on 28 September 2000. His visit was highly provocative to the Muslim community, and is often blamed for setting off the Al-Aqsa intifada. (*Below*) Muslims attend a rally at the Haram al-Sharif compound in front of the Dome of the Rock, their third holiest site after Mecca and Medina.

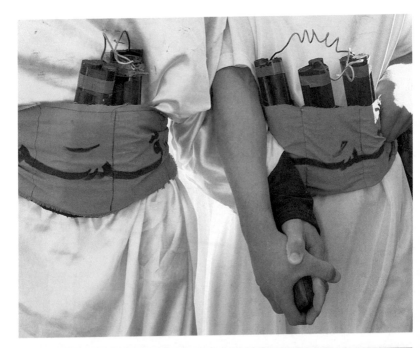

4. (*Above*) Members of the militant group Islamic Jihad, explosives strapped around their waists, march through Gaza City during a rally on 22 December 2000. (*Below*) An Israeli bus burning at Beit Lid junction near Netanya, 9 September 2001, after a Palestinian suicide bomber detonates his device.

5. (*Above*) A poster of Yasser Arafat behind an Israeli tank in Ramallah during Operation Defensive Shield, March–April 2002. In a sweeping invasion, Israeli forces reoccupied every major Palestinian town and city, causing numerous casualties and substantial damage. (*Below*) A Palestinian child cries amidst the devastation of the Jenin refugee camp, where the Israelis fought a hard battle with entrenched militants.

6. (*Above*) Israeli forces blow up a building in Yasser Arafat's compound in Ramallah, the *muqata*, where all but Arafat's own office was destroyed. (*Below*) Arafat inspects his debris-strewn bed after the nearby explosion.

7. (*Above*) At a rally in Jerusalem on 23 February 2004, Israeli high-school students look at pictures of Israelis killed by Palestinian militants. (*Right*) A Palestinian looks at a poster of Palestinians killed by Israeli forces.

8. (*Above*) The helicopter carrying the body of Yasser Arafat comes in to land at the *muqata* in Ramallah, amongst a howling crowd of tens of thousands of Palestinians, gathered to witness Arafat's burial. The helicopter had to hover for some time before the crowd parted far enough to allow a precarious landing. (*Left*) Abu Mazen (Mahmoud Abbas), elected as Arafat's successor, sits beside the empty chair of the former leader, whose portrait gazes over the Palestinian Cabinet's meeting room.

Arafat then had to be allowed to leave as well, so Albright invited him to her farm located about twenty-five minutes away. She recalls:

When we got there my two-year-old grandson had just woken up from a nap, and took one look at Arafat and screamed, and I thought this is the end of this. Then we sat by the swimming pool, and Arafat told stories . . . that he liked Tom and Jerry cartoons, and he cheered my other grandson diving off the diving board, and he kissed my granddaughter, and then we have this completely lunatic picture of Arafat standing among all these people in their bathing suits, and he is in his uniform, it looks as though we had a cut-out figure that just joined us.

Major Mohammed al-Daya, Arafat's bodyguard who accompanied the Palestinian leader on this visit, remembers how 'after lunch [Albright] took us for a tour round her garden and she told Abu Amar, "After I retire I will come and live in this house." And she told him: "You can make me the greatest Secretary of State in the whole world . . . if [you] sign the agreement [with Barak]." Abu Amar looked at her and smiled but didn't reply.'[55]

Back at Camp David, it was a quiet day – the negotiators went ten-pin bowling in Camp David's own bowling alley. *Gladiator* was shown in the cinema.

DAY 13: *SUNDAY, 23 JULY*

At 6.25 in the evening, a helicopter landed at Camp David and out of it came the President, with his daughter Chelsea beside him. He jumped into a golf cart and drove to Aspen. He was full of energy and waved to delegates he encountered, saying, 'Hey guys, I'm back, let's get back to work.' He sat with aides, then saw Arafat and Barak separately, and at 11.30 p.m. embarked on a marathon series of meetings. Some progress was made on security issues: on Israeli early warning stations in the West Bank after their withdrawal; on airspace use by the Israelis over the future Palestinian state; on co-operation in the fight against terrorism. There were mixed results on demilitarization of the future Palestinian state – the Israelis insisted on Palestine not having an army at all, but the Palestinians were adamant on having armed forces as do other independent states. There were also mixed results on the Israeli demand to have a presence in the Jordan Valley after their withdrawal and to have access routes in the West Bank in the event of a threat from the east.[56]

DAY 14: *MONDAY, 24 JULY*

They broke at 5.30 in the morning, resuming again later and continued throughout the day. It was no secret that the main stumbling block remained Jerusalem. The real moment of truth came that night, when at 9.30 the Israeli Shlomo Ben-Ami and the Palestinian Saeb Erekat joined President Clinton, his National Security Advisor Sandy Berger and Secretary of State Madeleine Albright to try to tackle this problem. If Jerusalem was out of the way, then everything else, it was thought, would fall into place.

DAY 15: *TUESDAY, 25 JULY*

It was past midnight when Clinton said to Saeb Erekat, 'How about I try to get you the following: sovereignty in the outer neighbourhoods [of Jerusalem]; limited sovereignty in the inner neighbourhoods; sovereignty in the Muslim and Christian Quarters of the holy city, with *custodial sovereignty* over the Haram.'[57] Erekat wrote this down and the President added, 'I have no earthly idea whether Barak can accept this.' The critical addition in Clinton's proposal was, of course, 'custodial sovereignty' over the Haram al-Sharif, and Shlomo Ben-Ami, listening attentively to the President's offer, was uneasy. 'This is too much', he said to Clinton; 'it goes beyond what Barak can accept.'[58] But for Saeb Erekat even that was not enough. 'President Arafat instructed me', he said to Clinton, 'not to accept anything less than Palestinian sovereignty over all areas of Jerusalem occupied in 1967, and at the forefront, Haram al-Sharif.'[59] Clinton said, 'Take the proposal to President Arafat and get back to me.'

Erekat left and Shlomo Ben-Ami stayed a little longer to talk to the President. 'Clinton looked tired', Ben-Ami recalls; 'he was wearing jeans, these sort of scruffy jeans, it was very late in the evening, and [referring to the time left for him in office] he said, "I don't have the time."'

Meanwhile the Palestinians reviewed the latest proposal and, according to Akram Hanieh, 'the proposal did not need much discussion', for without full sovereignty over the Haram al-Sharif they felt they could not respond positively. With that, they started work on a letter stating their response to the proposal, and the entire summit. At three in the morning Mohammed Dahlan and Saeb Erekat were sent to deliver the letter to Clinton. As Dahlan recalls,

Arafat chose me and Dr Saeb Erekat to deliver the message . . . it was raining, and we walked to President Clinton . . . Of course, President Clinton realized from the moment we walked in that we were carrying a rejection . . . from the way we looked . . . the way we entered, our performance, it was obvious, but it was a touching moment.

Albright recalls how 'when the answer came that Arafat does not agree to the ideas . . . the President . . . sank back into the chair, and he said, "I really – I don't like to fail and especially at something like this."' Seeing that Clinton was at the end of his tether, Saeb Erekat launched into an impassioned and dramatic appeal. 'Mr President,' he said,

what you did is unprecedented. I've been following this conflict, breathing it, all my life. I've never seen Palestinians and Israelis discuss Jerusalem, discuss the Old City, discuss borders, discuss refugees. We have broken so many taboos. Things that have been forbidden for us all our lives are now talked about. It's to your credit. What you did is historic. Wherever we go after this, we're not going to reinvent the wheel. It's going to be the Clinton Camp David.[60]

At around 3.15 in the morning Clinton reported Arafat's rejection to Prime Minister Barak, and half an hour later Barak asked to see Dennis Ross. He was solemn, predicting that the collapse of the summit would lead to a direct and violent confrontation with the Palestinians. He said he would now need urgent US support, and proceeded to list what was politically essential for him. He needed Clinton to declare that all ideas presented at Camp David were null and void, and he asked for something more to show the Israelis what he had really won for his co-operative gestures: a new strategic upgrade of Israeli–American relations and a package of new military support to show that Camp David had not weakened Israel; the US embassy to be moved from Tel Aviv to Jerusalem, to show that Barak's offers had strengthened, not weakened, the Israeli hold on Jerusalem; and a US commitment to fight a unilateral declaration of statehood by the Palestinians, including a guarantee of opposition to admission to the UN of that state if it was unilaterally declared. Ross promised to discuss these requests with Clinton.[61]

Clinton met Arafat and Barak at 10.30 in the morning; it was the first and only trilateral meeting at Camp David, but for all practical purposes the summit was over. Clinton now felt that it was time to help Barak, to shore him up politically, so the peace camp in Israel would not collapse after the summit and the peace process could continue.

Martin Indyk and Aaron Miller of the American team had been drafting a statement to be read by the President at the end of the summit since it had become clear failure was imminent the previous night. Their major concern was that the situation on the ground, particularly in the occupied territories, was going to ignite because of the disappointment on both sides, unless a positive spin could be put on events. Indyk and Miller wanted the President not to take sides and not to blame either Arafat or Barak for the failure of the summit. Thus their statement was balanced and did not assign blame to either side. But, as he reviewed this statement over breakfast, Clinton rewrote some of the passages and at the press conference his pitch came from his heart. He said he had enormous respect for what Barak had done and the Israeli public should be proud of their Prime Minister. There was no similar praise for Arafat. 'The language that was used', as Robert Malley recalls, 'was to say that Barak had shown real courage and vision and that Arafat had reiterated his commitment to peace, which was a way of saying that one showed courage and the other showed up.'[62]

Before going to Camp David it had been agreed among the parties, and had been guaranteed by Clinton, that whatever the results of the summit, Barak would continue to withdraw from areas he had already promised to Arafat and, in particular, he would transfer the three Arab villages near Jerusalem. But now Clinton said to Barak that, although he would not say so publicly, he did not expect Barak to withdraw from more land or transfer the villages. 'You were ready to cut your legs off for this guy,' Clinton said to Barak. 'If I were you I wouldn't have done the redeployment.'[63] The hint was clear.

9

Picking Up the Pieces

From the moment Camp David ended, Barak's mind switched to his next mission – crusade is perhaps a better word to describe it – to spread the word that the debacle at Camp David was Yasser Arafat's fault. On the plane back to Israel, Barak requested a world map and assigned people to go off and tell the world what *really* happened – how Barak was generous but Arafat turned down his big offers.

Barak had a bumpy landing in Israel, where the collapse of the summit was regarded as a personal defeat and all newspaper headlines screamed 'Failure'. Even a sympathetic appearance by President Clinton on Israeli television, in which he laid the blame for the failure of Camp David squarely at Arafat's door, did little to change Israeli public opinion. There was no such bumpy landing for Arafat, though, who was received in the Palestinian territories as a hero who had had the guts to stand up to a unified Barak–Clinton front.

It became a war of words, with Palestinian propagandists also taking up the cudgels and touring the world's capitals blaming the Israelis for the collapse. Finger-pointing became the Camp David legacy; the peace process took a break while the parties threw mud at each other.

'I HAVE A PARTNER, MY PARTNER IS YASSER ARAFAT'

Barak's aides were still putting pressure on him to meet Arafat, to make a gesture that might restart the negotiations. Eventually, Barak reluctantly agreed to see the Palestinian leader.

On 25 September 2000, a Black Hawk helicopter was dispatched to fetch Arafat and some of his colleagues and bring them to Barak's home at Kochav Yair. The Prime Minister was waiting for them at the gate. The two leaders then went through the usual process of hugging and kissing like old friends, before entering to enjoy Nava Barak's chicken casserole.

Just before the meeting Israel Hasson, one of Barak's peace negotiators, said to the Prime Minister, 'You just have to talk to [Arafat], take him and talk to him.' Barak asked, 'What am I to do with all the others [guests]?' Hasson replied: 'We will take care of them . . . and you will go out with Arafat.'[1] Barak did as he was told, and, as the Palestinian Saeb Erekat recalls, 'All of a sudden, they both stand up and say, "We're going to go outside." There was a veranda . . . They opened the glass gate, and then they shut the glass gate behind them and they took their plates with them. I had my dinner, but I never took my eyes off what was going on outside.' Thus, exactly two months to the day after Camp David ended, Barak and Arafat did something they had failed to accomplish throughout the summit – talk to each other. In an interview for *Elusive Peace* Barak recalls what he said to Arafat:

Look, Mr Chairman, we are dealing with perhaps the most complicated conflict on the planet today . . . but it will not be solved in heaven, it will only be solved by us here on earth, and it puts a great responsibility on us, because if we cannot do it, there is no one else who can make the decisions. We have not succeeded so far, and we have a final chance to make the decisions, and these are painful decisions, and if we do not make them then thousands of people will die on both sides, and we will not be able finally to explain our failure to our children, and our children's children.

They also talked about the recent announcement by the leader of the Israeli opposition, Ariel Sharon, of his intention to visit Temple Mount in Jerusalem. This was certain to be seen by Palestinians as provocative, particularly coming in the wake of the failed Camp David summit as it did. Arafat urged Barak to stop Sharon, otherwise, he will 'destroy everything', to which Barak replied, 'I'm a democracy . . . I can't prevent the leader of the opposition from doing what he pleases.'[2] Back in the sitting room, as the Israeli negotiator Gilead Sher recalls, Sharon's visit was also raised 'with a lot of concern by Abu Ala, who said, "You know it's very dangerous . . . it might result in serious bloodshed . . . this is not the moment, you have to do whatever you can in order to stop it."'

When Barak and Arafat returned from their tête-à-tête to join the guests they smiled, and told them they were committed to the 'peace of the brave'.[3] Forewarned of the meeting, President Clinton phoned from Washington, and talked to Barak and Arafat. 'Mr President,' said Barak, 'I have a partner, my partner is Yasser Arafat, and with him I am going to sign an agreement.' Arafat reciprocated by telling Clinton, 'I'll be Barak's partner as I was Rabin's.'[4]

The two leaders then announced the launch of a new round of talks, to take place in Washington, and, as Gilead Sher recalls, 'they said to us, "Go ahead, go to Washington, come up with an agreement, *inshallah*."'[5]

'THE PEOPLE ARE TIRED'

That very night the negotiators flew to Washington to start peace talks the next day at the Ritz Carlton Hotel.[6] Their task was to try to narrow the remaining gaps between them and incorporate the ideas raised at Camp David into letters of invitation for yet another summit of leaders. It was thought that even if such a summit was not convened, at least there would be principles accepted – which would be a historic achievement in itself.

But, as it was the night before, hanging over the talks like the proverbial sword of Damocles was Ariel Sharon's forthcoming visit to Temple Mount in Jerusalem. Mohammed Dahlan, the Palestinian negotiator, urged the Israelis and Americans to stop the visit. He said to Shlomo Ben-Ami that if the visit took place, then

It will be the beginning of clashes between Israelis and Palestinians . . . if Sharon visits the Haram there will be a crisis and no one could control it . . . the people are tired . . . and [Sharon's forthcoming visit] is a big excuse for [Palestinians] who [are] under pressure to react . . . if Sharon visits the

Haram then there will be a serious crisis between Israelis and Palestinians.[7]

From Washington, Israel Hasson phoned Jibril Rajoub, the Palestinian in charge of security in the West Bank. 'Jibril,' he said, 'we can't tell Sharon not to go to the Temple Mount, it's his right.' Rajoub replied, 'There is no way he should go into the mosques [which are on the Haram / Temple Mount].' Hasson said, 'Sharon didn't ask [to enter them].'[8] When Hasson finished talking to Rajoub he handed the receiver over to Shlomo Ben-Ami, to whom Rajoub said, 'I'm in control . . . if he doesn't enter the mosques everything should be OK.'[9] Gilead Sher recalls how, after the conversation with Rajoub, Shlomo Ben-Ami reported to them what Rajoub had just told him. Ben-Ami said:

He told me that if Ariel Sharon did not enter the mosques, then the situation would be acceptable. It would be bad, it would be difficult, it would be better if there was no visit, but if Sharon stayed only in the courtyard and did not enter the mosques, then Rajoub could deal with the situation.

It is perhaps worth mentioning that this version of events is contentious. Jibril Rajoub, in an interview for *Elusive Peace*, fiercely rejects Shlomo Ben-Ami's account.

The fuse had been lit, however, and the region was on the verge of a huge explosion.

10

Death at the Mosque

'TEMPLE MOUNT IS IN OUR HANDS'

On 28 September 2000, wearing dark sunglasses and escorted by more than 1,000 police officers, the leader of the Likud opposition, Ariel Sharon, paid a visit to Jerusalem 'to examine archaeological sites on Temple Mount'. Sharon's visit had more to do with domestic politics than archaeology, however, and by visiting Temple Mount he was attempting to do two things. First, to further weaken the already wounded Barak by showing a strong position on Jerusalem – that, unlike the Prime Minister, who put Jerusalem on the negotiating table at Camp David, Sharon would never sacrifice Jerusalem, would never negotiate it.[1] And second, to boost his political stature and steal the limelight from the former Prime Minister Benjamin Netanyahu, a potential rival for the Likud Party's leadership.[2]

Sharon was often dubbed by Arabs 'the butcher of Beirut', and his visit came close to the anniversary of the 1982 massacre of Palestinians at Sabra and Shatilla refugee camps during the Israeli invasion of Lebanon, of which Sharon himself, Defence Minister at the time, was the chief architect. These were factors that made the visit controversial and provocative to Arabs.[3]

Sharon toured the Temple Mount/Haram that fateful morning, and though he was careful not to enter the mosques in the compound, he declared to the press, 'Temple Mount is in our hands and will remain in our hands.'[4]

'STOP KILLING'

The visit itself passed more or less peacefully, with only minor skirmishes and stone-throwing, and for the Israeli and Palestinian negotiators in Washington this was a profound relief. Their relief was premature.

The day after Sharon's visit to Temple Mount, Palestinian demonstrations erupted, some organized by local leaders and others spontaneous. On the Haram itself, Israeli police responded harshly, using live ammunition against the rioters and killing and wounding many of them. These, we now know, were the first shots of the Al-Aqsa intifada although it had yet to gain that name.

At first the violence was confined to the West Bank. To ensure that riots did not spread to the Gaza Strip, Mohammed Dahlan, head of Preventive Security forces there, talked to the IDF's Chief of Staff Shaul Mofaz. Dahlan told the military chief, 'Stop killing . . . and don't do it here in the Gaza Strip. The Gaza Strip is something different than the West Bank. If you open fire [in the Gaza Strip], it will be a disaster.'[5] But when Palestinian demonstrations did spread to the Gaza Strip, the Israeli army reacted with massive force, killing scores of Palestinians. After that, Mofaz phoned Dahlan, inviting him for a consultation to see how they could work together to contain the growing violence. Dahlan, however, declined, telling Mofaz, as he recalls, 'No . . . No way. Maybe we'll meet after a year or two.'

Meanwhile, both in the Gaza Strip and the West Bank, the army used overwhelming force to disperse the riots; this led to great numbers of casualties among the Palestinians compared with very few on the Israeli side. During the first days of the riots, the Israeli army fired between 1 and 1.3 million bullets.[6]

Just two days after Sharon's controversial visit to Temple Mount, the world watched live on TV the agonizing death of a twelve-year-old Palestinian boy, Mohammed al-Dura, pinned down in crossfire between Palestinian snipers and Israeli troops. Mohammed was crouching in terror behind his father, Jamal, who struggled in vain to protect his son from the gunfire. Millions witnessed the moment the boy's life was snuffed out by a bullet, either Israeli or Palestinian. He died there, cradled in his father's arms, another martyr to fuel the rapidly escalating fires of the Al-Aqsa intifada.

'ON THE BASIS OF MY EXPERIENCE OF GUERRILLA WARFARE IN ALGERIA'

A week into the intifada, Secretary of State Albright called a summit in Paris to thrash out a ceasefire agreement. She had agreed with the French President Jacques Chirac that, although in Paris he was of course the official host, she would run the talks at the US ambassador's palatial residence in rue du Faubourg Saint-Honoré. It was also agreed, and this was a promise Yasser Arafat made specifically to the Egyptian President Hosni Mubarak, which Barak also accepted, that when an agreement was initialled in Paris, the official signing ceremony would take place in Sharm el-Sheikh in Egypt.

When the parties arrived in Paris they each first paid a courtesy call on President Chirac. Arafat was the first to go to the Élysée Palace. He told Chirac, 'Ehud Barak made a major mistake in letting Sharon go to the Plaza of the Mosques . . . all Muslims saw his visit as a provocation.' Arafat said that he would insist on three conditions during the Paris talks: observance of a ceasefire by the Israelis; their withdrawal from recently occupied lands; and the establishment of a commission of inquiry into the start of the intifada. Chirac, according to his Foreign Minister Hubert Vedrine, told Arafat 'not to lay out any prerequisites . . . that he should agree to talk with Barak and Albright without any prerequisites but at the same time [Chirac had promised that he] will try and get the Israelis to agree to a commission of inquiry'.[7]

While Arafat was visiting Chirac, Barak and his team were meeting Secretary of State Albright and Dennis Ross at the US ambassador's residence. Barak said to them: 'I'm not sure that Arafat wants to put an end [to the violence] . . . We're sure that he can put an immediate end to this [but he is not interested] . . . Arafat has to collect [illegal] weapons . . . if he can't, it's because he is a gang leader, not a political leader.'[8]

At noon Barak arrived at the Élysée. President Chirac first told him what Arafat had said but Barak denied it was his fault: 'It's all the fault of Arafat. He has given orders to fire [at us] . . . and even when he doesn't [give such orders], he turns a blind eye when his men open fire . . . All our army is doing is reacting.' When, as he had promised Arafat, Chirac asked Barak to agree to an international commission of inquiry into the events leading to the outbreak of the intifada, Barak simply said, 'We reject the idea.'⁹ Foreign Minister Vedrine said to Barak: 'A gesture has to be made as a first step. It would be good if, here in Paris, Israel made a gesture towards Arafat.'¹⁰ Barak replied, 'Today he's asking for one gesture, and tomorrow he'll ask for another one. Every time we make a gesture, he demands more.' Chirac then said:

I would like to point out that no countries and no media subscribe to the Israeli version of events. The whole world shares the same feeling, even Mexico . . . Sharon provoked these incidents and he did so with the consent of your government. The discrepancies have to be considered: sixty-four Palestinians and nine Israeli Arabs dead, 2,300 Palestinians wounded, while, on the Israeli side, only two civilians and one soldier were killed. No one can believe that the Palestinians are to blame for this chain of violence. On the basis of my experience of guerrilla warfare in Algeria, I know how to interpret this kind of imbalance. Using combat helicopters against stone throwers is unacceptable . . . It's up to Israel to make the first gesture.¹¹

To that long speech Barak replied by saying that 'Arafat must not be rewarded for his bad behaviour.'

Meanwhile Arafat went for his meeting with Secretary Albright. He said that it was 'out of the question that there should be no commission of inquiry'. Albright replied, 'Do you really need the French? The United Nations? Do you really want us to go back to the time of useless commissions of inquiry?'¹²

At three o'clock, the negotiating teams settled down in the American ambassador's residence. Progress was slow as 'there were frequent fireworks between Arafat and Barak . . . there was that animosity which was very clear'.¹³ Again, the main bone of contention was whether there should be an international commission of inquiry to investigate responsibility for the outbreak of violence. Barak was not willing to accept such an investigation, as the Israelis were always against internationalizing the conflict. He did not trust the UN, where there was a huge majority against Israel, and would accept only a US-led investigation. But Arafat insisted on a UN-led investigation 'with a senior figure like [Nelson] Mandela presiding over it'.[14]

'TWO POLAR BEARS'

They sat for hours trying to reach some kind of agreement in order to stop the violence. Barak told Arafat repeatedly that he must instruct his people on the ground to stop the riots. Gamal Helal, Secretary Albright's translator, recalls how 'Prime Minister Barak actually moved from his side of the table to Chairman Arafat's side and, in a serious, genuine way, tried to tell him, "Do your part and end this intifada."'[15] Barak urged Arafat to pick up the phone and talk to the people who were adding 'fuel to the fire' and instruct them to stop doing so. 'I couldn't hold back', Barak recalls in our interview,

and I said, 'Mr Chairman, perhaps you can make a phone call to Marwan Bargouti and Hussein al-Sheikh and tell them, with us listening, that you are instructing them to stop the riots.' Arafat looked at me and said, 'Who? Who?' with an expression of someone who was hearing the names of two polar bears. So I thought maybe my accent in Arabic is not good enough, so I repeated the names, this time with a pronounced, clear Arabic inflection – 'Mar-wan Bar-gou-ti' and 'Hu-sse-in a Sheikh' – and Arafat again, 'Who? Who?'

Even some of Arafat's aides could not stop themselves laughing at this, because, as Barak recalls, 'it was clear to them that he knew that I know that these are the two people who are organizing the riots'. Forced to drop the pretence, Arafat picked up the phone and talked to the two, instructing them in Arabic – just as the Israelis who were listening to the conversation hoped – to calm down the situation.

'SHUT THE GATES . . . SHUT THE GATES'

Secretary of State Albright now left the main room to consult with Barak, leaving Arafat on his own. As his aide Saeb Erekat recalls, 'Arafat then stood up, starting looking at paintings, looking at things.' When Robert Malley of the American peace team saw Arafat 'pacing and pacing and pacing' he went over to talk to him. He found a very angry man. 'You think I don't know what's happening?' Arafat shot out at Malley. 'You think I don't know what's happening? I know why I'm waiting. I know that you're on the phone and Barak is on the phone with Chirac to try to turn him against me, and I'm not going to accept this.' With this, Arafat turned on his heels and headed for the exit, followed by his ambassador in Paris, Leila Shahid. 'Before we knew it,' Robert Malley recalls, 'Arafat was storming out of the door.'[16] Barak's Chief of Staff, Danny Yatom, witnessed what happened next. 'Suddenly,' he recalls, 'I saw Albright . . . chasing Arafat. It was the first time in my life I ever saw her running. It was funny. Arafat running like a duck, Albright chasing him.' Still running, Secretary Albright shouted to the guards, 'Shut the gates . . . Shut the gates' to prevent Arafat's car from leaving the grounds. Albright recalls 'running [after Arafat] in my high heels'. Her aide, Gamal Helal, pleaded: 'Madam Secretary, please let him go, let him go, please, just let him go.' But Albright would not have it. 'No', she shot back, 'he's not going anywhere, we still have business to continue, and we have to have him back.'[17] Major Mohammed al-Daya, Arafat's bodyguard, recalls what happened next: 'She . . . stood by the car and knocked on the window . . . Arafat looked the other way . . . So she entered the car . . . and she sat next to Arafat in the car. And she started talking to him.' According to Albright: 'I got into the car with Arafat, and I said, "Look, Mr Chairman, we have come so far, we have gotten agreement on a lot of points, I'm sorry that I couldn't sit with you because I was trying to get the Israelis to agree, will you come back in?' Arafat complied and, as Erekat recalls, 'he kissed her hand and they walked back in and they reconciled on the way'.

With Arafat back, the trilateral meeting restarted. It was a relatively relaxed and even intimate discussion. They talked about how the violence had started in the first place with young Palestinians throwing stones at Jews praying at the Wailing Wall. Barak and Arafat had an animated discussion about whether it was at all possible for someone standing on the Haram to hit Jews praying just under them at the Wall. Arafat maintained, 'Nobody can throw a stone at Jews praying at the Wailing Wall.' Barak replied, 'How do you mean they can't throw stones? . . . of course they can throw stones . . . I've commanded the area and I know precisely how stones can be thrown there.' Arafat said, 'I know . . . I'm an engineer.'[18] Then Arafat recalled the conversation they had had ten days before. 'Ehud,' he said, 'I warned you at that dinner at your house. I told you not to let Sharon go to the Plaza of the Haram . . . Why did you give him permission for that visit? I've told you that he will destroy everything . . . I've told you that this is his intention.' Barak said, 'Listen, we're a democracy . . . I can't prevent the leader of the opposition from doing what he pleases.'[19]

In the meantime the negotiators and US officials worked on a two-page draft of a ceasefire plan. It included a timetable for an Israeli withdrawal from Palestinian areas the Israeli army had re-entered during this intifada, along with measures both sides would take to stop the bloodshed. However, the main bone of contention remained: the issue of an investigation into the start of the intifada. Barak preferred an American-led inquiry and refused to accept a UN-led commission as demanded by Arafat. However, by the end of the afternoon Arafat appeared to have dropped his demand.

'CHIRAC HAD A HUGE CHAIR OVERLOOKING THIS'

Throughout the afternoon and evening, President Chirac kept phoning the negotiators, inviting them to the Élysée to brief him. 'I was between these two groups,' Madeline Albright recalls, 'when I got a phone call from President Chirac and he said, "You are in my country and protocol is very important and I need to host you and this is the only time I can do it", and I said, "Mr President", in French, "this is a very important moment, this is not a really good idea, for us to come right now, we are about to finalize this document, and I would really appreciate it if you did not invite us right now."' But Chirac kept phoning and eventually, although the document was not yet finalized, Albright felt she had to accept the invitation. But she hated it. 'She was extremely upset at the invitation', the Palestinian Saeb Erekat recalls. 'She made her position clear to Arafat and Barak. She was agitated. She was extremely, extremely upset.' Albright had good reason to be. She felt they were on the verge of an agreement and, as it was still unsigned, any outside intervention might cause it to unravel. But Arafat believed President Chirac was on his side and a visit to him would better his position. So Arafat insisted that they should all return to the Élysée to report.

Albright agreed to a brief protocol meeting at the Élysée Palace. When they got there, however, they found that Chirac had organized a full-blown conference. 'There was', as the Palestinian negotiator Nabil Shaath describes, 'a setting for a proper meeting. There were chairs with names, "the UN" . . . "Palestine", "Israel". Chirac had a huge chair overlooking this.' Also present were UN Secretary-General Kofi Annan, his Middle East emissary Terje Roed-Larsen, Javier Solana, representing the EU, and others.

Chirac made his opening remarks, saying that he was glad Paris could be the venue for this meeting. Then, according to the French Foreign Minister Hubert Vedrine, Arafat took the floor and 'he was adamant that the commission [of inquiry] *must* be established [in liaison with the Secretary-General of the United Nations]'. Barak intervened. He said he did not consider the establishment of a commission of inquiry as 'the best way to restore trust and peace', but that nonetheless he would agree to accept a commission composed of 'distinguished Americans'. Chirac's next intervention, however, caused a stir on the part of the Americans and Israelis, as he clearly sided with Arafat on this most sensitive issue. He said, according to the French Foreign Minister, 'I'm sure the EU would indeed support such an inquiry and indeed take part in it if so required and that this would help make it credible.' He also said that 'it would be desirable for the Secretary-General of the United Nations to define and organize it.'[20] Rubbing it in even further, Chirac added: 'The incident of

28 September [Sharon's visit to the Temple Mount/Haram] must be the subject of an investigation. An explanation must be offered to local and international public opinion. Reality must be faced without fear. When there is an accident, it must be acknowledged, and an investigation must follow. This is the voice of reason.'[21]

These comments made some members of the American team, as Robert Malley recalls, 'feel that Chirac was undermining [them]'. After all, they had spent all day trying to get Arafat to drop the demand for a UN-led international investigation. Albright recalls how 'I was giving Chirac the dirtiest look, thinking, you know, you broke an agreement here and it made me realize that, as nice as it was to be in Paris, there was a down side to holding these talks in France.' Seeing her fragile agreement unravelling in front of her eyes, Albright snapped at Chirac. 'Excuse me, Mr President,' she said, 'this has been removed from the agenda ... there is an agreed paper ... it has been agreed between Chairman Arafat and Prime Minister Barak ... it has been accepted by both of them [not to have a UN-led investigation].' According to Robert Malley, 'Madeleine was furious at the French ... furious ... she really felt that they had stabbed her in the back.'[22]

'YOU'VE PROMISED ME TO STAY AND YOU WILL STAY'

The meeting at the Élysée took nearly an hour-and-a-half, and delegates did not leave the Palace until around midnight. As they left the meeting, Albright reminded Arafat of his commitment to return to the US ambassador's residence and put the final touches on the agreement – and initial the document before leaving for the official signing in Egypt the next day. But Arafat said to Albright, 'Fine, I've stayed with you all this time, we attended the meeting at the Élysée, but now I have to go to my residence at the Hôtel Meurice and you can continue [without me].' Albright was flabbergasted. 'You've promised me to stay and you will stay,' she said. Arafat replied, 'I've promised that *we* will stay, and Nabil Shaath, my Foreign Minister, will be staying here and continuing with you.'[23] Arafat then got into his car, adding, 'I will be in my hotel and you can call me any time and when you finish come to me – I'll come again.' Albright's aide, Gamal Helal, was nearby. 'I opened the car door,' he recalls, 'I said "Mr Chairman, you still have to initial the agreement. Please, you gave your word. Don't, don't run away."' Arafat said: 'No, no, no, no, I'm gonna leave Nabil Shaath and Saeb Erekat, they can do it on my behalf.' He then, as Helal recalls, 'instructed the driver to go, and he left'.[24]

Albright now insisted that Erekat and Shaath go and bring Arafat back so that they could proceed with the negotiations and initial the agreement. Barak's man Gilead Sher describes how 'We were waiting. We were exhausted. We were now sleeping on the sofa, on the carpet . . .' But Arafat's aides returned empty-handed.

By then it was already 1.30 or 2 a.m. Secretary Albright tried to salvage the summit by trying to put together something that Arafat would agree to initial. At around four in the morning, Erekat and Shaath went again to the Meurice Hotel to show Arafat the final draft. 'President Arafat was still awake', Nabil Shaath remembers, 'and he looked at the paper and said, "Fine, we have no problem with the paper, but the question is the venue. We've promised President Mubarak and we've got to go to Sharm el-Sheikh together, as agreed."' But he would not return to the US residence to initial the agreement as originally promised. When Shaath and Erekat returned to Albright to announce that Arafat would not initial in Paris, but 'had given his word' that he would do so in Egypt the next day, a furious Albright flared up at them, saying, 'Listen carefully, we are not your Chairman's puppets.'[25] But that was that.

The summit had collapsed. Arafat had unilaterally changed the ground rules – he was not going to be jumped by a mere Secretary of State, even if she was American. And if Arafat would not initial in Paris, then Barak would not sign in Sharm el-Sheikh. The day after the Paris summit, the Egyptians, Palestinians and Americans waited in vain for the Israeli team. No agreement was signed.

'THIS IS THE MIDDLE EAST NOT SWITZERLAND'

Back in Israel and the occupied territories, with no ceasefire the violence escalated. On 7 October 2000 at Joseph's Tomb, a Jewish holy site in Nablus, a single Israeli soldier was attacked but not killed by a Palestinian mob. Fearing that an Israeli intervention to save the wounded soldier would lead to even more violence at the tomb, Barak decided to ask the Palestinian Authority to rescue the soldier. Urgent calls were made to Jibril Rajoub, Chief of Palestinian forces on the West Bank, who promised to deal with the matter. But nothing happened and the soldier bled to death. The mob then broke into the site and burnt it down. Worse was to come.

On 12 October, two Israeli army reservists made a fatal error by taking a wrong turn into downtown Ramallah, where they were set upon and lynched. An Italian television crew happened to be there and filmed the event, which was seen by millions of shocked viewers in Israel and worldwide as the two were brutally murdered, and then their bodies were beaten even more. As the murder was carried out in a Palestinian police station near Arafat's compound it seemed to Israelis like an official act of the Palestinian Authority.

The Israeli opposition demanded a strong response, but in a Cabinet meeting some ministers urged Barak to show restraint. The Prime Minister banged the table and said, 'This is the Middle East not Switzerland . . . they are going to pay a heavy price this time around . . . We'll bomb them from Jenin [in the West Bank] to Jabalya [in the Gaza Strip].'[26] Now, for the first time in the intifada, Prime Minister Barak ordered an attack by helicopters against Palestinian targets. Giora Eiland, then Chief of the Operations Directorate in the General Staff, recalls how, 'I was called to Barak's office in Tel Aviv and he said to me, "OK, I give the green light to use attack helicopters, but don't do it until I speak to a few people."' The Prime Minister then phoned President Hosni Mubarak of Egypt and a few other leaders, explaining the situation and why he had to retaliate. He then gave General Eiland the order to attack. Cobra attack helicopters, already in the air, started the short flight towards their targets in the Gaza Strip and West Bank.

'THEY MIGHT LAUNCH AN ATTACK ON YOU WITH HELICOPTERS'

Meanwhile, in the Gaza Strip, Arafat was waiting in his Gaza office to receive CIA boss George Tenet, who was on a tour of the region. Arafat sent Mohammed Dahlan to fetch Tenet from the Erez Crossing. By the time Dahlan got there, news of the lynching had already reached them. Dahlan, in an interview for *Elusive Peace*, recalls the conversation with Tenet. Tenet said, 'I need an approval from the [Israeli] Prime Minister's office [to enter Gaza].' Dahlan replied, 'Come on, why?' Tenet: 'I think that something happened in Ramallah.' Dahlan: 'Yes, I know about that.' Tenet: 'They might launch an attack on you with helicopters.'[27]

Dahlan immediately tried to phone Arafat to warn him of the coming attack but could not get through. Knowing that Arafat always had Al Jazeera television on, Dahlan then phoned a friend at the channel, asking him to put him live on air. So it was that Dahlan warned Arafat on live TV that the Israelis were about to attack the Gaza Strip. Arafat got the message and went down to his bunker. 'Then,' as Dahlan recalls, 'I saw the four helicopters ... I saw them coming.' It was a devastating attack and a powerful example of what the Israelis could do if provoked. 'We barely used one per cent of our power', bragged Chief of Staff Shaul Mofaz.[28]

'COME ON MAN'

With violence getting out of control, President Clinton intervened personally by summoning an emergency summit on 17 October at Sharm el-Sheikh, to which Barak and Arafat were invited, along with President Mubarak, UN Secretary-General Kofi Annan, Jordan's King

Abdullah II and the representative of the EU, Javier Solana. Clinton hoped he would be able to bring the parties together to sign a ceasefire agreement to stop the bloodshed.

Arafat, Barak and Clinton met at the Jolie Ville Golf Resort with their security chiefs, while their foreign ministers met separately, all working to draft a ceasefire agreement. The foreign ministers' gathering was, a leading US diplomat recalls, 'the nastiest meeting I have ever attended in diplomacy. People were very angry . . . everybody was accusing everybody of bad faith and we all walked out through different doors.'

Barak and his aides attempted to formalize what had been discussed in Paris earlier in the month, but Arafat again reopened the issue of an international inquiry into the causes of the violence. After hours of persuasion, President Clinton eventually managed to cut a deal, which Arafat then tried to have reviewed yet again. As Gamal Helal recalls, 'We agreed a text of what we had achieved . . . then suddenly Arafat gets grumpy . . . Mubarak got angry with him, "Come on man, what more do you want, this guy [Clinton] came all the way from Washington, we've all been hammering away trying to get a deal, and now you want to revisit it?" '[29] But Arafat again, as he did in Paris, tried to leave without signing. When he was eventually brought back he still insisted he would not sign. So, reluctantly, it was agreed that instead of a signed agreement, President Clinton would read out the deal of the assembled leaders. Thus, after twenty-eight hours of talks, an oral ceasefire plan was announced and Barak and Arafat agreed to take immediate concrete measures to end the violence. It was also announced that a US-led fact-finding commission, chaired by an American and with representatives from Turkey, Norway and the UN, would investigate the causes of the violence and propose ways to prevent their recurrence.[30] But with violence continuing the Sharm ceasefire agreement simply collapsed.

'YOU SHOULD CONTACT THE NOBEL
PRIZE COMMITTEE'

On 2 November 2000, Prime Minister Barak dispatched his Regional Co-operation Minister Shimon Peres, and close aide Gilead Sher, to see Arafat to try once again to stop the violence. They flew by helicopter to the Erez Crossing and from there were taken by car to the meeting with Arafat. After a long discussion they agreed a ceasefire plan, similar in many ways to the one concocted at Sharm on 17 October. It was agreed that Arafat and Barak would simultaneously make a radio broadcast calling on their respective forces to stop fighting. Shimon Peres suggested, and Arafat accepted, that there should be a week with absolutely no violence to mark the forthcoming anniversary of Yitzhak Rabin's assassination.

With this ceasefire plan agreed, Shimon Peres and Gilead Sher returned to Israel – they came under fire on their way back – and then sat with Prime Minister Barak, the Chief of Staff and the Director of Military Intelligence to assess the agreement. When Peres finished his report, the Prime Minister, as Gilead Sher recalls, joked: 'Listen, if you've achieved a ceasefire with Arafat then you've done something historic. But if Arafat will not act according to what he is supposed to do then you should contact the Nobel Prize committee [Arafat was given a Nobel Peace Prize in 1994] and ask for Arafat to be given an Oscar instead.'

It was around three in the morning when Barak talked to Arafat about their speeches. 'Mr Chairman,' he said, 'I'm not going to mention anything about Zionism and stuff like that. I'll stick to the statement . . . word for word . . . and I hope that you'll do the same.'

At around 12.45 in the afternoon, Barak was already at the Ministry of Defence in Tel Aviv, waiting to deliver the agreed announcement at two o'clock. However, when his aide Gilead Sher phoned Arafat's Chief of Staff, Nabil Abu Rudeineh, he was told that 'there might be someone else . . . perhaps Nabil Shaath who would deliver the broadcast'. Of course, if Arafat would not broadcast, neither would Barak.

Instead, at half past two, a car bomb exploded at Hamashbir store in Jerusalem. A week or so later, on 9 November 2000, Hussein Abayat, a Palestinian the Israelis claimed was involved in attacks on them, was killed by a missile attack. This became Israel's first 'targeted assassination', marking the next stage in the escalating spiral of violence between Israelis and Palestinians.

II

Clinton's Last Stand

On 7 November 2000, George W. Bush was elected President of the United States. Bill Clinton remained in office until 20 January 2001 but he was now the proverbial 'lame duck'. Still, he had not given up on trying to make peace in the Middle East.

Just before Christmas 2000, Clinton called Israeli and Palestinian teams to the White House to present to them his formula for peace, the 'Clinton Parameters', one last attempt to try to resolve the Israeli–Palestinian conflict. Clinton's ideas were not the terms of a final deal, but guidelines for final accelerated negotiations that he hoped could be concluded in the coming weeks. 'There was', as Gamal Helal of the US peace team recalls, 'a sense of genuine excitement on the US side, because we felt that we really had a chance . . . that the parameters were fair, they were balanced, they took into consideration the needs of both sides.'

When Clinton entered the Cabinet room in the White House to present his ideas, he found familiar faces waiting for him: the Israelis Gilead Sher and Shlomo Ben-Ami, and the Palestinians Saeb Erekat and Mohammed Dahlan among others. The President was dressed casually in a sweatshirt and jeans and was holding a can of Diet Coke in his hand. He moved from one negotiator to another, shaking hands and exchanging some casual words. He then sat and read his plan while the delegates took notes, as no written text was presented.

On the territory that Israel should give to the Palestinians on which

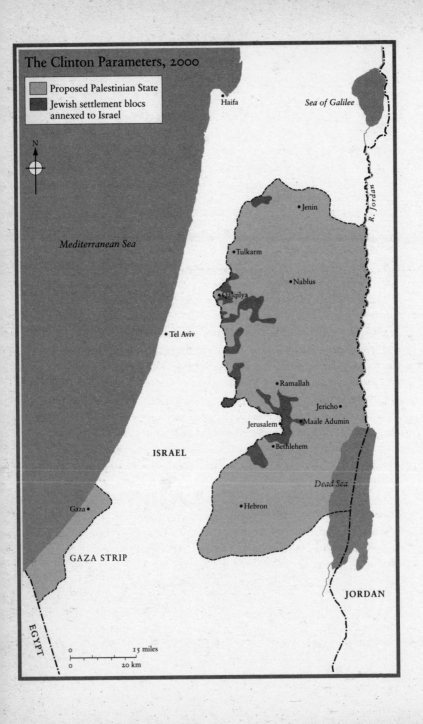

The Clinton Parameters, 2000

Proposed Palestinian State

Jewish settlement blocs
annexed to Israel

N

Sea of Galilee

Haifa

Mediterranean Sea

R. Jordan

Jenin

Tulkarm

Nablus

Qalqilya

Tel Aviv

Ramallah

Jericho

Jerusalem • Maale Adumin

ISRAEL

Bethlehem

Dead Sea

Gaza

Hebron

GAZA STRIP

JORDAN

EGYPT

0   15 miles

0   20 km

to establish their state, Clinton suggested that the figure should be 'in the mid-90 per cents, between 94 and 96 per cent of the West Bank territory'. For the 4 to 6 per cent of West Bank land that Israel would annex in order to incorporate big settlement blocs (all isolated settlements would be dismantled), Clinton suggested Israel should compensate the Palestinians with 'a land swap of 1 to 3 per cent'.

Regarding Jerusalem, Clinton said that 'The general principle is that Arab areas are Palestinian and Jewish ones are Israeli.' It was on the Camp David deal breaker – the question of sovereignty over the Temple Mount/Haram – that Clinton had an ingenious new idea. He said, 'I believe that the gaps are not related to practical administration but to the symbolic issues of sovereignty and to finding a way to accord respect to the religious beliefs of both sides.' He then offered two possibilities: Palestinian sovereignty over the Haram and Israeli sovereignty over the Western Wall and the space under the Haram sacred to Judaism; or, Palestinian shared sovereignty over the Haram and Israeli sovereignty over the Western Wall.

Regarding refugees, Clinton said, 'The Israeli side could not accept any reference to a right of return that would imply a right to immigrate to Israel in defiance of Israel's sovereign policies on admission or that would threaten the Jewish character of the state.' The solution he proposed was that, 'the guiding principle should be that the Palestinian state would be the focal point for Palestinians who chose to return to the area without ruling out that Israel would accept some of these refugees'. He added, 'I believe that we need to adopt a formulation on the right of return that will make clear that there is no specific right of return to Israel itself but that does not negate the aspiration of the Palestinian people to return to the area.' Clinton concluded by saying, 'I propose that the agreement clearly mark the end of the conflict and its implementation put an end to all claims.' He then added:

I believe this is an outline of a fair and lasting agreement. It gives the Palestinian people the ability to determine the future on their own land, a sovereign and viable state recognized by the international community, Al-Quds as its capital, sovereignty over the Haram, and new lives for the refugees. It gives the people of Israel a genuine end to the conflict, real security, the preservation of sacred religious ties, the incorporation of 80 per cent of the settlers into Israel, and the largest Jewish Jerusalem in history recognized by all as its capital.

When Clinton finished reading his text he said: 'This is the best I can do.' He then asked the negotiators to brief their leaders and tell him if they were prepared to come for discussions based on these ideas. If so, said Clinton, he would meet them separately the following week. But if these ideas were not accepted, Clinton added, then 'they are not just off the table, they also go with me when I leave office'.

It was a balanced package in the sense that both sides had to compromise and accept less than they had hoped for. The Israelis had to agree to have a smaller Jerusalem, and the Palestinians largely to give up on the right of return – their dream of sweeping Palestinian returns to Israel proper.

'I tried to ask a question', the Palestinian Mohammed Dahlan recalls, 'but Clinton told me . . . very nicely, very politely, "There is no space for clarifications, or questions or comments . . . you are here only as messengers for your leaders, and I thank you very much for your efforts as negotiators. In the last three months, you have crystallized situations that have helped me put forth these proposals." ' And as the Israeli Gilead Sher recalls, 'Clinton said, "This is not open to changes, to additions or reductions . . . all I want is yes or no, if this can serve as the basis for further negotiations for the final settlement." ' And as Clinton's National Security Advisor Sandy Berger recalls, 'There we were, very much used to a garrulous Bill Clinton who was always willing to talk another five minutes or ten minutes or maybe two hours if he thought that was useful. He put the offer on the table, he said, "I'm not taking any questions" and he left.' Dennis Ross then took charge and he went over the text again to ensure that each side had copied the points accurately. They had to come up with an answer by 27 December 2000.

'I DO NOT INTEND TO SIGN ANY AGREEMENT BEFORE THE ELECTIONS'

On 28 December 2000, Barak's government officially accepted the Clinton Parameters as a basis for ending the Israeli–Palestinian conflict. But rather than a genuine acceptance, it was Barak's attempt to 'leave the dead cat' on Arafat's doorstep, assuming – on the basis of previous experience with Arafat – that he would eventually reject the plan. In an interview for *Elusive Peace* Barak admits, for the first time, that saying 'Yes' to the Clinton Parameters was more of a trick to expose Arafat than a genuine acceptance of the proposals. Barak:

In order not to pass the responsibility [for the failure of the peace process] from Arafat back to us . . . [I convinced my] government to adopt [the plan] . . . and that was part of [my] crusade to fix the fact that what had happened at Camp David was not an [exceptional case] but rather part of Arafat's systematic unwillingness to enter into negotiations over a [peace] settlement.[1]

But three days later, and even before hearing from Arafat, in a midnight (Israeli time) phone call to Clinton, Barak turned the parameters down, telling the President that 'I do not intend to sign any agreement before the elections.' It was now Arafat's turn to respond to the Clinton Parameters.

'I'M AFRAID YOUR WATCH IS BROKEN, MR CHAIRMAN'

Arafat was received in the White House on Tuesday, 2 January 2001, and, although he had already missed the deadline imposed on both sides to respond to the ideas by 27 December 2000, President Clinton still hoped Arafat would accept his proposals.[2] Clinton did not tell Arafat that Barak had phoned the night before to turn the parameters down, presumably hoping that should Arafat agree to the plan he could then return to Barak and press him to rethink and perhaps accept as well.

Clinton was in for a disappointment, however. Dennis Ross, who was present in the meeting, relates that while Arafat said to the President, 'I accept your ideas', his reservations, in Dennis Ross's words, 'unfortunately, revealed his real answer'.[3]

Arafat rejected Clinton's suggestion that the Western Wall should go to the Israelis, agreeing only to give them the Wailing Wall, which forms part of the Western Wall.[4] He also rejected Clinton's suggestion that Palestinian refugees should generally go to the future Palestinian state rather than to Israel proper. 'If we reopen these issues,' Clinton said to Arafat, 'then we're going back to square one.' And he went on to explain, as Robert Malley, who was also present in the meeting, recalls, 'that we're creating a box. This is a box within which negotiations could take place ... We've set the parameters, and then you can deal with [Barak] within those parameters.' National Security Advisor Sandy Berger recalls the dramatic meeting:

We were in the map room, it's downstairs in the residence, it was a very small room that had been used, and Arafat simply was not able to say [yes I accept the parameters] ... The President was extraordinarily disappointed, and he said to Chairman Arafat, 'You know, they've always told me that you are someone who will wait until five minutes 'til twelve, but I'm afraid your watch is broken, Mr Chairman.'

The Clinton formula – his last-ditch attempt to reach peace between Israelis and Palestinians before leaving office – was rejected by both Barak and Arafat.

'I AM A FAILURE, AND YOU HAVE MADE ME ONE'

Just before Clinton left the White House for good, Arafat phoned him to thank him for his efforts. 'Arafat said to him', as Erekat recalls, ' "We will never forget you, Mr President. You are a great leader. You brought Palestinians and Israelis to where they are today, and wherever we go, it will be Clinton who planted the seeds." ' In *My Life*, Clinton recalls this conversation with Arafat, writing,

Arafat thanked me for all my efforts and told me what a great man I was. 'Mr Chairman,' I replied, 'I am not a great man. I am a failure, and you have made me one.'[5]

PART TWO

Sharon vs Arafat
2001–2004

12

Enter Sharon

'SHARON? I DEFEATED HIM IN BEIRUT'

In Israel's general election of 6 February 2001 Ariel ('Arik') Sharon, leader of the right-wing Likud Party, and renowned for his hawkish views and military past, won a landslide victory over Prime Minister Barak, receiving 62.5 per cent of the vote compared with Barak's meagre 37.5 per cent. Sharon's victory was a tremendous personal comeback. The disastrous invasion of Lebanon, which, as Defence Minister in 1982, Sharon had devised, had lost him his job in government and left him politically dead. But an electorate's memory tends to be short. The sheer disappointment at the failure of Barak's attempt to achieve peace led the Israeli people to vote overwhelmingly for Sharon. His military experience, toughness and determination, they believed, could perhaps provide them with the personal security to which they all aspired. Sharon's road to victory began four months before with his walk on Temple Mount/Haram al-Sharif, which triggered the intifada that made Israelis feel they needed a firm hand to end the violence.

Sharon established a coalition government between his Likud Party and Labour, offering their new leader, the 78-year-old veteran Shimon Peres, architect of the 1993 Oslo Agreement with Arafat, the post of Foreign Minister and giving the sensitive and prestigious Defence portfolio to another Labourite, Binyamin ('Fuad') Ben-Eliezer.

The most pressing problem on the new Prime Minister's desk was the war that was still raging with the Palestinians. To tackle this problem Sharon had to do something he hated – make contact with his nemesis Arafat. In spite of the revulsion he felt towards him, Sharon twice picked up the phone and spoke (in English) to the Palestinian leader. 'The theme', recalls Sharon's then aide Danny Ayalon, was 'Can Sharon work with Arafat? Can the Palestinians stabilize things enough?' Ayalon remembers that Arafat 'made his promises – but nothing happened' and the war continued.[1] On 8 February, 4 Israelis were injured by a car bomb in an orthodox neighbourhood in Jerusalem; three days later an Israeli was shot and killed in his car near Jerusalem; on 14 February, 8 were killed and 25 were injured when a Palestinian drove a bus into a group of people at a bus stop near Tel Aviv. These violent actions reflected Palestinians' anger and frustration with the continuation of the Israeli occupation – the harassment at checkpoints, the curfews imposed by the army, the humiliating searches, the continuing expansion of Jewish settlements on Palestinian confiscated land and the lack of any hope for a better future. The Israeli army retaliated and the vicious circle continued.

Next, the Prime Minister tried sending emissaries to meet Arafat. His son Omri and Yossi Ginossar, an ex-Shin Bet operator who had acted as a go-between with the Palestinians for former Labour prime ministers (Rabin, Peres and Barak), had two meetings at the *muqata* with Arafat and his Chief of Staff, Nabil Abu Rudeineh, and confidants Mohammed Dahlan and Mohammed Rashid. The Israeli message in these talks was the same: Arafat must first curb violence and stop the attacks on Israel before any progress could be made.

There was also international pressure on Arafat to curb attacks on Israel. Ron Schlicher, US Consul-General in Jerusalem – the official point of contact between the US Administration and the Palestinians – met Arafat soon after the February election. 'Mr Chairman,' he said, 'you have to stop the violence. Who'd have dreamt a year ago that Sharon would be Prime Minister?', to which Arafat responded, 'Sharon? I defeated him in Beirut and by God I'll defeat him again!'[2] Arafat often repeated this mantra to his aides as well. 'Whoever is afraid of Sharon can go home!' he would say. 'We will defeat him as we did in Lebanon!' His veteran negotiator Saeb Erekat once asked, 'How exactly did we win? [After all,] Sharon expelled us from Lebanon and we were exiled to Tunis for more than a decade!' To that Arafat just swore.[3]

Prime Minister Sharon made other overtures that February. At his farm in the Negev, he hosted two veteran Palestinian leaders – Abu Mazen, for many years Arafat's number 2, and Abu Ala, speaker of the Palestinian parliament and a leading negotiator. 'I have four years to reach peace', Sharon said to his guests, to which Abu Ala replied, 'There's no point in waiting for so long. It's possible to reach an agreement in six months.' In the same spirit Sharon even said that he could agree to a temporary Palestinian state being established on 42 per cent of the West Bank and Gaza Strip, in areas already under full or partial Palestinian control. This idea was not new; the logic behind it was that if a temporary Palestinian state was established, peace talks could be conducted between two legally recognized units – states – rather than between the state of Israel and a very legally intangible creature called the Palestinian Authority.

Follow-up meetings continued and by the end of February, even before Sharon's government was officially sworn in, a secret but written understanding had been reached. The jewel of this understanding was to be a first meeting between Sharon and Arafat at the Erez Crossing at the beginning of March 2001. In return for a pledge from Arafat to fight terrorism and condemn violence, the Israelis would withdraw to the positions held before the outbreak of the Al-Aqsa intifada. Discussions on a Final Status agreement would then open in April, with a renewal of security co-ordination between security chiefs of both sides and a symbolic release of forty Palestinian prisoners from Israeli jails. A senior Palestinian who was involved in these secret talks says, 'Everything was agreed and was ready down to the nitty-gritty, certainly the [Sharon–Arafat] meeting at the Erez checkpoint.'[4]

But Arafat was concerned about the timing of the planned meeting with Sharon. He intended to go to the Arab summit in Amman, Jordan on 27–28 March 2001 and thought it preferable to go to Amman with Sharon still being regarded as an enemy rather than as a new partner. So the Israeli–Palestinian understanding and the planned Arafat–Sharon meeting at Erez fell through. Arafat travelled to Amman without seeing Sharon and missed the first and, as it turned out, only opportunity to establish some kind of working relationship with his arch-enemy.

'YOU DIDN'T THINK YOU WERE GOING TO BE THE PRIME MINISTER'

Meanwhile, on 20 March, Sharon travelled to Washington for his first summit meeting with George W. Bush, who had been sworn in as President exactly two months before. They first met for lunch in the White House before emerging for a photo opportunity. 'The Prime Minister and I had met before', said Bush, referring to his visit to Israel in 1998 when Sharon, then Foreign Minister, had hosted a group of US governors. 'I took a tour of the West Bank by helicopter', Bush added, 'and he was the guide. It was a really interesting day for me. He's got a marvelous sense of history, and I learned a lot about our friend [Sharon] by touring the West Bank by chopper with you, Mr Prime Minister.' Then, turning to Sharon, Bush added, 'You didn't think you were going to be the Prime Minister and you probably darn well didn't think I was going to be the President. But here we are.' Sitting alongside Bush, Sharon made his intentions clear. 'The first thing and the most important one, is to bring security to the citizens of Israel . . . that is the first thing that we have to accomplish.'[5]

Sharon meant that fighting terrorism must come *before* any peace talks, and he expected the US not to interfere in any way which would break that rule. Bush could not have been more willing to agree. The two leaders' instincts were very much alike. Bush did not expect Sharon to negotiate under fire, and he also knew from the experiences of his predecessor in the White House that Arafat was a lost cause. Bush knew just how much Clinton had invested, and how much face he had lost, in trying to clinch a deal between Barak and Arafat. He had no desire to repeat that failure. He could not afford to lose face at the start of his presidency by investing in a hopeless case. A British diplomat, listening in on a call between his Foreign Secretary Robin Cook and the new US Secretary of State Colin Powell just after Bush became President, recalls how Powell said: 'We're going to stand back, and let things happen.'[6] That was to be the new US policy on the conflict.

Although Bush was determined not to intervene directly in the conflict, he had no desire to see things deteriorate further, and in their talks in Washington he made it absolutely clear to the Prime Minister that he should not kill Arafat. The Prime Minister, for his part, as his close aide Danny Ayalon recalls, 'undertook with Bush ... not to harm Arafat physically'. Sharon returned home satisfied with his first official visit to Washington. He said to Israeli reporters that President Bush shared his assessment that the approach of his predecessor Barak and former US President Clinton 'was not realistic'.

'A GENETICALLY MODIFIED IMPROVEMENT OF HIS FATHER'

In the meantime, the Israeli military continued to tighten its grip on the occupied territories, and the Palestinians, in their frustration, hit back – and hard. On 1 March 2001, an Israeli was killed and 9 were injured by a bomb detonated in a taxi in northern Israel; on 4 March, 3 Israelis were killed and 60 injured by a suicide bomb in Netanya; on 27 March, two bombs in Jerusalem buses killed 1 and wounded 28. And although the Prime Minister maintained in public that he would not negotiate with Arafat under fire, nonetheless, he discreetly tried to keep a line open with the Palestinian leader.

In mid-April 2001, Sharon dispatched his son Omri to Arafat. After changing cars and slipping through the back roads of Ramallah, Omri arrived at a house where he waited for Arafat. When the Palestinian leader showed up, the two embraced like good friends before withdrawing to a back room where they talked in private in English and Arabic, with Omri taking careful notes. The young Sharon carried a message to Arafat from his father: 'If you want peace then give us a period of absolute quiet.' Sharon left the meeting in high spirits. 'I felt happy', he recalls, 'that I had even tried to talk. It's good to feel that you've done something that is the right thing to do.' Arafat was equally satisfied. 'He's like my son', he said to aides after Sharon departed. 'He is a very broad-minded man ... a genetically modified improvement of his father.'[7]

But the violence continued, and even escalated, with Palestinian suicide bombs and Israeli military actions taking place on a daily basis. On 18 May 2001, a Palestinian suicide bomber killed himself and 5 Israelis and wounded over 100 at a shopping mall in the northern coastal town of Netanya. Sharon ordered a massive retaliation, and F-16 warplanes were used to attack Palestinian targets in Nablus and Ramallah for the first time.[8] Then, on 25 May, two suicide bombers blew themselves up, one at Hadera in the north of Israel and one at a security outpost in the Gaza Strip, wounding at least 65 Israelis. Two days later, 30 were injured by a bomb in Jerusalem. That month, meeting his Chief of Staff Shaul Mofaz, IDF deputy Chief of Staff Moshe ('Boogie') Yaalon and the Director of Shin Bet Avi Dichter, the Prime Minister said, 'We have to strike at the Palestinians everywhere ... simultaneously. The Palestinians should wake up every morning to realize that twelve of them are dead ... without realizing how this had happened.' Sharon made the war on the Palestinians the military's top priority, telling his Chief of Staff, 'That's your war. Don't keep your gear in warehouses for a future war with Syria. Your test is in victory over the Palestinians.'[9]

The violence reached its peak on 1 June, when Said al-Hutri, a Hamas operative from Nablus in the northern West Bank, blew himself up outside a popular seafront disco at the Dolphinarium in Tel Aviv. He killed 21 young Israelis and wounded more than 80. That night, a Friday, Sharon gathered his Cabinet, and the question on everyone's lips was what to do with the man they felt responsible for this atrocity – Arafat.

'WHO COULD BE WORSE THAN ARAFAT?'

Sharon felt that Arafat, far from trying to curb the violence against Israel, was in fact orchestrating it, either by directly encouraging the attackers or by looking the other way. The Prime Minister had always been obsessed with Arafat and was even more so now. According to Sharon's Defence Minister, Binyamin Ben-Eliezer, getting Arafat was 'almost the baby of Sharon from our first meeting'. 'Sometimes', Ben-Eliezer recalls, 'I got home telling my wife that still Sharon has an open account with Arafat ... going back to [the] 1982 [war in Lebanon].' Now, after the horrifying killing at the Dolphinarium, the Prime Minister urged his Cabinet to 'remove' Arafat – perhaps to expel him. But ministers were opposed. 'If you sent him out [of the country]', argued Ben-Eliezer, 'this would allow Arafat to roam the world and to move from one capital to another ... and we would have to go from one president to another ... to prime ministers ... to convince them that he is bad. We don't need that.' Deputy Chief of Staff Moshe Yaalon called for Arafat to be classified as 'an enemy', but this was also rejected. Eventually, the Cabinet decided only to define Arafat as someone who 'supports and activates terrorism' but not expel him – for the time being.

On 9 August 2001, a Hamas suicide bomber blew himself up in the crowded Sbarro pizzeria in central Jerusalem, killing 15 and wounding 130.[10] With that and more violence, the question of how to deal with Arafat continued to dominate Cabinet meetings. In one of these a minister said, 'Who could be worse than Arafat?' Foreign Minister Peres retorted simply, 'Hamas.'

'ALL IT TAKES IS FOR THE HELICOPTER PILOT TO HICCUP'

While careful not to harm Arafat physically, Sharon and his ministers had no qualms about taking out other Palestinian leaders. Thus, at around 9.30 in the morning of Monday, 27 August 2001, an Israeli helicopter-gunship fired two missiles through the window of the second-floor office of the Popular Front for the Liberation of Palestine (PFLP) in Ramallah, decapitating the faction's Secretary-General, who was sitting at his desk.

The 63-year-old Abu Ali Mustafa was the elected leader of the second biggest organization in the Palestinian Liberation Organization (PLO) after Arafat's Al Fatah, and a leading figure in the occupied territories. The military claimed that the strike was in response to the Sbarro pizzeria suicide bombing and shooting attacks for which the PFLP had claimed responsibility. The Israelis insisted Mustafa was personally responsible for directing the organization's terror operations.

It was – until 11 September 2001 – US policy to oppose political assassinations, and in Israel, straight after the killing of Mustafa, US ambassador Dan Kurtzer said to Sharon: 'You know that Washington is going to criticize Israel for the targeted killing [of Mustafa].' He added that in fact there happened to be twenty American families close to where the attack took place. Sharon said he had not known that but 'even if we had known, the fact is that we only killed Abu Ali Mustafa'. Kurtzer replied: 'All it takes is for the helicopter pilot to hiccup and the building gets destroyed [and Americans hurt].'[11] In Washington, State Department spokesman Richard Boucher condemned the assassination, saying, 'Israel needs to understand that targeted killings of Palestinians don't end the violence but are only inflaming an already volatile situation and making it much harder to restore calm.'[12] The Americans even threatened to halt the supply of spare parts for the Apache helicopters Israel often used for the assassinations.[13]

The killing of Mustafa shocked the Palestinian leadership to the core. Jibril Rajoub, head of security on the West Bank and a close associate of Arafat, recalls: 'I was in my headquarters ... and I could not move [it was like] ... I was paralysed [and I knew] that the assassination of Abu Ali Mustafa would have to provoke a huge Palestinian response.'[14] His colleagues Saeb Erekat and Nabil Shaath warned the US Consul-General in Jerusalem, Ron Schlicher, that the killing of a political leader such as Mustafa 'takes us up to a new level'.[15] They were right, but the assassination was soon overshadowed by an event far from the Middle East.

13

The Long Shadow of 9/11

'YOU'VE GOT TO BE MORE CATHOLIC THAN THE POPE'

On 11 September 2001, the militant Islamic group Al Qaeda, using hi-jacked airliners as flying bombs, destroyed the World Trade Center in New York and part of the Pentagon in Washington and left almost 3,000 dead. It was a massive terrorist attack which radically altered the US agenda, and had an equally strong impact on Israeli–Palestinian relations.

As the first airliner slammed into the World Trade Center, the Palestinian Minister of Information, Yasser Abed Rabbo, was at home in Ramallah having his siesta. He was woken by his wife to join her in watching 'an American thriller on television about a disaster in New York'.[1] As Abed Rabbo joined her he saw the second aeroplane strike, and it dawned on him that this was no thriller, but a real-life terrorist attack. Abed Rabbo jumped into his car and hurried to Gaza. Walking into Arafat's office, he found the Palestinian leader pacing up and down saying, 'Who could have been behind this?' Clearly, the worst fear for the Palestinians was that the attack had been carried out by one of them: TV screens around the world were already showing celebrations on the street in Gaza. But Arafat soon had an explanation. He said to Abed Rabbo, 'The towers are collapsing from the inside. These are not aeroplanes. Someone has put explosives in them. I'm an engineer! I should know!' He then added, 'This is an attack made by the Americans.'[2]

The down-to-earth Abed Rabbo understood that this was no time for conspiracy theories, and he urged Arafat 'to do something to counter that'. A symbolic act in front of television cameras was called for, perhaps for Arafat to donate blood. 'I'm an old man, I'm over seventy', Arafat insisted. Rabbo replied, 'This won't do you harm, it will be for your benefit, not just politically but physically as well.'[3] Eventually Arafat yielded, and the next day he joined Abed Rabbo at the Dar Ashifa Hospital in Gaza where, in front of the news crews gathered for the event, he gave blood. It was a PR success and did something to recover Arafat's image abroad.

That day, US Consul-General Ron Schlicher came to see Arafat in Gaza. 'From now on', Schlicher warned, 'the number one topic in the US Administration is going to be terrorism. The number one topic for *you* is going to be what you're doing to stop terrorism . . . You've got to be . . . more Catholic than the Pope.'[4] Schlicher explained to Arafat that the fine distinction between 'legitimate resistance', a term often used by Palestinians to justify their armed struggle against Israel, and pure 'terrorism' was non-existent after the 9/11 attack on America. *Both* had to be stopped.

'DO THE DAMN MEETING'

The US did also press Prime Minister Sharon to calm things down. President Bush was now contemplating a major assault on Afghanistan to oust the Islamic Taliban government there, which sheltered Al Qaeda. 'War on terror' became Bush's first priority. But for that to succeed he needed to quieten the Israeli–Palestinian problem. If Palestinian suffering was shown daily on television screens across the Arab world, it would be difficult for the President to get the Arab and Muslim allies he needed for his campaign against terrorism. The intifada must not divert attention from Bush's cause.

It was against this backdrop that the President asked Israel's Foreign Minister, Shimon Peres, to meet Arafat to work with him on a plan to reduce tensions. The meeting had, in fact, been suggested before 9/11 but Sharon had vetoed it. In his first telephone call to Sharon after 9/11, President Bush told him: 'It will be helpful for Peres to meet Arafat to show that some progress been made [on the Israeli–

Palestinian front].'[5] But Sharon sensed that the President was over-looking Israel's best interests in order to entice the Arab world to co-operate with him in America's war on terrorism. An official listen-ing in to the conversation recalls how 'the Prime Minister said "No" [and became] the first [world] leader to say "No" to the President of the US after nine-eleven'.[6]

The US ambassador in Israel, Dan Kurtzer, was then instructed to go and see Sharon and explain to him that the world had changed. He told the Prime Minister that the bottom line was that he should send Foreign Minister Peres to see Arafat. 'Do the damn meeting', he told him. But the Prime Minister still resisted, concerned that it would set a precedent for the US to ask further concessions from Israel in order to facilitate US foreign policy aims. 'First,' Sharon said to Kurtzer, 'it's a meeting [that you are asking for] and then [you'll ask Israel to do] other things as well.'[7]

Sharon was also under pressure to give the green light for the meeting from Shimon Peres himself. The Labour leader went to see Sharon at his farm in the Negev, and told him that 'in spite of all our disappointments [with Arafat] I want to try once more'.[8] Eventually Sharon gave in, perhaps because he felt that he had made his point and it was time to move on.

On 26 September 2001, Peres met Arafat in Gaza's Rafah airport and reached an agreement to resume full security co-operation. They agreed to make 'a maximum effort' to sustain a ceasefire and carry out all security obligations from previous agreements between them. Peres agreed that Israel would begin lifting curfews and redeploying forces away from areas occupied by the army since the start of the Al-Aqsa intifada. Arafat agreed to start collecting illegal weapons and to arrest suspected militants. Peres asked Arafat specifically to arrest Atef Abayat, a leader of the Al-Aqsa Martyrs Brigade militia in the West Bank town of Bethlehem, who was involved in incessant mortar fire at the Jewish suburb of Gilo near Jerusalem, and who had also, on 20 September 2001, shot and killed an Israeli citizen, Sarit Amrani, near Bethlehem. As Peres recalls, 'Arafat gave instructions to [his] commanders in my presence [to arrest Abayat].'

Peres, his hopes raised slightly, reported to the Prime Minister that

Arafat had made his promises and had already started making arrests. That evening, however, there was once again gunfire at Gilo, and on the next morning the Israelis spotted the 'arrested man' Abayat driving a jeep around Bethlehem. 'I phoned Arafat', Peres recalls in an interview for *Elusive Peace*, 'and said "You're making yourself look ridiculous, and you're making us look ridiculous."'[9] But the Israelis were no better at sticking to this agreement. Immediately after the meeting, the army moved into Rafah and destroyed the airport's runway as a punishment for an attack that destroyed an army stronghold and left four Israeli soldiers injured.

'ISRAEL WILL NOT BE CZECHOSLOVAKIA. ISRAEL WILL FIGHT'

Nine-eleven continued to cast its shadow. On 2 October 2001, in a dramatic break with America's previous policy, President Bush announced to a meeting with congressional leaders that he backed the creation of a state for the Palestinians. He said, 'The idea of a Palestinian state has always been part of a vision, so long as the right to Israel to exist is respected.'[10] This bold statement, Bush assumed, would remove many of the reservations Muslim countries in the region might have about supporting the US in its war on terrorism. Secretary of State Colin Powell, a moderate within the new conservative administration, and the driving force behind the statement, said, 'There has always been a vision in our thinking, as well as in previous administrations' thinking, that there would be a Palestinian state that exists at the same time that the security of the state of Israel was also recognized, guaranteed and accepted by all parties.'[11]

There was no immediate response from Prime Minister Sharon to Bush's words. In fact, just ten days before, on 23 September, the Prime Minister himself had given an important speech (at a place called Latrun; hence it became known as the Latrun Speech), in which he articulated *his* support for a Palestinian state. 'Israel,' Sharon declared, 'wants to give the Palestinians what no one else gave them – a state. Not the Turks, the British, the Egyptians, or the Jordanians gave them this possibility.' As an American diplomat comments, 'Sharon knew that he had opened the door' when he delivered his Latrun Speech, and so could hardly complain when Bush also backed the creation of a Palestinian state.[12]

However, Sharon was not quiet for long. In fact, he saw the President's speech in support of a Palestinian state yet another American attempt to try to appease the Arab world at Israel's expense. Furious, the Prime Minister now prepared a fierce response. His closest adviser, Danny Ayalon, recalls that Sharon wrote the speech himself on his farm in the Negev. 'We, his senior advisers, got it in Tel Aviv and we realized we could not make a single change. And he was going to say this. He felt that after nine-eleven Israel could easily be sacrificed to pacify radical Islam, become the fall guy. And he felt he could not allow that.'

On 5 October 2001 Sharon delivered his speech, in which he openly expressed his unhappiness with what he felt was America's willingness to sacrifice Israel. 'I call on the Western democracies and primarily the leader of the free world, the United States,' Sharon said. 'Do not repeat the dreadful mistake of 1938 when enlightened European democracies decided to sacrifice Czechoslovakia for a convenient temporary solution ... Do not try to appease the Arabs at our expense. This is unacceptable to us. Israel will not be Czechoslovakia. Israel will fight.'

Sharon's speech went down extremely badly in the US, where, as a senior diplomat recalls, 'we made very clear [to the Israelis] the level of our frustration [with Sharon's words]'.[13] Sharon's adviser Danny Ayalon got a call that night from the Senior Director at the US National Security Council, Flynt Leverett; it was, as Ayalon recalls, a 'tough' conversation. The White House's spokesman, Ari Fleischer, stated that the Prime Minister's comments were 'unacceptable'.[14] Bush was personally hurt by Sharon's harsh words – Sharon effectively compared him with Neville Chamberlain – and US–Israeli relations plunged to their lowest point in a decade. A diplomat who prefers to remain anonymous says in an interview for *Elusive Peace*: 'Bush *hates* Sharon, especially after the Czechoslovakia speech. He won't forgive him for that.'

The US ambassador to Israel, Dan Kurtzer, was soon instructed to fix it, so he spoke to the Prime Minister. He told Sharon that the objective now was to correct the damage and the way to correct it was as follows: the Prime Minister can say to the ambassador that he regrets his speech. He can put out a public statement that he regrets it. He can send a letter to the President that he regrets it. Paying lip service, a bland statement was released by Sharon's office in which the Prime Minister apologized, claiming his words were misinterpreted.

14

Spiralling Violence

'CHAIRMAN ARAFAT HAS MADE HIMSELF IRRELEVANT'

Meanwhile, in the West Bank, the PFLP had been plotting revenge since the assassination of their leader, Abu Ali Mustafa, on 27 August 2001. It came on 17 October.

That day, at the Hyatt Hotel in Jerusalem, two Palestinians, Hamdi Koran and Basel Asmar, watched Israeli Tourism Minister Rehavam Zeevi – one of Israel's most hardline politicians – having breakfast with his wife. Zeevi felt he was being watched, saying to his wife, 'There's an Arab giving me strange looks.' Soon after, at around seven in the morning, the minister returned to his room on the eighth floor, where Koran and Asmar were waiting for him in the corridor. Asmar called out 'Gandhi' – Zeevi's nickname – and when Zeevi turned to look, Koran shot him twice in the face. It was a political assassination, just like that of Abu Ali Mustafa.

While Sharon called an emergency Cabinet meeting, his Foreign Minister Shimon Peres phoned Arafat. 'What are you doing?! Are you crazy?!' he flew at him. 'If you don't arrest the people who did this we will have to use the severest means against the Palestinian Authority.' Arafat replied, 'I'll do my best.'[1]

Sharon blamed Arafat for the assassination of Zeevi – not only a Cabinet minister but a close personal friend of Sharon – and led his shocked ministers in issuing an ultimatum to Arafat to arrest and hand over to Israel the 'murderers and their senders' responsible for the assassination. 'If the PA does not comply with this demand', went the announcement, 'Israel will see the Palestinian Authority as an entity that supports terror.' On the next day, in a special Knesset session, Sharon stated, 'Everything has changed ... the responsibility is Arafat's alone, as someone who has carried out and is carrying out acts of terrorism and never took steps against it.'[2]

In the meantime, the army asked for permission to expand operations and direct them not only against the Islamic militants but also against Arafat's PA. 'We said,' a leading military commander recalls, 'those who carried out this act belong to the Palestinian establishment ... not to Hamas or Islamic Jihad ... So if something like that could be carried out by a part of the PA, then perhaps the time has come for us to expand our operations against the PA's security apparatus.'

In Ramallah, a stream of visitors was urging Arafat to take action against the perpetrators. Terje Roed-Larsen, the UN special envoy in the Middle East, pressed Arafat to condemn the assassination and take on the extremists. Arafat responded: 'The assassination is extremely damaging to the Palestinian cause.' Larsen insisted on more. 'Words are not enough', he recalls saying to Arafat. 'This time the PA must take vigorous action against terrorism.' Ron Schlicher, the US Consul-General in Jerusalem, also went to see Arafat to demand action. 'We will act on it', Arafat said, to which Schlicher replied, 'No, I need specifics, will you *arrest* these people?' Arafat: 'Yes, yes, it will be done.'[3] Assistant Secretary of State William Burns also travelled to Ramallah to urge Arafat to take on the extremists, and found the Palestinian leader trying to shift the focus to Palestinian grievances. Burns said, 'This is not the time for that ... You must understand very clearly just how the Administration feels about this kind of killing ... and take action.'[4] But Arafat did little. 'We have curfews', he complained to American and European visitors who came to urge him to act; 'I can't go anywhere ... my security forces can't do anything ...'[5] But it was never easy with Arafat at times like these, as Alastair Crooke, who served as Special Security Adviser to Javier Solana, the EU head of Foreign and Security Policy, explains:

Arafat at these times has a wonderful defensive mechanism ... 'You know, the Israelis have destroyed these Roman trees!' Papers come in, you get diverted. It's not even counter-attack, he just wanders off on to other subjects. I don't recall him really engaging on Zeevi. There were plenty of people who would come and wag fingers at him, and Arafat would tap his foot and look round rather sort of grimly, then suddenly the usual plot: someone would come in through the door and put some papers in front of him and he says, 'You will not believe it, the Israelis have just . . .' Then he'd read out something about a school being bombed or something. At many meetings people came away either thinking they had an agreement when they didn't, or they were frustrated because they had ended up talking about the Christian church in Nazareth. He was good at that.[6]

President Bush wrote Arafat a strong letter in mid-November 2001, the bottom line of which was that Arafat had failed to act decisively on the Zeevi assassination and to root out terrorism. Violence continued, with the Israeli military tightening its grip on the occupied territories – deploying checkpoints, separating one village from another, doing searches and imposing curfews – and the Palestinians hitting back. On 27 November, two Palestinians killed 3 Israelis and wounded 30 others in Afula in northern Israel, and two days later, 3 more Israelis were killed as a suicide bomber exploded a bomb on a bus near Hadera in northern Israel. This was followed, on 1 December, by a double suicide bombing attack at the Ben Yehuda pedestrian mall in Jerusalem, which killed 11 people, mostly teenagers, and injured 180.[7] On 2 December, 15 Israelis were killed in the suicide bombing of a bus in Haifa, and on 9 December another Palestinian suicide bomber struck again in Haifa.

In December 2001, Aaron Miller of the State Department went to see the Palestinian leader with a list of thirty-three militants linked to terrorism, whom the US insisted that Arafat put behind bars. 'Arafat', as Miller recalls, 'exploded and began to cry, and had to leave the room for about ten or fifteen minutes, saying, "You are humiliating me . . . you are humiliating me." '[8] He knew the US could not have prepared the list itself, and so he was effectively being asked to take orders from Sharon. When Arafat returned to the room, as Miller recalls, 'he was kissing our hands, kissing us, and apologizing for his outburst'.

On 12 December 2001, an attack on an Israeli bus near the settlement of Emanuel on the West Bank left 10 Israelis dead and 30 wounded. For Prime Minister Sharon this was the last straw. He picked up the phone and called Defence Minister Ben-Eliezer and ordered retaliation, *there and then*. The military hit back hard, bombing Arafat's headquarters in Gaza and other government facilities, and destroying Arafat's entire helicopter fleet. In Cabinet, Prime Minister Sharon and his ministers decided that 'Chairman Arafat has made himself irrelevant . . . no contacts will be maintained with him.'[9]

'OH MY GOD WE'VE CAPTURED AN EMPTY SHIP'

However, Arafat *was* still very relevant, at least in Palestinian eyes. In Ramallah, on 16 December 2001, he called 'for a complete halt to all operations, especially suicidal operations [against Israel]', and went on to warn that 'we will punish all those who carry out and mastermind such operations'. It led to an almost total end to attacks on Israel (except on settlers and settlements in the occupied territories, which were regarded as legitimate targets) – including those by Hamas and Islamic Jihad.[10] As a result, there was a dramatic drop in the number of casualties on both sides: in December 2001, before Arafat's ceasefire, 69 Palestinians and 39 Israelis were killed; after, in January 2002, the number of Palestinians killed dropped to 30 and Israelis to 17.[11]

This ceasefire did not indicate a strategic change of mind in Arafat, however. Far from it; he was still very much prepared to use violence to achieve his aims, as was about to be dramatically demonstrated.

The *Karine A*, previous known as the *Rim K*, was a ship flying the convenience flag of the Pacific island of Tonga.[12] Omar Acawi, a colonel in the Palestinian Naval Police, was its commanding officer, and it had a crew of thirteen. The ship was purchased in Lebanon by Adel Mughrabi, a major buyer in the Palestinian weapons purchasing system, with the assistance of Hezbollah to the tune of $400,000. With Iranian help, Fuad Shubaki, Head of the Finance Administration in the PA and Arafat's confidant, arranged the $15 million necessary to pay for the fifty tonnes of arms and ordnance which were loaded on to *Karine A* on the Iranian island of Kish. The destination of the ship and its vast arsenal was the PA.

According to the 1993 Israeli–Palestinian Oslo Agreement, the Palestinians were limited to certain numbers and types of weapons and ordnance for their security, and although they had more arms than the agreement permitted, the Israelis had looked the other way as long as the excess weapons were limited to small arms. But on the *Karine A* there were 80-kilometre-range rockets, 122 mm mortars, anti-tank and anti-aircraft missiles, Katyusha rockets, and explosives. All of these went far beyond what Oslo permitted and, if turned on Israel, could have inflicted serious damage. Smuggling this consignment into Palestinian land constituted a serious violation of the Oslo Agreement.

The Palestinian plan was for the *Karine A* to unload its weapons in sealed barrels close to the shores of Gaza, from where the cargo would then be collected by the commander of the Palestinian Naval Police, Juma'a Ghali, and his executive Fathi Ghazem.

Israeli intelligence had found out about the *Karine A* as early as the spring of 2001 and kept an eye on her whereabouts. When she was seen sailing for the Suez Canal on her way to her final destination, the Israelis decided to board the ship. First, though, they had to be absolutely sure that this was the right target – seizing the wrong ship would have been very embarrassing. Therefore, as Chief of Staff Shaul Mofaz recalls in an interview for *Elusive Peace*, 'I demanded a hundred per cent identification of the ship . . . [My Naval Intelligence people] . . . asked me, "What do you mean by a hundred per cent identification?" I said, "I want to see a ship with the name *Karine A* on it."' Twenty-four hours later, Naval Intelligence put a picture on his desk and said: 'Sir, you have a picture, this is the ship, it has the name *Karine A* on it.'[13] With the ship's identity certain, Mofaz took personal charge of the operation from a command aircraft overhead. He recalls, 'I sat between the Commander of the Air Force and of the Navy . . . we had monitors that gave us a picture . . . and when we identified the ship [among many others sailing in the Red Sea] and we saw the name [*Karine A* written on it] and it fit the name we had from our Intelligence, I gave the green light for the operation.'

Still, there were a good many unknowns: it was the right ship, but were the weapons on board? Would the crew resist an attempt to take it over? Were the smuggled weapons, if they were there at all, booby-trapped to explode in the faces of the Israeli commandos? With all these questions hanging in the air, Operation Noah's Ark began.

In the early hours of 3 January 2002 Israeli navy commandos swooped down on to the deck of the *Karine A* from their helicopters. The takeover went smoothly, with no exchange of gunfire at all. But for Chief of Staff Mofaz, watching in his flying headquarters, there were still some tense moments:

Our troops ran to the storage rooms . . . the first storage room was empty, then the second storage room was empty and our hearts started to beat very fast. I said, 'Oh my God we've captured an empty ship.' But the third and fourth storage rooms were full; first they saw mattresses and toys but after the troops took away these mattresses and clothes and toys someone yelled out, 'Here we have found the first rockets and the Sagers and the mines and explosives', and only then did everyone breathe.

The ship was taken, but for now its capture was kept secret. The Chief of Staff did not want the news to get out until the *Karine A* and its naval escort were safely in Israel's territorial waters.[14]

'THE SPIDER AND THE FLY'

Meanwhile, Secretary of State Colin Powell's Special Advisor, General (Ret.) Anthony Zinni, was in Israel trying to take advantage of the quiet – the ceasefire called by Arafat two weeks before was still holding well – to bring Israelis and Palestinians together. His mission, which had begun in November 2001, was to try to get both sides to implement a security plan drawn up the previous June by CIA director George Tenet, aimed at creating a lasting ceasefire. Zinni's task was to try to move this along.

However, when he landed at Ben-Gurion Airport near Tel Aviv on Thursday, 3 January, Zinni was in for a surprise. He was met by Israeli security officials, who took him aside and told him in general terms about the *Karine A*. Early the next day, Zinni, accompanied by his deputy Aaron Miller, met the Prime Minister at his farm in the Negev and, as Zinni recalls, Sharon said to him, 'I have something very important to tell you.' The Prime Minister then went on to give Zinni more details about the *Karine A* operation. He told him that when the ship crossed into Israel's territorial waters, around midday, Israel would announce her capture. Zinni, who was on his way to Ramallah, realized that the announcement would take place during his meeting with Arafat, so he asked Sharon, 'Mr Prime Minister, I would like to be able to break the news to him . . . I want to look at Arafat's face and see the reaction.'[15] Zinni thought this might give him some leverage with Arafat, as he could say to him, 'You know, now you've been caught with your hand in the cookie jar . . . it's time to get serious.' Aaron Miller, present at all Zinni's meetings, remembers that 'The body language was like the spider and the fly . . . Sharon in this meeting was not only calm but extremely confident . . . assuming it was going to be successful.'[16] After consulting with his military advisers, Sharon gave Zinni the green light to break the news to Arafat, but he warned 'Don't do it before noon.'

In Ramallah later that day, Zinni met Arafat, saying to him, 'After lunch, Mr Chairman, I would like to see you privately.' Zinni planned to break the news in this tête-à-tête. Arafat, as Zinni recalls, said 'Fine, fine, after lunch we can talk.' But the lunch overran and, as Zinni recalls, 'All of a sudden people started running in, cell phones were going off and I knew right away when the cell phones started ringing and people got up that it had been announced, and it had been revealed. And then people came up to [Arafat] and started whispering, and I could pick up enough of the Arabic to know it was the *Karine A*.' Zinni watched for Arafat's reaction; he looked 'both confused and dismissive . . . "it's nothing", he said. "This was not our ship. It's an Israeli plot. This is an Israeli set-up."'

At their private meeting, Zinni said to Arafat, 'I don't advise you and I don't think it's wise for you to say it was somebody framing you, or a set-up. I think you should handle it very wisely, very openly, very honestly.' Pulling the Palestinian chief negotiator, Saeb Erekat, over to him, Aaron Miller said, 'Look, this is a very serious issue. You are smart enough to understand that whatever black arts the Israelis use, this isn't a set-up. So you have to condemn it, you have to credibly launch an investigation, and you need to ensure that those responsible for it are not only prosecuted but actually made accountable.' Erekat, Miller recalls, 'only did a lot of shucking and jiving and dancing around'. But what more could Erekat do or say? After all, his boss Arafat was denying any knowledge of the ship.

As for the Israelis, they played their cards carefully, doing their utmost to milk the affair for as much political advantage as possible. 'Usually', General Zinni explains, 'the [Israelis] just went in there with brute force. This time [however] they put the Palestinians on the defensive in a really slick way.'[17] Israeli Naval Intelligence Commander Admiral Yehezkel Mashita and Head of Research in Military Intelligence Yossi Kuperwasser, both former military attachés, travelled to Washington to brief the American Intelligence community – the Pentagon, Naval Intelligence, the CIA – on the *Karine A* affair and Arafat's PA link to it. Chief of Staff Mofaz also travelled in person to the US, bringing with him intelligence linking Arafat *personally* to the *Karine A*, and he explained to the Bush Administration how, as Mofaz recalls in an interview with *Elusive Peace*, 'Arafat reached a personal agreement with the Iranian leadership about receiving the weapons in return for allowing Iranians a foothold in the Palestinian territories.'[18]

And Arafat? He continued to play his cards badly, writing a letter to President Bush denying any link to the *Karine A*. According to a leading US diplomat:

[Arafat's] letter was met with a great deal of scepticism [in Washington] because it . . . flew in the face of the evidence that we had before us. And it deepened the sense on the part of the President and others that Arafat was playing a double game. And the commitments, the rhetoric that he had used at some point in conversations with us about wanting to try and stop violence, was simply not borne out in the actions he was taking.[19]

This letter, the diplomat adds, 'was what sunk [Arafat] there . . . The President wrote him off after that letter. It was a straight line downwards from there.'[20] Another US diplomat agrees. 'In Bush's mind', he explains, 'that was the ultimate disaster for Arafat. Disaster number one was not doing anything in response to the Zeevi [assasination]. Number two [was] the *Karine A*.' Indeed, the President took it as a personal affront that Arafat would lie to him and this really was the point of no return for Arafat as far as President Bush was concerned.

'WE ARE NOT ASSASSINATING THEM . . . WE'RE REMOVING THEM FROM OUR SOCIETY'

The Israeli military and Shin Bet, meanwhile, were preparing a preemptive strike against the man they accused of murdering twelve Israelis between January and December 2001. A particularly horrific example was the case of two Israelis who, having mistakenly wandered into the West Bank town of Tulkarm on 23 January 2001, were taken to a nearby field and killed in cold blood.

Raid Karmi was twenty-eight, charismatic, brave and hugely admired by young Palestinians in Tulkarm. But for Israeli Defence Minister Ben-Eliezer he was a real headache. 'I have spent many months working on him', Ben-Eliezer recalls; 'his name never went off my desk.' According to Chief of Staff Mofaz, 'Raid Karmi was a terrorist with blood on his hands . . . he was involved in many terrorist attacks against us . . . he used explosives, machine-gun fire against the army and striking civilians . . . we had to either arrest him or kill him.' The decision that was taken was to 'put Karmi on a cross' – to kill him.[21]

It was not easy to do, however, as Karmi was elusive and had already survived one attempt on his life, on 6 September 2001. 'He used costumes, he moved from place to place, he hid, changed locations, changed women. The information [about him] did not last more than twenty minutes', recalls Ben-Eliezer. But the Israelis finally discovered a weakness: he used to visit the same mistress every day before lunch, the wife of a Fatah official in Tulkarm. On his way back to his hideout, Karmi would always use the same route along a cemetery wall. 'And once we found out that this was a regular habit with a regular time schedule then things became simpler,' recalls

Ben-Eliezer. Then one day Shin Bet reported to the Defence Minister, 'We have him now and we know that today between this hour and that hour he will leave the house of this lady . . .'[22]

The Defence Minister knew that killing Karmi would wreck the fragile ceasefire declared by Arafat on 16 December 2001. So, despite a prime opportunity to take out a dangerous enemy, he opposed the operation. At the meeting of military leaders and Shin Bet where the decision was to be taken, he argued that 'if we are going to kill him . . . we are also going to kill the ceasefire'. The Chief of Staff and the Director of Shin Bet were in favour of taking Karmi out, the latter claiming that Karmi was a 'ticking bomb'. Prime Minister Sharon was very keen on these special operations. He called the Palestinians on Israel's wanted list 'dogs' and was often the driving force behind a strike.[23]

Finding himself in a minority, the Defence Minister reluctantly agreed to allow the operation to go ahead, but he said to the Prime Minister, 'Arik . . . I want you to know that I am not certain of this . . . I'm going to do it, but my heart is not totally in it. Because right now we are in the middle of a ceasefire . . . it is clear that it will end the ceasefire.'

With the green light given, the Israelis planted a bomb at head height in the wall of the cemetery on Karmi's route home in an eastern neighbourhood of Tulkarm. And on Monday, 14 January 2002, at eleven in the morning as Karmi walked past the cemetery, the bomb was detonated. He was killed instantly. Abu Hamid, the Al-Aqsa Martyrs Brigade commander in Jenin and a colleague of Karmi, recalls how after the assassination, 'We all went down to the streets and had a small meeting together. We thought there should be a response from the Al-Aqsa Martyrs Brigade. We co-ordinated with the leadership on what our response would be.' After this consultation an official response came, saying, 'The so-called ceasefire is cancelled, cancelled, cancelled . . . You [Israel] have opened hell on yourself. You will be burned by its fire.'[24] The ceasefire was indeed over and the violence was resumed.

Some two weeks later, on 30 January 2002, Prime Minister Sharon hosted a dinner at his residence in Jerusalem. Arafat, of course, was not invited, as Sharon would not talk to him. But the guests included Arafat's closest advisers, Mohammed Rashid, Abu Mazen and Abu Ala. They dined and talked for four hours and Rashid recalls it as 'an amicable meeting'. In the course of the conversation Abu Mazen said to Sharon, 'You should stop the targeted assassinations', whereupon the Prime Minister replied, 'We're not assassinating them ... we are just removing them from our society.'[25]

15

Operation Defensive Shield

'THIS IS MY PROPOSAL'

March 2002 ('Black March') was a bloody month, claiming the lives of 239 Palestinians and, in 17 separate suicide bombs, 133 Israelis. Determined to stop the bloodshed on both sides, which diverted attention from his war on terror, President Bush announced in a Rose Garden speech on 7 March that, 'because of our commitment to peace, I'm sending General Tony Zinni back to the region next week to work with Israel and the Palestinians to begin implementing the Tenet work plan'. It was to be yet another stab at trying to deal with the security problem.[1]

When Zinni arrived in Israel he gathered together the Trilateral Committee group, consisting of security experts from Israel, the occupied territories and the US, which had been set up by George Tenet to deal with security co-ordination. This committee was the only point of engagement between the parties and it seemed to be the best venue for any attempt to put the Tenet plan into effect. They started work on 14 March 2002 and 'over the next few days', as Zinni recalls, 'I sensed a far more serious focus and readiness than ever before to make the process work'.[2] Indeed, in subsequent meetings, the parties succeeded in dramatically shrinking gaps on the implementation of the Tenet plan, and they were close to striking a deal. Some gaps remained – thirteen issues which concerned the Israelis and three which worried the Palestinians. On 26 March, with time running out – it was feared that any major attack on Israel and a strong retaliation could easily derail the talks and unravel the fragile understandings which were starting to emerge – Zinni decided to offer his own proposal, what he called a Bridging Proposal, based on his understanding of the needs of the parties.

That day, at 7 p.m., Zinni faxed his proposal to both sides, explaining in a follow-up telephone conversation that 'this is my proposal . . . and I think it's practical . . . I think it's feasible . . . I think it's balanced.'[3] Zinni asked the negotiators to take the proposal to their respective leaders to see if they would be willing to implement it. After studying the document, and before they had even taken it to Arafat, the Palestinians said, 'General . . . this plan is in fact a new plan and not just an implementation of the Tenet work plan.' They felt that the original Tenet plan was, in fact, more favourable to them than the new Zinni proposals and insisted that they should focus on how to implement the previous Tenet plan rather than introduce a new one.[4] 'OK,' Zinni said, 'then you don't accept the proposals.' Not wanting to be blamed for wrecking the talks, the Palestinians said, 'We are not opposed to them. We just need to talk further about them.' Zinni replied, 'We've got to hurry! We've got to hurry! We need an answer!' According to the Palestinian negotiator Saeb Erekat, Zinni said, 'How much time do you need to review the paper?', to which Erekat said, 'I have to take it back to my leadership, and then we have to hold a session with the Higher Negotiating Committee headed by President Arafat, Abu Mazen, Abu Ala and the others. And then, I hope that I can get back to you in twenty-four hours.' Zinni said, 'That's too long. We don't have time. Can you do it quicker?' Erekat promised, 'I'll do my best.'[5]

'PUT UP OR SHUT UP'

Erekat phoned Arafat from his car, telling him that 'General Zinni submitted a paper to us. It's very important Mr President that you call all your colleagues and the Higher Negotiating Committee.'[6] Later that night Erekat took the committee through the Zinni proposals, which disappointed them, as they felt that the paper made unrealistic demands by requiring them to stop Palestinian militants and collect weapons *before* the Israelis made any equivalent gestures. The Palestinians wanted a parallel rather than sequential approach, both sides acting at the same time. Arafat instructed Erekat to produce a formal Palestinian response that included all their reservations. It was far from a straightforward yes or no.

Meanwhile, the Israeli negotiators – General Giora Eiland and his deputy Eival Gilady – went off to see Chief of Staff Mofaz and the Defence Minister, and got their approval to go straight to the Prime Minister and tell him, 'the Ministry of Defence thinks you should accept [Zinni's proposals]'.[7] It was the day before Passover, one of Israel's biggest holidays, and the Israeli negotiators wished the Prime Minister to accept the Bridging Proposal with no reservations, to give Zinni a clear yes, for if there were any reservations the whole thing would have to be delayed until after the week-long holiday. At 8 p.m. on 26 March, Eiland and Gilady phoned the Prime Minister's office and were given an appointment to see him in three hours' time.

Later, in Jerusalem, they waited nervously for Sharon to finish a meeting with the Israeli ambassador to Belgium and his wife. At midnight the two finally walked into Sharon's office holding the detailed Zinni Bridging Proposal, written in English. They had the hard task of persuading a very suspicious Prime Minister to accept it. The Prime Minister insisted on going over each and every paragraph and Gilady read it out loud to him. Giora Eiland recalls: 'Sharon made us work very hard to convince him that this paper should be acceptable . . . he asked a lot of questions not about what was written, but about what was not written there . . . What if, what if, what if the Palestinians . . .'[8] Sharon was particularly concerned about the lack of sanctions should one side fail to carry out its obligations, as he suspected the Palestinians would not stick to the letter of the agreement. But Eiland and Gilady insisted that the Prime Minister should approve the entire deal as a package and not open any issue, lest the Palestinians demand to open other issues as well. Eventually, at two in the morning, Sharon said, 'OK, I approve this, but I want you to know that I'm really not happy with this section and this section, but I am accepting your recommendation, and I accept the plan.'

Delighted, Eiland and Gilady considered what to do next. Should they wait until daybreak to break the news to the Americans? As Eiland recalls, 'I said, "Well, it's two o'clock in the morning, we can wait until morning, it's not that urgent", but my deputy [Gilady] said "No, we have sat here until two o'clock in the morning, and kept the Prime Minister busy, we'll get Zinni busy as well."' Gilady then phoned Zinni at his hotel, waking him up to tell him, very formally, 'The State of Israel accepts your proposals and we are ready to implement them from tomorrow [27 March].' Zinni said, 'You've got to be kidding, you accept it?'[9] By then fully awake, Zinni consulted his deputy Aaron Miller, urging him, 'You gotta push as hard as you possibly can [with the Palestinians].'[10] Miller phoned Erekat. 'Look,' he said, 'we need an answer. And we need an answer quickly.' But Erekat started arguing about this clause and that clause and an impatient Miller said to him, 'This is not the time for academic arguments . . . the seminar is over.' He added, 'You tell Chairman [Arafat] to put up, or shut up. Because if you don't, in combination with *Karine A*, and the ditch you've already dug yourself with this Administration, it will be over . . . You will have no one left. And the Chairman has to understand he will have no one left. He will be alone. Put up or shut up. And tell the Chairman to do the same – with no excuses.'[11] Erekat replied: 'Aaron, it's two-thirty in the morning. It has to be tomorrow. But I promise you it will be tomorrow.'

The following morning, 27 March, Erekat was still at work in a room in the *muqata* on the Palestinian response with the young lawyer Ghaith al-Omari. By that time, however, Zinni had started to lose patience, fearing the whole fragile plan would soon collapse. 'I have this sixth sense,' he explains, 'the hair on the back of my neck is going up, that we are going to get hit – hit hard, someone in here is going to upset this whole plan . . . and Passover is about to start.'[12]

'TOMORROW . . . YOU WILL BE IN PARADISE'

While all of this was taking place, a Hamas operative was on his way to Israel, dressed as a young woman, with a belt full of explosives around his middle.

Muhammad Abd al-Basset Oudeh was a 25-year-old Palestinian from the West Bank town of Tulkarm. He was a deeply religious and angry man whose wish to travel to Jordan to marry his fiancée had been blocked by the Israelis. He thus decided to join Hamas, become a *shahid* (a martyr) and kill himself in a suicide bombing mission, taking as many Israelis as possible with him. Al-Basset Oudeh was recruited into Hamas by Muammar Shahrouri under the auspices of Abbas Bin Muhammad al-Sayyid, the leader of Hamas in Tulkarm.

With the Jewish Passover round the corner, the would-be *shahid* met al-Sayyid and Shahrouri in the apartment of the latter's grandfather in Tulkarm to make the final preparations for the bombing mission. They brought a video camera to record the *shahid* as he read his farewell statement and Will in front of a Hamas flag, and an M-16 assault rifle. This recording would later be used to publicize the mission all over the Palestinian territories.[13] Al-Basset Oudeh read:

Our blood Sharon isn't cheap and our homeland is not easily invaded and no one will protect you from our bodies' shrapnel nor Arabs neither non-Arabs, and your entity will not be saved by initiatives or by unlimited Western support.

In an exclusive interview conducted in an Israeli jail for *Elusive Peace*, Muammar Shahrouri recalls: 'We videoed him ... with the M-16, the way we always do it, and he read his Will [saying] ... that he was going out to do an operation of revenge.' Next, al-Sayyid equipped Abd al-Basset Oudeh with a belt that contained approximately 20 lb of explosives and included pieces of shredded metal to increase the carnage, and demonstrated how to detonate the belt using a switch.[14] They then helped the bomber to dress. As Muammar Shahrouri recalls:

Abd al-Basset bought the clothes himself – they had to fit properly. He bought a sweater, and he bought a wig, a blonde wig. He was a nice looking guy, and so the most appropriate thing for him was that we dress him like a woman ... we shaved him, we gave him a haircut and he put on the wig, and we made him very pretty ... and he was carrying a bag, and he had sunglasses ... he looked like a foreign woman.

By that time, Hamas already had the posters of the bomber ready to be distributed. The posters announced the death of the martyr Muhammad Abd al-Basset Oudeh, and featured a quote from the Koran saying, 'A better life in Paradise is promised to those Muslim believers who kill infidels in the name of Allah.' In the centre was the picture of the *shahid* holding an M-16 assault rifle in his right hand, a Koran in his left and with an explosive belt around his body.

With the preparations complete, the group then spent the last moments praying and joking. 'Those were the last moments of his life', Muammar Shahrouri recalls:

Abd al-Basset kept smiling . . . and was optimistic . . . Abbas [al-Sayyid] said to Abd al-Basset 'Today *inshallah* (God willing) you are going to become a *shahid*, and tomorrow . . . you will be in the garden, you will be in paradise . . . Abd al-Basset . . . was calling to God, he was praying, he was asking forgiveness . . . he was reading the Koran a lot, he was praying, I prayed with him, he and I and Abbas . . . and there was an air of freedom . . . of happiness in the room, because Abd al-Basset was going out, and he had joked around with us, and he knew he wasn't going to just die, he was going out to get close to God, and that he was going to do it in the best way, the best way possible . . . Yeah, he was happy . . . Yeah, he had waited eight months for this moment.

His wait was nearly over. Soon, Fathi Raja Ahmad Khatib, the man who would drive Abd al-Basset Oudeh to Israel to look for the right place to fulfil his mission, arrived and they all said their farewells.[15] Muammar Shahrouri:

Abbas [al-Sayyid] said goodbye to him, and hugged him, and said to him 'We'll miss you', and me, I don't know exactly what I did . . . I felt hot . . . I showed him warmth, and I hugged him and I kissed him, and I said to him 'You are going to paradise, and I hope to come some time', and he said, 'Hopefully, God willing.'

It was around two o'clock in the afternoon on 27 March that Abd al-Basset Oudeh left. The first hurdle was an Israeli roadblock. The driver, Fathi Khatib, remembers: 'We were able to pass through these roadblocks because I had a blue fake Israeli identity card . . . and the suicide bomber with me had a driving licence of a Jewish girl and he was dressed like the picture . . . the suicide bomber himself was very calm . . . very happy.'

They drove to the village of Nazlat 'Isa where they switched to another car, and crossed into Israel proper. 'The goal for us', recalls Fathi Khatib, 'was [to find a gathering of Israelis who] wore military uniforms so that we would be able to specifically get the people who kill us. And we were not able to get to those areas where there was an Army base so we tried to find [a target] for about four and a half hours.'[16] They drove towards Herzliya, just north of Tel Aviv but, failing to find a target, headed to Tel Aviv. Again, they could not find a target and they then headed to the northern coastal town of Netanya. 'We hardly talked', recalls the driver Fathi Khatib. 'He was just praying to God saying, "Let me be successful."' When they got to Netanya the bomber got out of the car next to the seaside Park Hotel, where he had once worked. It was crowded with people celebrating the Passover.

'ARIK LISTEN . . . A CATASTROPHE HAS OCCURRED'

It was around seven in the evening when Abd al-Basset Oudeh entered the Park Hotel and walked into the main dining hall where guests were sitting around the table in the middle of the Seder, the feast ritual with which Jews celebrate Passover. He stopped in the middle of the hall, pressed the switch on his explosive belt and blew himself up, instantly killing 29 and wounding close to 150. It was the most devastating single suicide bombing since the outbreak of hostilities in September 2000.

Defence Minister Ben-Eliezer was celebrating the Passover with troops at the Gilo School on the West Bank. He recalls how they had just finished the prayers and he asked, 'Well – when are we eating?' At that moment he was pulled to one side and told that a few minutes before a bomb had exploded at the Park Hotel in Netanya and there were many casualties. Ben-Eliezer recalls, 'I rushed directly to the Ministry of Defence.' He phoned the Prime Minister. 'Arik listen,' he said, 'a catastrophe has occurred.' Sharon, as Ben-Eliezer remembers, was 'boiling . . . boiling. He said, "Listen! We have to destroy, destroy! I hope this time there will be no question about getting rid of Arafat!" '[17]

In Jerusalem, around the same time, the American envoy General Zinni and his deputy Aaron Miller were guests for the Passover dinner at the home of one of Sharon's political advisers. 'We were at the point', Miller recalls, 'when they were reciting the ritual in which God's ten plagues were visited on the Egyptians and it's customary to take a finger and dip it in the blood-red wine, and recite each plague, not in order to gloat, but to mourn the deaths of so many innocent Egyptians and convey the seriousness of God's wrath.' Just at that point, one of the security guards came in and whispered something in Miller's ear. Zinni, looking at his deputy, as he recalls, 'knew . . . that something major had happened'. Miller went over to Zinni and said, 'I've got to talk to you *immediately*.' They stopped the Seder and Miller took Zinni aside and told him of reports about a big explosion at the Park Hotel. Zinni soon received confirmation from Defence Minister Ben-Eliezer. 'General Zinni,' he said, 'there is going to be strong retaliation. The only hope now is if the Palestinians accept your proposals [and do that] immediately . . . that is the only way we can mitigate the Israeli reaction . . . If they don't accept this now, and we go into this operation at the scale that's being planned, your plan will be dead.'[18]

Zinni phoned Arafat. 'I pleaded with him . . . pleaded with him,' he recalls. 'I said, "Tell me no, or tell me yes on the Zinni Plan, tell me you want to restart this." ' But instead of giving a straightforward answer or commitment, Arafat started shouting so loudly Zinni had to hold the receiver away from his ear. 'I'm against the deaths of innocents . . . We have nothing to do with this, you have to understand we are in a confrontation with the Israelis and people are frustrated.' Zinni phoned Arafat's chief negotiator Saeb Erekat, hoping that perhaps *he* could pressure Arafat into accepting his proposals. But, as Zinni recalls, 'He would not give me an answer, he just waffled around it . . . just hemmed and hawed.' General Giora Eiland, a leading Israeli negotiator, also talked to General Zinni that night. 'This is the end of the co-operation between Israel and the Palestinian Authority,' he said, 'and as far as we are concerned, there is no hope that we'll continue to work together to try to solve the security problems. These days are over.' Zinni, as Eiland remembers, 'realized that his [Zinni Bridging] proposal was dead . . . that his mission was over'.

'PEOPLE WERE DRESSED VERY SMARTLY'

Back in Tel Aviv, at 11.30 p.m., Defence Minister Ben-Eliezer gathered his military chiefs and, as his Military Secretary Mike Herzog recalls, 'People were dressed very smartly – not in military uniform [because they came straight from their Seders]. The atmosphere was very heavy. It was obvious to everyone that we had crossed a threshold.' In the discussion, the Defence Minister talked in terms of a limited operation to be directed against Hamas, whom they knew to be behind the bomb. But his military chiefs argued that more radical action was required. Deputy Chief of Staff Moshe ('Boogie') Yaalon said that the problem was not Hamas but Arafat's PA, which was allowing Hamas' violence to continue. The only way to stop this 'crazy tidal wave of violence', as Yaalon put it, 'was to recapture the Palestinian cities . . . to take security matters back into our own hands. If this means neutralizing the abilities of the PA both politically and in security matters, then it's better to do this, because in the end trusting them would prove to be one big mistake.'[19] Besides, argued the generals, Hamas was too elusive to be pinned down and had no hard targets which the army could go after. The military was calling to reoccupy all the territories given to Arafat to run under the 1993 Oslo Agreement. As Chief of Staff Mofaz recalls in an interview for *Elusive Peace*, 'it was clear to me that we would have to go into the centres where the terrorist organizations were located . . . inside the Palestinian cities, inside the refugee camps'.

The military chiefs won the argument. The next question was whether the attack should be focused only on the West Bank, or directed against the Gaza Strip as well. It was agreed that the focus should be on the West Bank where, unlike the Gaza Strip, there was

no fence or other obstacle to stop terrorists from cro
and carrying out attacks such as the one at the Park H

When they had made these decisions, the military
Security Cabinet meeting chaired by the Prime Ministe
which immediately accepted their plan. It was decided,   ...on's
adviser Danny Ayalon recalls, that 'from now on we do not rely on
Palestinian promises to fight terror, we do not rely any more on
Palestinian steps, and we don't expect anything from the Palestinians
to stop the terror . . . we have to take it upon ourselves'. According to
Ben-Eliezer's Military Secretary Mike Herzog, although final govern-
mental approval was still needed, it was at that small Cabinet meeting
that 'the decision was made . . . to reoccupy the [Palestinian] cities'.
When the meeting was over, instructions were given to military units
to start preparations and for some to advance to forward positions.

'I DON'T WANT ANOTHER JESUS STORY ON OUR SHOULDERS'

One day after the bombing, on the night of 28 March, Sharon gathered
the entire government and his military chiefs to discuss Israel's
response to the horrific attack at the Park Hotel. The meeting lasted
eight hours, and the atmosphere was very stormy. On the agenda
was what should be done with Arafat. Some ministers suggested expelling him. However, the powerful intelligence chiefs opposed this. The
head of Mossad, Ephraim Halevi, the head of Shin Bet, Avi Dichter,
and the Director of Military Intelligence, General Ahron Zeevi-
Farkash, argued that Arafat in exile might cause more damage than
Arafat in Ramallah. There was also the fear that Arafat, who always
carried two guns, might resist any attempt to expel him and perhaps
even be killed, which would inevitably increase Palestinian violence.
Chief of Staff Shaul Mofaz thought otherwise. He explained to the
meeting that with Arafat around it would be difficult to calm the
situation, and they should not pass up this opportunity to get rid of
him once and for all. Mofaz, as General Eiland recalls, said that timing
was of the essence, and that under the shock of the 'horrible massacre

...at the hotel in Netanya . . . it would be much easier [to expel Arafat], and to justify it, than in any calmer situation'. Mofaz himself recalls: 'My recommendation to the government [was that] Arafat should be exiled from the Palestinian territories and sent somewhere overseas.' The Prime Minister himself agreed, telling ministers that it was finally time to expel Arafat.

It was easy for Sharon to take this extreme line because he knew quite well that other members of his coalition, notably the Labour Defence Minister Ben-Eliezer and Foreign Minister Peres, would oppose it. 'I prevented Arafat's expulsion all along', Shimon Peres recalls in an interview for *Elusive Peace*:

I said 'I don't want another Jesus story on our shoulders.' I thought there was no point in expelling Arafat, because Arafat outside could be no less effective than Arafat inside. On the outside he would be seen, appear to be persecuted and the television would be all over him . . . and what would we achieve by that? Arafat is also a political leader, and not just the leader of a former terrorist organization . . . he was also elected and we have an agreement with him . . . I prevented his expulsion.

Expulsion was not the only option discussed. Another idea, as General Giora Eiland recalls, was to 'begin [the operation] with a one-tonne bomb on [Arafat's] *muqata* in Ramallah [as] the very first move'. But, attractive as it was to some ministers present, the US had vetoed killing Arafat. A leading American official told *Elusive Peace* how he passed a message from the President to Sharon, making it absolutely clear to the Prime Minister that 'they mustn't touch Arafat'.[20]

After a long argument the government meeting decided to compromise. Arafat (though not the PA) was defined as 'an enemy' and he would be 'isolated' physically at his headquarters 'at this stage'. The last three words were added by the Prime Minister to leave his options open for further steps against Arafat. As Defence Minister Ben-Eliezer explains, 'the conclusion was that we were getting very very close to the *muqata*, so close we could see it with the naked eye. But . . . without harming [Arafat].'

The die was cast. Operation Defensive Shield, a full-scale invasion of the West Bank, would begin immediately. The IDF would enter Palestinian towns and cities under Arafat's control on the West Bank starting with Ramallah, 'the capital of the terror', as Defence Minister Ben-Eliezer dubbed it. General Giora Eiland recalls explaining to ministers that the army will need 'complete freedom to operate according to operational considerations with absolutely no political constraints . . . [for a period of] at least a month'. This was needed, the military chiefs explained, in order to round up suspected militants, find the laboratories where weapons were illegally produced and to impose tight control over the West Bank on a 'door to door basis'. Thirty thousand reservists were to be called up – the biggest mobilization in twenty years.[21]

'THESE TANKS ARE NOT COMING FOR A TOUR TO RAMALLAH'

In the meantime, the American envoy General Zinni had kept up the pressure on the Palestinians to provide him with an answer to the Bridging Proposal. On 28 March, at 11 p.m., the PA's chief negotiator, Saeb Erekat, at last phoned Ron Schlicher, the US Consul-General in Jerusalem, to say that 'the answer is ready'. Schlicher said, 'I'll send a car to the checkpoint at the outskirts of Ramallah. Just hand whoever will be there the letter.'[22] Around 12.30 on the morning of 29 March, Erekat handed the letter over to the driver of the American car. When Zinni and his deputy Aaron Miller opened the envelope back in Jerusalem, they were very disappointed. The answer, as Aaron Miller recalls, was another ' "yes but" . . . in a way that highlighted the clean Israeli "yes" by comparison'. Zinni describes the Palestinian response as 'a whole mish-mish . . . not an answer that we could use'.

Erekat – no fool – understood that with the Palestinian failure to give a clear response to the Zinni proposals, the game was up – and an Israeli operation was coming. Thus, once he had handed over the letter, he went straight to Arafat in the *muqata*, at 1.30 in the morning, and said, 'Mr President, I think things will happen here tonight. And if you want me to stay then I'll stay with you. I have brought my shirts, my socks.' Arafat said, 'No. If this happens you're no good to me here. I want you outside.'[23] At 1.45 a.m., Erekat left the *muqata* and drove to his home in Jericho. At the bypass road minutes from Ramallah, he saw a huge column of Israeli tanks, armoured vehicles and ambulances. Erekat immediately phoned Arafat's office to report. 'Look,' he said, 'these tanks are not coming for a tour to Ramallah. They're in for a big thing in Ramallah. They will enter Ramallah.'[24]

Later that day, Palestinian leaders started gathering at the *muqata* where, as Mohammed Rashid recalls, they found Arafat 'in his khaki fatigues . . . ready . . . very cautious . . . alert'. Arafat asked each of his aides where they intended to stay. Rashid recalls how 'Arafat said to Yasser [Abed Rabbo] "Where are you going to stay?" He said, "My house." Arafat said, "Keep in touch from there and don't leave your house without instructions." He then asked Jibril [Rajoub]. Jibril said, "My house." Arafat said, "You stay here or go to your headquarters. You are in charge of the forces." He asked me. I said, "I'll stay here or go to a hotel." Arafat said, "Go to a hotel and stay in contact with me and try to organize an information campaign about that attack." And he asked Mohammed Dahlan to do the same.'[25]

By then, Operation Defensive Shield was already under way. The Israeli forces had reached the outskirts of Ramallah, and had started taking control of other West Bank cities and towns.

'THE LEMON LEAVES . . . WHEN YOU FRY THEM, THEY BECOME LIKE WOOD'

The attack on Arafat's compound in Ramallah, when it came, was devastating. Surrounded by tanks and troops, the compound's walls were crushed, along with the cars in the parking area, and a tight siege was imposed with Israeli troops taking up positions just fifty metres away. Israeli troops occupied the buildings next door to Arafat's, taking positions on rooftops. From the basement of his headquarters, with the Israelis closing in on him, Arafat talked to CNN by telephone: 'They have destroyed completely seven of our buildings . . . Completely surrounding my office and firing at my office with all their armaments.'

In the coming days, Israeli forces moved into other towns. In Bethlehem, just south of Jerusalem, their attack was particularly fierce. 'It was quite different from all the previous invasions', Mazzin Hussein, a Palestinian militant in Bethlehem, recalls. 'Usually we can get into the Old City and that's it, they can't follow us. But this time, they were all over ... shooting ... tanks ... everything. So there wasn't really time to make decisions – we just ran.'[26] Crucially, an Israeli special forces unit – the Shaldag Unit – had not deployed in time to block the entrance to the Church of the Nativity, built on the birthplace of Jesus Christ. Palestinian militants flooded into it, including many on Israel's wanted list. Father Parthenius, a Greek Orthodox priest resident at the church, recalls how 'We finished our prayers then went over to find out what was going on. We spoke to them. They were very tired, nervous and scared. They wanted something sweet, so we made some tea.'[27] From that moment on, the Palestinians – more than 200 of them – were locked inside the church and surrounded by Israeli troops, under a tight siege, just like Arafat in Ramallah. With so many people gathered in the building conditions soon deteriorated. Mazzin Hussein recalls that food was so tight that 'We [were reduced] to eating leaves and grass – lemon leaves ... we ate anything that could have been eaten, we ate wood. The lemon leaves ... when you fry them, they become like wood.' From outside the church the Palestinian Chief of Police in Bethlehem, Ala Hosni, tried to help with some food. He recalls: 'I arranged for us to throw bread from house to house until it got to the houses near the Church [of the Nativity], and then someone would lob it into the courtyard.'[28]

The siege of the Church of the Nativity would continue for many days prompting – as some Palestinians hoped when they entered it in the first place – an international outcry over the treatment of such a holy place.

16

The Holy Land Defeats America

'IF YOU THINK ABOUT THE OTHER THINGS THAT
WE WANT TO DO'

With Defensive Shield under way, in Washington, the National Security Council – the President's main forum for considering national security and foreign policy matters – met in the White House Situation Room. The President was there as well as all the NSC principals. On the agenda was what the United States could, and should, do to defuse the escalating conflict in the occupied territories and Israel. Defense Secretary Donald Rumsfeld was particularly opposed to any US engagement. In his eyes the Israelis were conducting a fight against terrorists, and it would be inconsistent with the President's war on terror for America to try to rein in Ariel Sharon. Rumsfeld also argued that the situation between Israel and the Palestinians was so far from resolution, and the Palestinian side was so corrupt and beyond repair, that there was really no basis on which the United States should try to intervene diplomatically until the Palestinian leadership changed. When Secretary of State Colin Powell suggested he should at least go to the region to try to calm the situation down, Rumsfeld said, as Powell recalls in an interview for *Elusive Peace*, 'Well you know, Colin, I'm not sure this is the best use of you this time . . . It's not clear what can be accomplished under this set of circumstances.'[1]

Powell disagreed. He said that the United States had no choice but to intervene, as the violence had reached such intolerable levels that US credibility in the region was at stake unless there was a visible high-level American initiative to try to improve the situation. The President listened to the debate and, somewhat uncharacteristically, ruled against Secretary Rumsfeld. He leaned over the table, looked directly at Rumsfeld and said, 'If you think about the other things that we want to do in this region', namely to topple the Iraqi leader Saddam Hussein with the support of as many Arab states as possible, 'then it is really important that we be seen as on the right side of the Palestinian issue.'[2] It was settled that there would be a high-level American initiat-ive led by Secretary of State Powell. 'At the end of the meeting, after a very extensive discussion,' Colin Powell recalls in an interview, 'the President and I were walking out and upstairs towards his office, and he was to my left and he glanced over at me with a slight smile on his face and said, "This is going to be painful. You're going to have a tough time over there and you're probably going to lose a few layers of skin, but you can stand it, you can afford this." ' Powell replied, 'You got it Mr President.'[3] They then discussed the plan. First the President would make a speech outlining the new policy to get Israeli–Palestinian negotiations restarted. Arafat would have to denounce terrorism unequivocally, and Prime Minister Sharon would have to halt Defensive Shield and get out of land recently occupied. Then – although this was still just a suggestion – there would be a regional international conference of foreign ministers (rather than heads of state, which would effectively enable Arafat to be kept out of the picture as he was not a foreign minister). The logic of a regional ministerial conference – an idea pushed strongly by the British Prime Minister Tony Blair, who needed to demonstrate to his sceptical public that he was getting something in return for his support for Bush in Iraq – was that it would bring together ministers from Europe and elsewhere and underscore Arafat's commitment to the international community to try to do more to stop terrorism. In fact, the idea of a regional conference was also raised by Prime Minister Sharon, who thought that it could reinforce the importance of key Arab players doing *their* part in pressing Arafat to stop attacks on Israel.

Acknowledging just how difficult it would be to make the plan work, even just to stop the Israeli military operation, Powell said to the President, 'Do you understand what you're saying to the Israelis?

You're going to have to look Sharon in the eye and say "get out".[4] Bush replied that he understood.

'I MEANT WHAT I SAID'

Soon after, on 4 April 2002, President Bush stood in the White House Rose Garden and announced that he was sending Secretary Powell to the region. He said:

Israel is facing a terrible and serious challenge. For seven days, it has acted to root out terrorist nests. America recognizes Israel's right to defend itself from terror. Yet, to lay the foundations of future peace, I ask Israel to halt incursions into Palestinian-controlled areas and begin the withdrawal from those cities it has recently occupied.[5]

In Israel, meanwhile, US ambassador Dan Kurtzer was asked to visit the Prime Minister to back the President's demand for a withdrawal. He was to tell him that in the view of the US, there was still legitimacy to the Palestinian Authority. The message was, 'OK, you did your military stuff and now find a way to gracefully back away.'[6] But Sharon would not have it, as the army had not yet had anywhere near enough time to achieve their aims, which were to occupy Palestinian territory, round up suspected militants, find all the laboratories where weapons were illegally produced and impose tight control over the West Bank. Danny Ayalon, Sharon's close aide, recalls how the Prime Minister explained to the ambassador that 'We are in a struggle, a very difficult struggle, an existential struggle against a murderous terror, and to stop the operation against the terrorists before the mission has been accomplished will be counter-productive and will allow the terror to return in a stronger form in the future.'

With Sharon stonewalling, an exasperated Bush repeated his message on 9 April, saying, 'I meant what I said to the Prime Minister of Israel.'[7] But domestic criticism of the President grew, and the pressure on him to draw back from his warning was intense. The neoconservatives in his Cabinet, like Dr Paul Wolfowitz and Vice President Dick Cheney, felt the Israeli Prime Minister was leading his country in a just fight against terror, as Bush was leading America after 9/11. And evangelical Christians, key in electing Bush, also attacked him for pressuring Sharon; the White House received 100,000 angry e-mails from the Christian Right.[8] Soon, there were massive demonstrations supporting Israel in Washington, organized by the American Jewish lobby, and top Republicans in Congress also added their voices against the President's new policy. Encouraged by this support, Sharon simply ignored the President, allowing his forces to carry on with Operation Defensive Shield, and maintain a tight siege on both the Church of the Nativity and Arafat's *muqata* in Ramallah.

'THE SMELL! IT WAS KILLING, KILLING'

Ramallah, usually lively, now became a ghost town. Inside Arafat's *muqata* the situation was worsening. 'It was horrible', Yasser Abed Rabbo, whom the Israelis let in and out of the *muqata*, recalls:

The smell! It was killing, killing. They had perhaps five or six toilets for three to four hundred people in there. And not always working. And often no water, perhaps some water for drinking. And they had no underwear to change. I went into the *muqata* pretending I had documents, but really I had cigarettes and underwear from my home. This was the request of the people. And once my wife insisted I should take all the meat from the freezer, some chickens, beef, seven kilos. And Arafat jumped, 'What's that?' I said, 'Just something maybe to boil up, to make some soup.' But Arafat said, 'No, it's not enough for everybody, so we can't have it.' I said, 'It's up to you – give it to the weak and sick.' The next time I went, they said, 'All the meat is rotting!'[9]

Into this grim scene, on 5 April 2002, walked Secretary of State Powell's envoy, General Zinni, paving the way for the Secretary's trip. Originally Sharon had refused to allow the visit, but Zinni pushed it through, saying to Sharon that as the representative of the US Administration, and ahead of Powell's visit, 'I'm going to go and see Arafat', and, to his surprise, the Prime Minister approved. 'Go, OK,' he said.[10]

'GOD, WHAT AM I GOING TO FIND IN ARAFAT'

Taking his security men with him in two armoured cars, Zinni went to Ramallah, which looked, as he remembers, 'like something out of World War II on the Eastern Front . . . the place was all shot up, the IDF forces had surrounded it'. Thorough co-ordination was required to avoid mistakes in the tense stand-off between Israeli troops and the nervous Palestinian guards. The State Department's Arabic translator, Gamal Helal, joined General Zinni for the visit to see Arafat. He recalls that 'The arrangement was to really put the car that carried General Zinni's team as close as possible to the staircase where we actually entered the *muqata*.' In order to avoid mistakes, Helal proposed that he would get out of the car first and talk to the guards in Arabic. With Israeli forces backing off a bit, Zinni and his small convoy pulled up into the narrow strip of no man's land, and then Helal told the Palestinian guards, 'I have General Zinni, and I have the American delegation, and we're coming to see Chairman Arafat.' They got out of the cars and climbed through the rubble to the door, which was half boarded up so only one person could file in at a time to the *muqata*. Aaron Miller remembers how they 'were led single file through this darkened *muqata*. The first thing that hit you was the stench . . . overpowering . . . There were . . . European peace activists [who had managed to enter the *muqata*], who were prepared to put themselves in harm's way to demonstrate solidarity and provide deterrence. They were lining the walls, yelling at Zinni and trying to shove petitions into his hand. And we were led up the stairs and into Arafat's office.' Zinni recalls,

I looked through the passageways and there were all these people that looked like they hadn't eaten, obviously hadn't used the bathroom, there was no water. As I made my way through and up to the second floor, where Arafat was, I saw some of his staff there, and they looked really horrible . . . unshaven, they had lost weight, really haggard, and I thought, God, what am I going to find in Arafat.

Walking into Arafat's room, Zinni found him at one end of a table with a small lantern and an AK47 assault rifle. 'Mr Chairman, how are you?', Zinni said and, as he recalls, 'Arafat looked up and he looked better than I had ever seen him. He looked more alive, alert, bright.' Arafat said, 'I am under siege, you know, I'm under siege!' And Zinni thought to himself, as he recalls, 'This is the environment he loves – this is the old revolutionary, he is in his element.' Zinni said, 'The Secretary is coming to see you, you've got to do more to arrest people . . . help the Israelis.' Arafat replied, 'Well I'm a prisoner. I'm a prisoner in my own *muqata*. How can you justify this, how can you rationalize this?'[11] Then, in a typical Arafat move, he pulled out a folder of photographs of damaged and defaced Christian holy sites. 'Look,' he said to Zinni, 'this is what the Israelis are doing! Can you believe it? Can you believe it?' over and over again.[12] Sticking to his guns, Zinni kept trying to persuade Arafat to take concrete steps to convince the Israelis to release the pressure on him. But, looking Zinni in the eye, Arafat just said, 'I'm a General like you . . . I'm the only undefeated Arab General.' Zinni could see there was no progress to be made, and walked away with only a list of items Arafat said he needed, including a demand that the Israelis restore electricity and water. As Zinni climbed into his car to return to Jerusalem, he left, as he recalls, 'with the impression that Arafat's own personal legacy was maybe more important [to him] than this process. It was going to be difficult for him to compromise.'

'THEIR WORLD IS AN EMPIRE OF LIES – ARAFAT'S LIKE OSAMA BIN LADEN'

Meanwhile, Washington was pressuring Sharon to make a goodwill gesture ahead of Powell's visit. In long and frantic telephone conversations between Sharon's aide Danny Ayalon and National Security Advisor Condoleezza Rice, the Israelis eventually agreed to withdraw from two Palestinian cities.

Powell came to the region and saw Sharon on 12 April 2002, finding the Prime Minister in no mood to listen, let alone to compromise. From the off, as Assistant Secretary of State William Burns, in Powell's entourage, recalls, they realized that this was going to be a tough sell.

Powell said to Sharon: 'I hope you've noticed what the President said. He thinks it's necessary for us to bring this to a conclusion.' Sharon, Powell recalls, 'understood that . . . but [said] that he had an obligation to defend Israelis and the operation would continue for some period of time, but clearly it was not an indefinite operation . . . he felt there were some objectives that still had to be achieved.'[13] Sharon then added, 'Their world is an empire of lies – Arafat's like Osama Bin Laden. Why do you apply different standards to Arafat than to Bin Laden, or the Taliban?' Powell replied, 'No, it's a different situation.' But Sharon remained unhappy about Powell's proposed visit to Arafat until Powell assured him that 'I'm going to be clear as day with Arafat, tell him the facts.'[14] When Powell asked Sharon about the siege of the *muqata*, the Prime Minister, as his aide Danny Ayalon recalls, told the Secretary of State that, 'the siege had a purpose . . . to bring those murderers, those terrorists to justice'. He would lift the siege only if Arafat would 'hand to us the terrorists and the murderers'. Sharon named six wanted men who were sheltered in Arafat's *muqata*. Five were involved in the assassination of Tourism Minister Rehavam Zeevi, the two gunmen and three more accomplices; the sixth man was Fuad Shubaki, whom Israel believed to be behind financing the *Karine A*, the weapons ship caught by Israel in January. Powell told Sharon that, after calming the security situation down, the US intended to have an international conference in the region to jump-start the political process. But, although in the past Sharon himself had raised this idea with the Americans, now he was reluctant, feeling that it might be regarded by Arafat as a reward for violence. 'We will just have to see about the conference', Sharon told Powell.[15]

Powell's visit to the region included the usual Israeli helicopter tour, this time of the Golan Heights, the disputed land Israel seized from Syria in 1967. On the day he was due to fly there was a major suicide bomb in Jerusalem's central market, which killed 6 and injured more than 50. Powell directed the helicopter to fly over the scene. One of his officials described it as 'a pretty sobering experience'. The Secretary of State gave Arafat an ultimatum: 'Our meeting will not take place until you denounce the bombing.' Keen to see the Secretary, Arafat obliged the following day. 'We condemn strongly,' Arafat said, 'all the attacks which are targeting civilians from both sides and especially the attack that took place against Israeli citizens yesterday in Jerusalem.' This did the trick. After the 24-hour delay, Powell's convoy rolled into Arafat's battle-scarred headquarters in Ramallah. 'This was certainly the most heavily armed motorcade I ever rode in during my career in government service', Flynt Leverett of the NSC, who travelled with Powell, recalls. 'I remember getting a briefing that morning from diplomatic security before I got in the car in which I would be riding. They were trying to alert, to give us a sense . . . if there was an explosion outside the building where the Secretary and Arafat would be meeting, here were the ways out. They had some elaborate contingencies laid out and, in the end, the security person who was in my car said, "You know, if anything happens, just sit tight, and we'll get you out."' On the morning of Powell's visit the Israelis had turned the electricity and water back on, so that the Chairman and the others holed up with him in the *muqata* could take showers in his honour.

Powell's motorcade picked its way through the tanks, knocked-down buildings, crushed cars and Israeli army checkpoints to the *muqata*. When they got there, as Aaron Miller recalls, 'We walked into the room, and there was Arafat and his aides, and we sat down, and [Arafat's] automatic weapon was still on the table, and the Secretary started the meeting and he tried to set the rest of us and Arafat at ease.'[16] Arafat received them in the dining room and he did his best to play host, offering his American guests some water, tea, a little bit of cake. They talked for three hours and Powell was forthright, frank and direct. In an interview for *Elusive Peace* Powell recalls:

I made it very clear to Chairman Arafat . . . [that he had to] use his position . . . to speak out against terror in no uncertain terms, without any hedging, and to make it believable to the whole world . . . I also made it clear to him that many people in my government, and in the United States, and elsewhere in the world, suspected his motives; we didn't believe that he was really serious about [rooting out terror] . . . 'and, so, Mr Chairman . . . You've got to act against terror by word and deed. One hundred per cent word, one hundred per cent effort . . .'

Powell explained just how bad the Chairman's standing was in Washington, and that there was a real risk that the Bush Administration would soon reach a point where it would no longer deal with him at all. He urged Arafat to start taking serious steps to fight terrorist violence and restore the kind of security co-operation the Palestinians had had with the Israelis in the past. The reward, Powell told Arafat, would be the political process – a peace conference – but this was entirely dependent on Arafat's compliance with these demands. 'I have a good deal of political capital and standing in the United States', Powell urged Arafat, 'and I am prepared to spend it for this purpose.'[17] Arafat said, 'Look, I am sorry to say that they are escalating their military activities again and stole our cities and towns and villages and camps ... You can see for yourself the humiliation which our people are facing on all the checkpoints.' One of the members of Powell's party, Flynt Leverett, recalls that there was a somewhat surreal quality to the conversation, with considerable stretches of Arafat's speech that seemed random and disconnected. Arafat told Powell, for instance, about his critical role in resolving tensions between India and Pakistan, by brokering the Simla Accord, claiming it was often referred to as the 'Arafat Accord'.[18] 'We sat there,' Flynt Leverett recalls, 'drank our tea and listened, and then waited for Arafat to come back to the point.' But when it got down to what he would do to stop attacks on Israel, Arafat promised little, insisting that he needed to be able to move around the West Bank and to go to Gaza to deal with the territories that he was being asked to pacify, which Powell knew Sharon would never accept. Arafat also insisted that the Israelis should first withdraw from recently occupied areas and end targeted assassinations.

Realizing that he was not getting far with Arafat, Powell said to him in a tête-à-tête away from the main meeting, as Gamal Helal, translating, recalls, 'Mr Chairman, this is the last time you will be able to see me. There is nothing that I can do for you if you do not do your part.' It was a clear-cut condition: 'If violence continues, we will not be able to help you.' But Arafat was unmoved. 'Well,' he said to Powell, 'what is it that I can do? Look around you. I am under siege by the Israelis. I cannot make a phone call. I cannot do anything.'[19]

On the margins of the meeting, at least a couple of senior Palestinians, Abed Rabbo, Dahlan and others, expressed concern that, once the Secretary of State had left, the Israelis would storm the *muqata* and kill Arafat. Leverett remembers that 'at the end of the meeting, before they left, Arafat began to speak in a fatalistic way about the possibility of his own death'. But Powell calmed the Palestinians down, explaining that 'the President had made it very clear to the Prime Minister, and the Secretary had underscored to Prime Minister Sharon, that the Administration did not want the Israelis to kill Chairman Arafat, that we believed that would be, to say the least, counterproductive, and the Administration had drawn a strong red line with Prime Minister Sharon on that'.[20] At the end of the meeting, Arafat accompanied Powell to the front door, but he would not emerge. His adviser Erekat explains, 'Arafat did not come out for security reasons. You see the Israeli snipers were all around. We were not going to take that risk.'

When he emerged from his meeting with Arafat, Powell had very little to say to the press except for the usual diplomatic mantra: 'We had a useful and constructive exchange . . . we exchanged a variety of ideas and discussed steps on how we can move forward.' But Powell knew quite well that he had got very little from Arafat. When he saw the Prime Minister later that day, Sharon was still insistent on his demand that Arafat must first give up the six wanted men with him in the *muqata* and take other steps to curb Palestinian terrorism.

'I AM SPEAKING TO YOU AS A BROTHER, PLEASE LISTEN TO ME'

On 15 April, Powell returned once more to Arafat. In their meeting he 'begged Arafat', according to an official in Powell's party, to give him 'something [Powell] can work with to show [that Arafat was] dealing with these extremists', and also to extradite to Israel the wanted people with him in the *muqata*, a request Arafat had previously turned down. 'Usually Arafat would say, "Of course, I'll do that!"' explains this official. 'But this time, he was more careful – he didn't make any promises like that because he knew we knew [the wanted men] were right there in his *muqata*.' Powell now asked to see Arafat alone, and Saeb Erekat, who translated for Arafat, recalls how

The Secretary spoke with an open heart, and with a passion. He said to Arafat, 'I am so aware of the Palestinian people's suffering, I am so aware of the Palestinian people's plight, and they deserve better, they deserve independence, they deserve freedom, they deserve their own state, but you need to do something, you just cannot continue sitting doing nothing, you just cannot continue allowing the parallel authorities . . . I am speaking to you as a brother, please listen to me. Many people in Washington do not want this meeting to take place between you and me . . . I came despite all of this, give yourself a chance, give your people a chance, take my advice . . . nothing will happen without you moving . . . the steps must come from you now.'[21]

Powell said to Arafat, 'Without you stopping the suicide bombers I can't help you', and Arafat stuck to his mantra saying, 'how can I stop suicide bombers when they are destroying the same authority that you want me to stop suicide bombers with?' But Powell could not accept this argument. He said: 'I know the Israelis have destroyed some of your facilities, they've destroyed a lot of your security cars, and other equipment, but you still have influence and authority that doesn't come just from police cars, it comes from who you are, and the position you occupy within the Palestinian Authority and the Palestinian community, and that's what we're looking for you to use. And we're not sure that you are prepared to do that, and if you're not, then you're going to find the road ahead very difficult with respect to your relations with the United States.'[22] The Americans left feeling sad and frustrated. As one leading American diplomat on this mission recalls, 'Arafat seemed confident he'd survive.'[23] He had failed to agree to extradite the six wanted men in the *muqata*, or to any of Sharon's other demands. The Secretary of State left the compound empty-handed.

'I WILL BE DISCUSSING THIS IDEA WITH PRESIDENT BUSH'

To make up for his lack of progress, Powell needed to end his visit with some positive message, to show a way out of the impasse. At his hotel suite in Jerusalem, Powell and his small team of advisers drafted the farewell statement that would set out Powell's multilayered vision on how to approach the Israeli–Palestinian crisis. If there could be a resolution to the security impasse – that is, if Arafat curbed violence, and Sharon withdrew from the areas recently seized by the army – America would step in. They would organize an international conference within the next few weeks to try to jump-start the political process.

However, Powell was in for a surprise. While he was at work in Jerusalem, the neoconservatives were at work in Washington. That night, one of Powell's team members, Flynt Leverett, took a call from National Security Advisor Rice's deputy, Steve Hadley. Leverett recalls:

Steve called to tell the Secretary he was not going to be authorized to give a statement that included explicit reference to a political process, political horizon, a possibility of an international conference . . . He said there was considerable interagency disagreement, primarily from the Secretary of Defense [Rumsfeld] and the Office of the Vice President [Cheney], who were not willing to support this idea, that they were also taking a lot of heat over this domestically from the pro-Israel community and from the President's conservative base and that, therefore, the Secretary should not go forward with a statement that talked about a political process at this point.

This was swiftly followed by a telephone call from Dr Rice herself. It was Leverett who once again took the call. Rice said even more clearly that the Secretary of State did not have authorization to give a farewell statement which would lay out the possibility of an international conference or a restarted political process.[24]

On his return to the main room where Powell was sitting, Leverett conveyed the message from Rice, adding that this, in the end, was the word from the White House. Powell knew he could not hold a conference without very strong backing from the White House, and now he realized just how much the neoconservatives had turned the President against him. This was further reinforced when, from Washington, Powell's deputy, Richard Armitage, phoned him to say that the neoconservatives – people in the Defense Department and the Vice President's office – 'are really eating cheese on you, they're putting your shit in the street'.[25] A member of Powell's team says that Powell was upset and angry; he felt completely undercut 'and he got very exercised, very agitated'. The change of heart in Washington was a massive blow for Powell, not least as it had come just after a preliminary press briefing in which he had mentioned some of his intentions, so it would be obvious to the press that he had been overruled. There was nothing he could do – Powell was instructed not to commit the President to any political process or international conference. In his eventual statement Powell said: 'A number of leaders with whom I have spoken have expressed interest in convening a conference on the Middle East in the near future, a conference with international backing ... I will be discussing this idea with President Bush ... upon my return to Washington.'

17

Massacre in Jenin?

America had failed to stop the fighting. In the West Bank town of Jenin, 'the martyrs' capital', and the adjacent refugee camp, the battle was particularly fierce. Between October 2000 and April 2002, the Israelis suspected at least twenty-eight suicide attacks had been planned and launched from Jenin. Now, it was the army's prime target.

The Jenin refugee camp, occupying approximately one square kilometre, was established in 1953 and was the second largest refugee camp in the West Bank, home to some 14,000 Palestinian refugees. It was a hotbed of Palestinian militancy, and on the eve of the Israeli invasion it was home to some 200 armed men from different Palestinian factions, including the Al-Aqsa Martyrs Brigade, Tanzim, Islamic Jihad and Hamas.

For the Israeli Defence Force it was a tough nut to crack. Unlike many other West Bank towns and cities, in Jenin, and particularly in the refugee camp, the Palestinians were well prepared. Palestinian militants, although from several different factions, co-operated and were led by one commander, Abu Jandel, who divided the camp into ten sections, each with twenty armed men to defend it. The Palestinians also booby-trapped houses and fields to slow down the advancing army and had snipers ready on the rooftops.

With its forces encircling the refugee camp, the army requested Defence Minister Ben-Eliezer to allow them to finish the job by bombing the camp from the air.[1] However, fearing the large numbers of civilian Palestinian casualties that approach would cause in the densely populated camp, the minister refused, giving orders only for a conventional battle and a house-to-house search. The Israeli army entered Jenin on 3 April 2002.

Progress was slow, so from 5 April attack helicopters joined the battle, locating and firing at groups of armed Palestinians. On 10 April, thirteen Israeli soldiers were trapped and killed by Palestinian militants. The army then became much more aggressive, shifting tactics from house-to-house searches and the demolition of selected houses of known militants, to a wider bombardment with tanks and missiles. The troops now moved only after armoured bulldozers, supported by tanks, had cleared the area of mines, a tactic which led to massive destruction as the gigantic D9 bulldozers flattened everything in their path. In some cases, troops used civilians as human shields to accompany them during operations to search houses, check suspicious subjects, or just to stand in the line of fire from militants.

With the battle raging the army declared Jenin a closed military area and prevented all access, imposing a round-the-clock curfew and prohibiting the press from entering the town and refugee camp. The army began mass arrests. They took hundreds of Palestinian men out of Jenin for questioning, before releasing non-militants. Left in towns often miles away from Jenin, and with no papers, it took these men days to get home. In the meantime, reports of hundreds of people missing – presumed dead – circulated. Rumours of atrocities in Jenin were further fuelled as Palestinian leaders, notably the PA's chief negotiator, Saeb Erekat, talked on television about 'a massacre' and 'war crimes' being committed at Jenin.[2]

With growing international concern about events at Jenin, the energetic UN envoy Terje Roed-Larsen sprang into action. He approached General Giora Eiland, the head of Planning Division in the General Staff in Tel Aviv, and said to him, 'Giora, this is going to be a terrible scandal. You have to put into motion search and rescue missions. This is a must. This is not going to look good. If there are people killed or injured there, we have to go in and help them. It's not only a moral duty but you are also obliged to do so under the provisions of international humanitarian law.'[3] When the Israelis showed no sign of changing tactics, UN Secretary-General Kofi Annan phoned Larsen, instructing him to go in person to Jenin to investigate. By now, 15 April, the battle was over and the Israelis were allowing people in. Larsen was one of the first foreigners to go to Jenin after the battle. He went to the centre of the refugee camp, which had been systematically levelled – it was soon nicknamed Ground Zero – and, standing there, surrounded by rubble and destruction, he talked to reporters. 'I am shocked at the sight and smell of corpses and destruction,' he said. 'This is horrifying beyond belief. Just seeing the area, it looks like there's been an earthquake here, and the stench of death is over many places where we are standing. The scene is absolutely unbelievable . . . No military operation could justify the suffering we are seeing here.'[4] Destruction was indeed substantial, particularly at the centre of the refugee camp, where an area some 200 metres in diameter had been levelled. Ten per cent of the camp was totally destroyed, with approximately 150 buildings razed to the ground and many others left structurally unsound. Some 4,000 Palestinians became homeless. In this battle 23 Israelis were killed; the Palestinian dead numbered 52.

'HANI, I KILLED ONE DOG'

These were not huge numbers, but the scenes at Jenin were horrifying. Abu Hamid, the Al-Aqsa Martyrs Brigade commander in Jenin, remembers how 'After the Israelis withdrew some of us came out . . . you could smell death everywhere. Some people were vomiting, it was shocking. You could see heaps of bodies. An arm here . . . a leg there . . . sticking out of the rubble.' Scenes like this had a strong effect on Palestinians, galvanizing many of the younger generation to join the ranks of militants ready to fight the Israelis. Here is the testimony of the Palestinian veteran leader Hani al-Hassan on the effect of the Jenin events on one Zakaria al-Zubaidi, who had fought there and had seen his family's house destroyed and his young sister killed. 'He came to me,' Hani al-Hassan recalls, 'and asked for compensation for the destroyed house. We gave him $2,500 – we give that to anyone. First he bought a Kalashnikov for $1,500. And he used the rest of the money to recruit other persons. Since that time he is the strongest fighter against the Israelis. Sometimes he calls me and says, "Hani, I killed one dog [an Israeli]. I need another ninety-nine in revenge for my little sister." They made him mad.'[5]

'WE HAVE NOTHING TO HIDE'

Amid growing calls for a UN investigation into Jenin, the Americans, who would usually support Israel in the UN, but knowing how difficult it would be to veto such a proposal, went to talk to the Israelis. Assistant Secretary of State William Burns met Sharon's aides Danny Ayalon and Uri Shani, advising them that 'an inquiry [into the Jenin events] is going to [be] set up and it's in the interest of Israel to try and shape that as best you can, and the United States will do everything that we can to ensure that this is shaped in a fair way'. After this meeting, as Ayalon remembers, 'I contacted the Prime Minister, told him about it, and he didn't object to there being an investigating committee, a professional one that would come to the area, and would tell exactly what had happened.' Foreign Minister Peres recalls how 'Danny [Ayalon] told me that the Americans phoned and said that it's very hard for them to veto this matter, and they suggest . . . to have an agreed-upon committee whose conclusions are not binding on us . . . I've agreed.' In an interview Peres explained: 'The problem with Jenin was that the pictures were horrible . . . the pictures could not be justified. And I thought an objective investigation could put an end to it.'

On 19 April 2002, the UN Security Council unanimously adopted resolution 1405 (2002), which called 'to develop accurate information regarding recent events in the Jenin refugee camp through a fact-finding team'.[6] This resolution was, in fact, tabled in the Council by the US delegation, and later that day in Jerusalem, Raanan Gissin, the Prime Minister's spokesman, talked to the press, saying, 'We have nothing to hide and we will gladly co-operate with this UN inquiry.'

On 22 April, UN Secretary-General Kofi Annan established the fact-finding team, composed of Martti Ahtisaari, Sadako Ogata and

Cornelio Sommaruga. Headed by Mr Ahtisaari, the team's members also included four senior advisers: Major General (ret.) William Nash, as Military Adviser; Deputy Commissioner Peter Fitzgerald, as Police Adviser; Ambassador Tyge Lehmann, as Legal Adviser; and Helena Ranta, as Medical and Legal Adviser. Several of these people had backgrounds in the former Yugoslavia in human rights work. The team was also provided with technical expertise in military, security and counter-terrorism issues, as well as forensic science and general support staff. They gathered in Geneva on 24 April and began to prepare a work plan based on three elements: (a) events in Jenin in the period immediately prior to Israel's military operation; (b) the battle in Jenin during Operation Defensive Shield; and (c) efforts by humanitarian workers to gain access to the civilian population in Jenin after the end of hostilities. They would move to the occupied territories to start work on 25 April.

However, back in Israel, Sharon's aide Ayalon remembers, 'When we saw what kind of a mandate . . . the terms of reference that they are preparing . . . and the make-up of this committee, that there were no professional military people, but more people with legal forensic background . . . [then] we understood that here they can trap us . . . and this was our great fear.' The Israeli army itself was strongly opposed to such an investigation. General Giora Eiland of the IDF's Planning Division met Chief of Staff Shaul Mofaz to explain why Israel should not agree to an international investigation.[7] First, he said, 'because an inquiry committee would not be professional, it would be very political, and many of its conclusions would be predetermined'. Second, it would set a precedent, and 'once an operation of ours becomes the basis for an investigation by the UN, any other operations we make could enter this category and this would . . . remove the right to self-defence from our hands'. The third reason, 'and the most important', was the legal aspect. If the UN committee insisted on interrogating soldiers and officers who had participated in Defensive Shield, and if the committee concluded that they had committed crimes against humanity, or other crimes that required them to be tried, then they might be called for trial in an international court – something Israel (like America) was loath to have happen to its soldiers. Eiland's arguments persuaded Mofaz. Mofaz told *Elusive Peace*, 'I was against it completely and I thought that just the very fact of sending in an external team was an accusation against Israeli soldiers . . . It did not require any external investigation and I was adamant, as Chief of Staff, because I felt it would harm the soldiers and the State of Israel.' Defence Minister Ben-Eliezer agreed. The three approached the Prime Minister and presented the 'far-reaching consequences a committee like this could have'. As Giora Eiland recalls, 'The Prime Minister accepted our assessment completely.'

The Israelis contacted UN Secretary-General Annan to express their reservations. He agreed to listen to their concerns and engage in a 'clarificatory process'. But with opposition to the inquiry growing in Israel, General Eiland phoned the Secretary-General's special envoy Terje Roed-Larsen. As Larsen remembers, '[He] informed me that a decision had been made not to co-operate [with the UN investigation].'[8]

'NEAR-DEATH EXPERIENCE'

Meanwhile across the Atlantic, on 25 April 2002, Crown Prince Abdullah of Saudi Arabia arrived at Bush's ranch in Crawford, Texas. He had one aim – to deliver a blunt message to the US President that he must use all his muscle to rein in Prime Minister Sharon and end the siege of Arafat's compound in Ramallah.

The Prince was one of the few Arab leaders Bush really admired, and was the only leader except Tony Blair whom Bush had invited to his ranch until then. The Saudi Prince was very straightforward with the President. He said that Bush had to act to end the Israeli occupation. 'If I don't get you to deliver on this and put pressure on the Israelis,' he said, 'then there is a very serious risk to me and all the other [moderate] Arab leaders from our peoples. We will be in danger from our own people. You have to release [Arafat].'[9] The Crown Prince mentioned specifically the danger to the regimes in Bahrain, Egypt and Jordan, which could go up in flames, as he put it, if the Israelis continued with their harsh treatment of the Palestinians and the siege against Arafat. The Prince shocked everyone when he issued an ultimatum to his host. As Secretary of State Powell recalls in an interview, 'The Crown Prince said, "If I don't get [the release of Arafat from the siege] then this trip will have been to no avail and I will be subject to more criticism . . . And Mr President I say this to you as a brother and as a friend, if I don't hear something that I can use, then *I might as well leave now.*" ' This statement, Powell comments, 'put a chill on the desert service'.[10]

Bush kept saying he had told Sharon to end the siege against Arafat, but that failed to convince Prince Abdullah, who was determined to leave and go home. Powell recalls what happened next: 'Bandar [the Saudi ambassador to the US] and I went outside and had a more intense conversation about this matter. I said, "You know, the President cannot just snap a finger at a sovereign government like Israel who responds. This will take some time. The President is engaged and we'll get this resolved and [the Crown Prince] can't simply leave and get in [his] plane and fly away." '[11] It was after that talk that Prince Abdullah decided to stay, and he and the President then had a two-hour tête-à-tête. According to an American official, in his meeting with the President the Crown Prince talked about '[Palestinian] women and children getting shot and killed [by the Israelis] . . . he brought pictures, and he said, "This is making the US look really bad"'. The pictures of dead Palestinian children – a small boy with a bullet wound to his head, a child cut in half – shocked the President to the core. He said: 'I want peace. I don't want to see any people killed on both sides. I think God loves me. I think God loves the Palestinians. I think God loves the Israelis. We cannot allow this to continue.'[12]

The meeting ended with both leaders promising to deliver the other side: Abdullah pledged to rein in Arafat and Bush to rein in Sharon and release Arafat from his siege. It was a real coup for the Saudi Prince. One of the Americans at Crawford explains: 'Abdullah got an incredible deal to end the siege on Arafat. He saved Arafat. He was prepared to jeopardize US–Saudi relations to get him released!'

Just how strong the impact of this visit and meeting with the Prince was on the President and his aides we know from Flynt Leverett, who recalls a post-Crawford debriefing at the NSC:

I remember . . . the President literally rolled his eyes when the subject came up and said, 'Boy, we don't want to do anything like that ever again.' And Secretary Powell referred to it as the 'near-death experience'. And just watching the President, Secretary Powell, Condi [Rice] in the Situation Room, it was very clear, from the expressions on their faces, from their body language, and of course what they said, that this had obviously made a big impression on them.

The principals returned from their 'near-death experience' at Crawford and swiftly reconvened in National Security Advisor Condoleezza Rice's office. Everyone who was at Crawford agreed that the President needed to make a major statement laying out his plan for resolving the Israeli–Palestinian conflict. But first they had to work with the Israelis to release Arafat from the siege on the *muqata* as soon as possible – this was a pledge to the Crown Prince of Saudi Arabia which the Americans were determined to honour.

18

Double-dealing in Ramallah and Bethlehem

Two days after the 'near-death experience' at Crawford, on 27 April 2002, Secretary of State Powell phoned the Israeli Prime Minister urging him to end the siege against Arafat, and National Security Advisor Condoleezza Rice phoned Sharon's aides, saying to them that the siege on Arafat had to stop *at once*. In response, the Israelis came up with a surprising package deal: if the US vetoed the investigation into the Jenin events at the UN, which the Israelis were keen to block, Israel would lift the siege on Arafat. Washington accepted. As the Israeli General Giora Eiland, who was involved in talks with the Americans on this package, puts it, 'Although it was not considered an official linkage, everyone knew that the [ending the siege against Arafat in the] *muqata* and the [UN inquiry] committee [into the Jenin event] were linked.'

To make sure that the Israelis did not drag their feet, Washington made it absolutely clear that if the Prime Minister wished his pre-scheduled visit to Washington in ten days' time to take place, then both the sieges of Arafat in Ramallah and of the Church of the Nativity in Bethlehem had to end *before* the visit. As a leading American diplomat put it, 'Condi [Rice] said this directly to Sharon, Bush also, but less sharply.'[1]

However, Israel still wanted to capture the Palestinian militants sheltering with Arafat at the *muqata* and several others at the Church of the Nativity. For the deal emerging between the US and Israel to come off, a solution had to be found that would let Sharon back down without losing face. Help came from a surprising quarter – the British.

'THINK ABOUT IT, ARIK, THINK'

During a tour of the Middle East, the previous November, the British Prime Minister Tony Blair dropped in on Prime Minister Sharon at his residence in Jerusalem for lunch, arriving in Israel by helicopter from Amman. As the British ambassador to Israel, Sherard Cowper-Coles, recalls, Blair pulled Sharon aside by the grand piano as the guests were departing. Ambassador Cowper-Coles hovered 'because I thought there might be something rather interesting coming out of this', and he heard Blair saying to Sharon that extraditing the terrorists in the *muqata* to Israel would be politically impossible for Arafat and, therefore, as a way out of the impasse, Britain could help by monitoring the terrorists in a Palestinian jail. Cowper-Coles recalls Blair saying, 'Remember, Arik, we are ready to help with monitors or observers.' Sharon sort of shrugged, and then, as Cowper-Coles remembers, 'Blair jabbed his finger and said, "Think about it, Arik, think about it, Arik, the offer is on the table."'[2]

Now, in April 2002, Blair's offer came back to Sharon's mind as he sought a way to remove the siege. As Cowper-Coles recalls, 'On a Saturday night ... my phone rang at home ... and it was Danny Ayalon, Sharon's foreign policy adviser, and he began straight off by saying, "My Prime Minister has been thinking about what your Prime Minister said to him in Jerusalem last November about the offer of monitors and observers. Is that offer still on the table?"' The ambassador replied that he 'had no reason to think that we had withdrawn the offer or changed it'. Cowper-Coles rushed back to the embassy that Saturday night and sent a cable to London, saying that Sharon had seemed 'to have taken the bait, and we needed to respond immediately'. Blair took the point. Within a week, on the morning of 30 April 2002, the prison expert Andrew Coyle, who had handled terrorist prisoners from Northern Ireland when Governor of HM Prison Brixton, landed in Israel.

British and American diplomats gathered in Jerusalem in the sitting room of the British Consul-General, Geoffrey Adams. He recalls: 'We needed a piece of paper which would set out on one side what we were proposing to do. So we sat there and wrote it. I remember thinking this was real-time diplomacy, we were actually creating something there and then.'[3]

The British and American ambassadors then had to sell the idea to the Israelis. They had a long and difficult meeting with Sharon's Chief of Staff, the lawyer Dov Weisglass. 'We took Weisglass through that stage by stage,' Cowper-Coles recalls, 'and he was . . . very sceptical.' The main bone of contention was the fact that the ambassadors were not in fact proposing that the *British* would guard the prisoners, but that they would make sure that the *Palestinians* set up a proper prison regime, whose integrity they would guarantee and monitor. According to Cowper-Coles, 'Weisglass's main worry was how this was going to look in domestic political terms and it was the deep instinctive distrust of most Israelis towards international involvement in solving their problem, particularly European involvement.' The ambassadors left their ideas with Sharon's man, who said he would put them to the Prime Minister.

'YOU'RE NOT GOING TO ARGUE WITH PALESTINIAN LAW ARE YOU?'

In the meantime, British prison expert Andrew Coyle went down to Jericho. There he inspected an old police building from the British Mandate period, like many others spread over the country from the 1930s. The building also served as a prison and, as it was quite isolated and remote from the heart of Jericho, it would be an ideal place to keep the six *muqata* wanted men. Coyle had to tread carefully between Israeli and Palestinian demands. He describes his dilemma: 'The Israelis wanted these people chained up and pinned to the wall, and the Palestinians wanted them in a five-star hotel. I argued with Erekat [the Palestinian accompanying Coyle] about where the prisoners were to be held,' Coyle recalls, 'particularly Shubaki [the *Karine A* paymaster] and [Ahmed] Sadat [the leader of the PFLP, whose people assassinated the Israeli minister Zeevi]. These guys were senior officials who one day might come back and Saeb [Erekat] was anxious that they be treated well. Erekat wanted them under house arrest with offices and the like. I had to say to him, "It's not going to be like that, Saeb." ' Coyle then asked to see the Palestinian prison law, which he knew was based on the British prison law. 'You're not going to argue with Palestinian law are you?' he asked Saeb Erekat. And Erekat, as Coyle recalls, was 'wise enough to fight with me to the brink and then pull back'.[4]

'LOOK, WE'RE NEARLY THERE'

In Tel Aviv, later that afternoon, the British ambassador Sherard Cowper-Coles got a telephone call saying that Sharon would like to go over the ground again with him and with Dan Kurtzer, the American ambassador. Cowper-Coles decided that it would be a good thing if they took Andrew Coyle with them as well, 'to have him in our back pocket'.

The ambassadors got to Sharon's office late in the evening, at 10.30 or 11, and first had another round of difficult discussions in the Cabinet room with Sharon's aides Dov Weisglass and Danny Ayalon. Again, what concerned the Israelis was how robust the prison regime would be. If it descended into farce, with the Palestinians accused of the murder of minister Zeevi and financing the *Karine A* roaming free, Sharon would be left open to accusations of being soft on terror. 'There is a little door from the Cabinet room through to Sharon's small study', Cowper-Coles recalls, 'where he sits and directs operations, and every so often Weisglass and Danny Ayalon would go through this door and consult Sharon, and then come back out and talk to Dan Kurtzer and me.' The negotiations were long and tough, with the Israelis wanting to cover every minute detail of the proposed regime. At one point, Ambassador Kurtzer got up and said to the Israelis, 'Well, that's it, we've had enough, I'm going back to Tel Aviv. This is ridiculous.'[5] However, Cowper-Coles pulled him by the sleeve, saying, 'Look, we're nearly there, I think they are going to bite on this, let's just give it another go round the course once more, and explain to them what is on offer.' Eventually, they were told, 'Well, come in and see the Prime Minister.'

'OK, OUT!'

The two ambassadors marched into Sharon's office. Cowper-Coles remembers: 'Sharon was sitting beside his desk, as usual, very courteous, but he said something like, "You realize how difficult this is for me, explaining to the Israeli people that I am going to allow the prisoners out, hand them back to Palestinian custody, and then have Brits monitor that custody."' Sharon listened carefully as the two ambassadors talked him through their plan, explaining that the operation would be designed and overseen by a man who had enormous experience of handling terrorist prisoners. Cowper-Coles remembers how 'I probably embroidered for Sharon's sake just how tough the regime was in Brixton, how dangerous the prisoners were there, and I also said a bit about Northern Ireland and Sharon was humming and hawing, and so, getting slightly desperate, I remember saying, "Well, if you want to see, or hear for yourself what we have in mind we have got the man himself sitting outside."'

Andrew Coyle was waiting patiently outside and, as he recalls, 'Suddenly, really late, [Ambassador] Sherard [Cowper-Coles] comes out of Sharon's office and says, "He wants to see you."' Before walking in, the British ambassador explained to Coyle that 'Sharon's English isn't that good, so you need to set things out very clearly and slowly to him.' Then, as they entered the Prime Minister's office, Cowper-Coles quickly whispered in Coyle's ear, 'Tell him exactly what it's like in Brixton for an IRA prisoner.'[6]

Sharon asked Coyle, 'If someone had assassinated a Cabinet minister in the UK, how would they be treated?' Coyle, shifting the conversation, said, 'I can't guarantee everything – but I can guarantee to tell you what is going on [namely by monitoring the Palestinians guarding the prisoners].' Ambassador Cowper-Coles recalls how 'Andrew Coyle came in and explained to Sharon how he would deal with Category A prisoners.' After a very long discussion, the Prime Minister eventually said, 'OK, we'll go with it', at which Cowper-Coles jumped to his feet and, determined to bank Sharon's words before he changed his mind, he immediately said to Ambassador Kurtzer and Coyle, 'OK, out!'

'YOU'VE JUST GOT TO DELIVER THIS!
YOU'VE GOT TO!'

However, would Arafat accept the deal? After all, he could consider it a concession of sovereignty to allow foreigners in to monitor Palestinian behaviour.

The job of delivering Arafat fell to the UK Consul-General, Geoffrey Adams, and the US deputy Consul-General, Jeff Feltman. While Kurtzer and Cowper-Coles were negotiating with the Prime Minister, Adams and Feltman were on their way to meet a Palestinian minister, Yasser Abed Rabbo, whom Arafat had appointed to negotiate on this for him in Ramallah.[7]

They sat in a long and tortuous meeting with Abed Rabbo, whom they found 'extremely sceptical'.[8] At one point, as Adams recalls, 'I went into a side room to take a call from [British ambassador] Sherard [Cowper-Coles] sounding incredibly excited ... and describing the scene to me. He'd just been called in to see Sharon, and he'd taken Coyle in with him, and they'd convinced Sharon to go along with this.' When Adams told the British ambassador how reluctant Abed Rabbo was, Cowper-Coles said, 'You've just got to deliver this! You've got to!' Adams recalls, 'I remember thinking ... Sherard was having this very sophisticated negotiation and I'm sitting here under curfew in Ramallah, gunfire outside, tat-tat-tat-tat-tat-tat-tat, with these [Palestinian] guys who are just not on the same planet at all ... this is tough, I felt under huge pressure.' When he returned to the room where Feltman was still sitting with Abed Rabbo, Adams said: 'Look ... we now really need to sort it out.' Abed Rabbo said, 'Well, I'll have to consult my President on this. I can't possibly decide this myself, now.' Adams asked, 'Could you go now and say to President [Arafat] we need to do this now?' Abed Rabbo: 'No, I can't possibly. Sorry, you've got to go. I can't possibly go! I can't get from here to the *muqata*. The streets are full of tanks!' Adams insisted, 'We'll take you there.' A reluctant Abed Rabbo set out for the *muqata* in a British car flying the Union Jack to see if he could persuade Arafat to accept the deal. But about twenty minutes later they came back white in the face.

They had come up against an Israeli tank and Abed Rabbo had said to the British driver, 'Right, that's it, turn around!' The meeting ended at 2.30 a.m. The diplomats returned disappointed to Jerusalem.

'YOU CAN HAVE THEM. TAKE THEM. TAKE THEM NOW'

However, they were back the next day. This time Adams was joined by the US Consul-General Ron Schlicher, and they went straight to see Arafat in person at noon, taking him step-by-step through the paper which they called 'The Ramallah Agreement'. At the heart of the proposed package was the idea that Israeli forces should withdraw from the *muqata* and 'generally from the town of Ramallah', and Arafat would then be allowed to travel – to go abroad and come back. In return, Arafat would agree to the removal of the six detainees to a jail in Jericho. Adams recalls how 'for the first hour and a half I thought we were sunk. I was incredibly depressed. We started in English. We then went into Arabic. I took him through it really slowly, saying each word in turn. And he would just pout and look at the floor . . . very sullen.' They covered the same ground over and over again, with no movement from Arafat. 'I felt we were just about to have to go', Adams remembers. 'It was getting embarrassing.' Then, after consulting his colleagues, Arafat said: 'You can have them. Take them. Take them now. Are you going to take them now?' This was, of course, impossible as arrangements still had to be made, but the diplomats were truly delighted. Just before they left Arafat turned to Schlicher: 'One more thing, your Excellency,' he said. 'Please remember not to forget that it is not me that is important but the Church of the Nativity, this is important.' Arafat was concerned not to appear to be more interested in ending his own siege than the one in Bethlehem.

With both Sharon and Arafat agreeing to move the six wanted men from the *muqata* to Jericho, final preparations got under way to ensure a smooth transfer.

'I'M NOT GOING IN THERE! IT'S A CELL!'

On 1 May 2002, the British prison expert Andrew Coyle met IDF and Shin Bet officials and talked logistics for six hours. They discussed how exactly the *muqata* wanted men would be transferred and, more importantly, how Coyle and his team would even know they had the right six prisoners. Eventually, the six wanted men were transferred to the Jericho prison, each in a different vehicle, with a British guard on one side and an American on the other. Hundreds of Jericho citizens had gathered to welcome the men. Here is what happened next, as Coyle remembers: 'We got the six of them in and gave them something to eat. And the Palestinians, including Saeb [Erekat], had another go – they were always checking to see how serious we were about the seclusion thing. So everyone was trying to open things up again.' The six were due to have a medical inspection. Coyle recalls: 'This man in a white coat told me he was a doctor, so I decided he would do. So they went out one-by-one; there was no trouble with the first four.' Then Shubaki, the mastermind behind the *Karine A*, went in to see the doctor. After about fifteen minutes Coyle realized Shubaki had not come out, and started to get worried. Coyle walked into the 'examination' room where, as he recalls, 'Shubaki was sitting there with his shirt rolled up – this was a medical, after all – smoking a huge cigar. He was holding court to the "doctor", the governor of the prison, and a few others.' Coyle said to the governor: 'What are you doing here? This is a medical.' The governor replied, 'This is my prison; I can do what I like.' Coyle said, 'Haven't you heard of medical confidentiality? In no prison in the world can the governor sit in on a prisoner's medical.' Reluctantly, the governor left. Coyle then took Shubaki to his cell, but when he saw it the Palestinian said, 'I'm not going in there! It's a cell!' Luckily, Shubaki decided to look round the cell and point out everything that was horrid about it. 'And I', Coyle describes, 'planted myself in the door, so he would have to climb over me if he wanted to get out. He turned to me and said, "There is no way I'm staying in here!" And I said, "Well, there's no way you're getting out now", and we locked the door.' Coyle later spotted out of the corner of his eye someone taking tea and biscuits to Shubaki. Coyle said, 'Ahem, what are you doing? . . . You can't do that. It's after 10 p.m. Every prison in the world is locked up at 10 p.m. and you can't open it until the morning.'

The Palestinian negotiator Erekat tried once again to get Coyle to relax the regime, asking, 'Can they have a fridge? Can they have a TV?' Tired of the nudging, Coyle said, 'Look – I really don't care what they have. My job is to see to it that they are *locked up*. That is all.' When Coyle went back to the prison the next morning the prisoners already had satellite TV and refrigerators in their cells. From the prison Coyle phoned the Israelis to say, 'Right, these people are locked up to my satisfaction', upon which Sharon's aide Ayalon said, 'Good, thank you very much.' After making the call, Coyle walked back to the monitors' office to watch on TV as the tanks outside the *muqata* in Ramallah revved up and pulled out. It was 2 May 2002 and the siege of the *muqata* was over. The same day, UN Secretary-General Kofi Annan released a statement saying,

The Secretary-General is today disbanding the Fact-Finding Team into recent events in the Jenin refugee camp . . . The Secretary-General has written to the Council President, the Government of Israel and the Palestinian Authority communicating this decision . . .[9]

The US–Israeli deal was done. The US had flexed its muscle in the UN, blocking the inquiry into Jenin, and Israel had removed the siege on Arafat.[10]

'OH ALASTAIR!'

There was still another siege to be ended, however. Since the beginning of April the Church of the Nativity in Bethlehem had been home to some 200 Palestinians, several of whom were on Israel's wanted list, trapped there by Israeli forces. The US, having blocked a UN inquiry into Jenin, now expected Israel to act soon to end her siege on the Church of the Nativity. So far, efforts to end the siege in Bethlehem had been carried out by low-level negotiators, mainly an

IDF Lieutenant-General, Leor Littan, and Saleh Tamari, a member of the Palestinian parliament. Now, however, with a new urgency given to the talks, senior negotiators were appointed: Brigadier Eival Gilady of the IDF's Planning Division and the Shin Bet District Commander of Jerusalem and the West Bank for the Israelis, and Mohammed Rashid for Arafat. Also involved were the CIA's Tel Aviv Station Chief Jeff O'Connor and the British MI6 agent Alastair Crooke, representing the EU.

Gilady and Rashid conducted their talks at the King David Hotel in Jerusalem, where the formula that emerged was a mixture of deportations of wanted Palestinians to Europe and the Gaza Strip, and the release of Palestinians not involved in terror.[11] Gilady's intelligence reports gave him a fairly good idea of who was in the church, but he still insisted that Rashid should come up with a comprehensive list.[12] Mohammed Rashid was reluctant to do this, preferring to deal with the number of people to be expelled rather than with specific names. He sought the advice of Alastair Crooke, who recalls how 'I told the Palestinian negotiating team that despite their reluctance to do it ... quite clearly we had to have a list. Once you start trying to remove people from a place like that, the only way that we could proceed without the thing breaking down ... is to have a list.' Arafat personally phoned the people in the church and instructed them to prepare the list. This was collected by Crooke, whom the Israeli army allowed to walk up to the Door of Humility, the entrance to the church, to receive the envelope containing the names. As Crooke recalls, 'someone handed me an envelope and told me this was the list. It was just a plain envelope, and it was sealed ... I intended to leave it sealed and to return it to the Palestinian negotiating team unopened.'

Every day after negotiating with Gilady, Rashid would return to Ramallah with the Israeli demands of who they wanted exiled, and consulted with nine other Palestinian leaders tasked to deal with the matter. But because the deportation of Palestinians was hugely unpopular, Rashid often found himself isolated even among his own colleagues. He recalls how on one occasion he joined Arafat in his room, and 'Arafat was standing and I was standing beside him, and I told him, "Don't worry, I am going [to conclude the deal], even if I have to do it alone, I will bring this agreement to success." So Arafat turned to me, and I could see a tear in his eye, and he said, "Well, I thank you for that, especially since your friends refuse to co-operate with you." '

The issue which dominated the talks was how many wanted Palestinian militants would be deported to Europe and how many to Gaza, a lesser form of exile. As Rashid recalls, 'I went to the King David Hotel, [where] we held the last meeting. I insisted that the number be seven [to be deported to Europe]. Eival [Gilady] asked to increase the number to thirteen.' On Gilady's insistence, it was agreed that 13 Palestinians accused by Israel of having 'blood on their hands', having been directly involved in killing Israelis, would be flown to Cyprus; another group of 26, considered less dangerous, would be expelled to the Gaza Strip; and the remaining 84 people would be released (the Israelis had by now released several groups from the church, mainly teenage boys).

It was a dramatic moment when the prepared lists of who would go where were turned over to those inside the church, where the besieged Palestinians would learn their fate. Mazzin Hussein, on Israel's list of wanted people, recalls how 'Abdullah Daoud [the most senior Palestinian in the church] got the list and started reading out the names. When he got to my name, and I was to be deported to Gaza, there was a chair behind me and I kicked it over . . . I was so angry . . . I had never been to Gaza. I had often dreamed I might visit Gaza – but not like this, for this reason!'[13]

On the brink of resolving the stand-off, another stumbling block emerged – the fate of the weapons held by the militants inside the church. Here is Ala Hosni, then Chief of Police in Bethlehem:

The Israelis wanted the weapons, and I said, 'No. They are ours.' They said, 'OK, we will check all the weapons. If they have a serial number [which showed that they were held legally by the Palestinians] then, you can have them, if not, we will take them.' Arafat himself called and said, 'We must have those weapons.' Then the US guy [the head of the CIA station in Tel Aviv, Jeff O'Connor] asked me what I thought. I said, 'You need to take responsibility. You take the guns.' He said, 'OK! We will take all the guns.' The Israelis agreed and we agreed. It was resolved.

The Palestinians left the Church of the Nativity, dropping their guns behind a screen and proceeding to buses which would take some of them straight to the Gaza Strip, and thirteen of them to the airport, from where they would be flown to Cyprus. Alastair Crooke was there to oversee the operation for the EU. He recalls:

The Israelis took them to a dramatic hangar. There were thirteen chairs in the middle of this hangar ... people with weapons all around ... tanks everywhere ... the [prisoners] were formally handed over to me. They all came out and said, 'Oh Alastair!' I knew at least half of them! I thought I was going to end up on a fourteenth chair. Some of the Israelis, whom I didn't know, gave me very evil looks. [British Ambassador] Sherard [Cowper-Coles] was there, he sorted out the British Hercules [that would take the Palestinians to Cyprus]. The thirteen [Palestinians] were just so tense until the gate went up, and then everyone breathed. They had still thought it was a trap, a trick. Then it was like a schoolboys' outing in Cyprus.

19

Dumping Arafat

Even before a deal had been concluded to end the siege of the Church of the Nativity, the Israeli Premier, on 5 May, was on his way to Washington. Sharon came carrying a dossier, which he referred to 'as a dossier documenting Chairman Arafat's involvement in support for terrorist actions against Israelis'.[1] During the meeting, as Assistant Secretary of State Burns recalls, 'Sharon piled through a fair bit of his dossier on Arafat and the President listened a little impatiently, not because he didn't believe it, but because it was a prolonged presentation.' They talked about Arafat, and it was apparent that President Bush agreed with Sharon that the Palestinian leader was an obstacle and part of the problem.

Sharon's aide Danny Ayalon, present at the meeting, recalls how the President 'looked around the room as he spoke [and said] that the office is bigger than the man [i.e., more important than Arafat]'. Another official on Sharon's team recalls that 'We were rather surprised, rather happy, to realize how the President considered Arafat as an obstacle to peace . . . the President used rather strong language when he referred to Arafat's role in the continuation of the conflict, saying, "He's a leader who has failed, hasn't fulfilled any of the functions as a leader of a society, socially, economically, he is dedicated to a mode of terrorism."'[2] This view of Arafat was by now accepted by all in Washington, even Secretary of State Powell, who explains: 'It was clear that it was time to let the world know that we couldn't deal with Arafat, to let the world know that the Palestinian people needed reformed leadership ... Somebody that we could work with and the Israelis could work with, because we found it impossible to work with Arafat. There was no disagreement about that aspect ... Arafat is not a partner we can work with.'[3]

We should recall that after the dramatic meeting between President Bush and Crown Prince Abdullah of Saudi Arabia, in Crawford, Texas on 25 April, Bush had committed himself to do two things. The first was to make Israel end the sieges in Ramallah and Bethlehem. The second, more long-term idea was for the President to make a major statement that would lay out his vision for resolving the Israeli–Palestinian conflict. With the first task completed, the Americans wanted to use Sharon's visit to Washington to deal with the second. As an official on Sharon's delegation recalls, '[in the visit to Washington] we heard for the first time of the President's intention to speak in the coming few weeks about the Middle East conflict'. But, unlike the Palestinians, the Israelis were to be intimately involved in creating the Bush plan and the speech which would kick-start it. Thus, already during this May visit to Washington, National Security Advisor Rice had invited the Israelis 'to raise ideas about what they thought the President's speech should address'.[4]

Sharon's visit to Washington ended rather dramatically on 7 May. One of the Israeli bodyguards was seen making all kinds of nervous gestures. Sharon's Chief of Staff, Dov Weisglass, approached him and, after a brief conversation, hurried over to the Prime Minister and the President. He said in English, 'We have reports that there has been a suicide bomb in Israel.' Sharon left for Israel immediately. The bomb at a Rishon Lezion club had killed 16 and wounded 60.

'MIAH BIL MIAH'

With the President and his team already working on the big speech, Assistant Secretary of State Burns and the NSC's Flynt Leverett went to see Arafat in Ramallah in May, to advise him that it would be in his interests to show he was serious about curbing terrorism. 'Every demand we put to him,' recalls Leverett, 'every requirement that we put on the table he accepted "Miah bil miah", meaning one hundred per cent.' On his return from that trip, Leverett briefed a White House Principals Committee meeting, telling them 'both of us would have felt better about that conversation if Arafat had told us he only agreed with sixty per cent. We knew, when he told us he agreed with us "Miah bil miah", that nothing significant was going to happen before the President would be giving his speech.'

Terje Roed-Larsen, the UN envoy to the Middle East, was also involved in trying to make Arafat stop attacks on Israel ahead of Bush's speech. 'We knew well in advance', Larsen recalls, 'that this was going to be a serious speech. So I told Arafat, "I know there is going to be a speech on 24 June, and you had better make sure there is nothing unpleasant in the run-up to that speech, because this could affect you for the rest of your life."' But, on 5 June 2002, a car packed with explosives blew up next to a bus near the Megiddo junction in northern Israel at 7.15 local time, killing 16 Israelis and wounding 50. Islamic Jihad claimed responsibility, as did the Al-Aqsa Martyrs Brigade, linked to Chairman Arafat's Fatah organization. Still, Washington kept the pressure on Arafat to curb violence ahead of the President's speech. The Saturday before the speech, the State Department translator and Middle East expert Gamal Helal was instructed to pass on an ultimatum to Arafat. Helal called Nabil Abu Rudeineh, Arafat's right-hand man, and gave him hell, in Arabic, swearing like a trooper down the line. He said to tell Arafat that he had thirty-six hours to move on security or it would all be over. After five or ten minutes, Yasser Arafat himself piped up – he'd been listening in on the call since the beginning and had heard everything.

'DROP ARAFAT'

In Israel, meanwhile, following National Security Advisor Rice's fore-warning of Bush's speech, 'folks kicked into high gear to influence its outcome', as a leading American diplomat recalls; 'they did a good job'.[5] What the Israelis did, among other things, was to throw mud at Arafat. A lot of it stuck. A week before the President's planned speech, at a critical Principals Committee meeting in the White House Situation Room, the participants had in front of them a document supplied by the Israelis, titled, *An Intercepted Conversation Between a Known Fatah Terrorist Leader and Another Individual*. In these transcripts of intercepted telephone conversations, the 'known Fatah terrorist', Mohammed Naifa, a militant from Tulkarm, said that he had just received a certain amount of money – $20,000 – from Yasser Arafat as reward for committing terrorist acts, and he signalled his intention to carry out more terrorist operations that would kill Israelis. Vice President Dick Cheney said that the transcripts were a 'smoking gun' – proof that Arafat was supporting and funding terrorist attacks against Israelis. Cheney argued that preserving the integrity of President Bush's global war on terror was the most important foreign policy objective for the Administration at that point. This meant that the US had no choice but to 'write off Arafat', who now had 'to be treated as a terrorist, as a corrupt and ineffective leader who, because of his terrorist connections, could no longer be dealt with by the United States . . . the United States [should] drop Arafat as an interlocutor . . . the President should make it clear in whatever speech he gave that we no longer considered Arafat a fit partner or a fit interlocutor.'[6]

Secretary of State Powell, although recognizing that 'it was impossible to work with Arafat', thought there was still no alternative to working with the Palestinian leader. He argued that dropping Arafat, as Cheney was recommending, would make it very difficult to move forward in any kind of positive way. Powell added that, while he appreciated the need to empower other Palestinians, in the end 'Arafat was the elected leader of the Palestinians . . . he was still the living symbol of their national movement.' Powell was supported in this critical NSC meeting by William Burns, who said that if the main thrust of the President's speech was going to be dumping Arafat, then they had to lay out very clearly what was in it for the Palestinians. As Burns put it, 'We need to say to Palestinians, "Here is the deal. Here is the two-state solution that you get. This is what the United States is prepared to support, but we're not willing to do it with that guy." '[7] But these moderate voices stood no chance, particularly as Palestinian attacks on Israeli civilians continued unabated. On 18 June, a suicide attack on a Jerusalem bus killed 19 and wounded 74 Israelis, and on the next day another attack in Jerusalem killed 7 and injured 50.

In his speech on 24 June 2002, with Powell, Rice and Rumsfeld standing beside him, President Bush delivered the *coup de grâce*. He simply dumped Arafat:

For too long the citizens of the Middle East have lived in the midst of death and fear. For the sake of all humanity, things must change in the Middle East. My vision is two states, living side by side, in peace and security. There is simply no way to achieve that peace until all parties fight terror. Peace requires a new and different Palestinian leadership, so that a Palestinian state can be born. I call on the Palestinian people to elect new leaders, leaders not compromised by terror.[8]

So, as Flynt Leverett put it, 'the speech emerged with a very clear call for new Palestinian leadership, but nothing on final status'.

'OUR JAWS DROPPED'

Prime Minister Sharon watched Bush deliver the speech live on TV in his office in Jerusalem. As his aide Danny Ayalon recalls, 'Sharon kept a straight face throughout, no display of any emotion'. Sharon's Chief of Staff Dov Weisglass, also in the room with the Prime Minister, recalls that 'It wasn't like a soccer game . . . but we were very pleased.'

There was no rejoicing in the Palestinian camp. Unlike the Israelis, the Palestinians had not been invited to contribute at all. And it was only on the morning of the day of the speech that news started trickling through that something was awfully wrong. Nabil Shaath, the Palestinian in charge of foreign affairs, recalls how 'I received a direct call from the Saudi embassy in Washington saying, "Warning, warning, red light! Problems coming . . ."'[9] Diana Buttu, Legal Adviser of the PLO Negotiations Affairs Department, recalls how 'I was with Nabil Shaath sitting in his hotel room. The whole Palestinian delegation was watching [Bush's] speech and our jaws dropped. We knew it was going to be harsh [following the warnings from the Saudi embassy] but did not expect *that* harsh.'[10] The response from the Palestinians was swift.

Saeb Erekat said on CNN: 'It is only for the Palestinian people to determine who their leaders are.' Others tried to put on a brave face. Diana Buttu recalls how 'sitting there Shaath got a call from Arafat and we were told that a Cabinet decision had been taken in Ramallah to be very positive about the speech – to try to turn lemons into lemonade'. But it was clear to all that for the Palestinians, and particularly for Arafat, the speech was a sheer disaster.

'WE HAVE SHEHADEH AND IT MAY BE POSSIBLE TO KILL HIM'

In his ruined *muqata* in Ramallah, Arafat, as stubborn as ever, showed no intention of relinquishing the reins of power, nor of curbing the violence. On 16 July, Palestinian militants ambushed a Jewish bus near the West Bank settlement of Emanuel, killing 9 and wounding more than 18, and on the next day two suicide bombers killed 5 and injured 40 in a double suicide bombing in Tel Aviv. In response, the Israelis decided to go after Salah Shehadeh, one of the founders of Hamas and the commander of its military wing in the Gaza Strip, wanted for the deaths of scores of Israelis.

When the opportunity to strike came, on 23 July, Defence Minister Ben-Eliezer was in London. He was in a cab on his way to Heathrow airport when he received a call on his mobile from his Military Secretary Mike Herzog, who told him: 'We have Shehadeh and it may be possible to kill him.'[11] Ben-Eliezer said, 'Tell me just one thing. Who is with him?' Herzog replied: 'No one except his wife and two other dirties.'[12] Ben-Eliezer asked, 'Are you sure? Has everything been calculated?' Herzog: 'Yes, calculated.' Ben-Eliezer asked again: 'No innocent people there?' Herzog: 'No.' Ben-Eliezer replied, 'OK. God bless you.' Operation Daglan got under way.

The assessment of the Israeli Air Force was that 'a bomb smaller than a tonne would not necessarily . . . kill him', as they planned to strike him while he was inside a building. They proposed to use more fire-power than they normally would in a targeted assassination, but in this case it was deemed necessary. 'A one-tonne bomb', Defence

Minister Ben-Eliezer explains, 'has an element of certainty. You can be sure it takes a person out, for sure . . . We have tried other bombs, and it turned out that there was greater chance of surviving with a quarter-tonne and half-tonne. And here the person [Shehadeh] justified use of a bomb of this kind.'

But when the one-tonne bomb was dropped on an apartment block in Gaza City it caused colossal damage, killing not only Shehadeh, his wife and daughter but with them fourteen other innocent people. When a shocked Ben-Eliezer landed in Israel, he found out that the operation was based on an intelligence 'fuck-up', as he put it, and 'intelligence they had about a neighbouring house which was supposed to be completely empty was wrong, meaning that there were people there and therefore they were killed'.[13] No remorse though from the Chief of the Air Force, Dan Haluz. When he met the crew of the plane that had dropped the one-tonne bomb which killed so many innocent people, he said, 'Guys, you can sleep well at night . . . I do . . . Your execution was perfect . . . Perfect.'[14]

Neither the killing of Shehadeh, nor other military operations, put an end to Palestinian attacks. On 30 July 2002, a suicide bomber blew himself up in Jerusalem, injuring 5, and on the next day, 7 were killed and 86 injured by a bomb planted in a cafeteria at the Hebrew University in Jerusalem.

It seemed that the plan laid out by President Bush in June to resolve decades of spiralling conflict between Israelis and Palestinians was having little effect on the ground. However, his plan was soon to receive a little extra boost, enough to give the peace process some new momentum. This came from yet another unexpected direction – the young King of Jordan.

20

The King, the President and
the Roadmap

King Abdullah had a vested interest in Bush's vision of a Palestinian state becoming a reality. Jordan was home to 1.7 million Palestinian refugees, and were the situation in the occupied territories to deteriorate they could well target their frustrations against Jordan's government and the King himself.[1] Therefore, after President Bush made his 24 June speech, the King conferred with his Foreign Minister, Marwan Muasher, and, as the latter recalls, 'We agreed that the [Bush] speech laid down a vision, a very important one, but that the vision in itself would not do much if it were not followed by practical steps.'[2] The King, who was due to visit Washington, was determined to press President Bush to come up with a practical plan to turn his vision into a reality.

Thus in Washington, on 31 July 2002, ahead of the King's meeting with the President, Foreign Minister Muasher had a preparatory meeting with the President's National Security Advisor, Condoleezza Rice. He said that while the President had demanded the Palestinians perform on security and stop attacks on Israel, 'for the Palestinians to co-operate on security they need to know they will get their state. So while it is important to stress security, it cannot be an end in itself.' Muasher pressed on: 'Condi, your plan is all sticks and no carrots. You're not giving the Palestinians anything on the carrot part: a vision, an endgame, a political horizon of a Palestinian state and the end of the occupation.' Rice rejected the argument. She said, 'We ask the

Palestinians to perform on security, and if they do we will see what happens next.'

Trying another tack, Muasher said Jordan assumed that the United States would be taking military action in Iraq to overthrow Saddam Hussein's regime in the wake of 9/11 and the US war on terrorism. Jordan, he said, was prepared to do whatever it could to assist America in that endeavour, but, 'in order to provide political cover for the King', the Americans needed to go further than just one speech. What was needed, Muasher said, was 'a roadmap . . . for getting to the two-state solution that the President talked about in his speech'.[3] The word 'roadmap' was to stick, but for now Rice was not budging. US policy was still to steer as far clear from the Palestinian mess as possible.[4] She also feared that a roadmap involving extensive diplomatic activity might dilute the thrust of the President's speech. 'There won't be any follow-up plan,' Rice said. 'There won't be any roadmap.'[5]

Muasher reported back to his King, who had arrived at the Four Seasons Hotel in Washington. 'Your Majesty,' he said, 'we're going to have a very difficult meeting tomorrow with the President . . . I just saw Rice . . . I presented the idea [of a roadmap] . . . She is not buying this argument.'[6]

'WHAT DO THE PALESTINIANS WANT FROM ME?'

However, the King was not put off that easily. At the White House the next day he put his plan to the President in person.[7] Their discussion first focused on Iraq and Saddam Hussein. Bush stated:

There is a huge amount of hyper-ventilation about Saddam [Hussein]. We can discuss this later. My opinion has not changed. History has called us. Thirty years from now I don't want people to say that Bush had the opportunity for peace but did not do it. We should not be threatened by thugs. I'm very passionate about this issue. I have to deal with the Europeans. They don't get it. What is happening in Iraq is a crime against humanity. I will not allow it to go on.

The King remarked that the President's mind seemed to be set on action, and then he shifted the discussion to the Israeli–Palestinian conflict. He repeated the argument his Foreign Minister had made to Condoleezza Rice the day before. 'We are going to support you in Iraq ... We assume you're going to take military action [to topple Saddam Hussein] ... We will do everything we can to support you, but we need more cover on the Palestinian issue. We need a roadmap on how we're going to get from where we are now to realizing the vision that you, the President, have laid out [in your 24 June address].'[8] The President still demurred. Secretary of State Colin Powell recalls what the King then said: 'Look, it's one thing to have a speech and vision, but you're not laying out *how* you get there ... You have to have a path, you have to have a way to get there.' Bush replied: 'What do the Palestinians want from me? I gave them a vision [in my speech]. What more can they want? I gave them the vision of a state.' The King then turned the floor over to his Foreign Minister Muasher:

MUASHER: 'Frankly, Mr President, most Palestinians are sceptical that this vision will be realized. All we are asking for is to take this exact vision of yours and translate it into steps. We are not asking for any commitments that you have not already given.'

BUSH: [Pause] 'I have no problem with that.' [Looking at the Assistant Secretary of State for the Bureau of Near Eastern Affairs, William Burns] 'Why don't you two work something out?'

MUASHER: 'There is clarity in the short term regarding what needs to be done on the political, security arenas. We are working with you on this. But we need to inject some clarity for the period after so people can have some hope.'

BUSH: 'Dealing with security, institutions and the constitution will give us the confidence to move to the next stage. The initial stage is more important than the final stage for now, which will include such issues as settlements and Jerusalem. We must first be happy with the Palestinian government which emerges. More than outlining steps, we need progress on the ground first.'

MUASHER: 'We need to assure people of our seriousness. We need to define a roadmap. That starts with security, institutions, dealing with the humanitarian situation, but also outlines the remaining steps till mid-2005, so that people can know exactly what they are getting, so that we can thus have more support for our work on security.'

BUSH: 'I thought that was clear in my speech. If it is not, we are willing to work with you in outlining these steps. I have no problem with that. After security and institutions, we will finalize issues such as settlements, occupation.'

BURNS: 'We can take the speech and translate it into steps.'

BUSH: 'I have no problem with that.'

The King was obviously delighted when he walked out of the Oval Office. So was Secretary of State Powell, who saw a new opportunity for the US to use its weight to solve the conflict. 'Powell', as Muasher recalls, 'was elated ... He came to me after the meeting and said "Congratulations."' Less happy was National Security Advisor Condoleezza Rice, who had to swallow her words, saying to Muasher, 'We will work something out ...' The roadmap was born.

The NSC's Middle East expert Flynt Leverett was then instructed to start drafting the roadmap. It was to lay out the actions that needed to be taken by the Israelis and the Palestinians to turn Bush's 24 June 2002 vision into reality and establish a viable Palestinian state, existing side by side with Israel.[9] Crucially, and unlike all former peace plans, the requirements of the roadmap were to be carried out *simultaneously* by each side – in *parallel* rather than sequentially. This, it was hoped, would prevent either side from stalling the process. The roadmap was to be released by the end of 2002 under the auspices of the 'Quartet' – Russia, the UN, the European Union and America, all as equal partners.[10]

By July, a first draft was ready to be shown to Arab ambassadors in Washington and to the Israelis. The Arabs were largely satisfied – it took as its basis a historic peace plan put forward by Saudi Arabia four months earlier, in which all Arab states would normalize relations with Israel in return for full Israeli withdrawal from all occupied territories, including Jerusalem, and a Palestinian right of return to Israel proper. The Israelis said it was 'horrifying'. Not only was it based on the Saudi plan, which they had rejected, but they felt that it was far more conciliatory towards the Palestinians than even the original Bush speech had been. Aided by his allies in Washington, Prime Minister Sharon started pressing the Administration to change it. His main concern was to ensure Israel did not have to fulfil its requirements under the plan until the Palestinians had eradicated terror attacks on Israel – in other words, to make the roadmap sequential.

As Israeli diplomatic activity to change the draft gained momentum, the Jordanians, who had been the driving force behind the initiative, became increasingly concerned that the US would lose its nerve. Flynt Leverett reassured Jordan's Foreign Minister Muasher. 'Don't worry,' he said, 'we are going to put the roadmap out. Sharon will have input, as other parties do, but he won't have a veto, and we will put it out before the end of 2002, well in advance of any military action we might undertake in Iraq.'[11]

That at least sounded encouraging.

21

Locking Arafat Up Again

On the ground the vicious circle of violence continued. The Israeli army proceeded with its operations – imposing curfews, deploying checkpoints, conducting searches – and Israel continued to expropriate Palestinian land for building settlements. The Palestinians, in their frustration, fought back. On 4 August 2002, a suicide bomb on a bus near Haifa killed 9 and injured 50, and close to the Damascus Gate in Jerusalem's Old City, 2 more were killed and 16 injured in a shooting incident. On 18 September, an Islamic Jihad militant killed himself and an Israeli policeman in the north of the country, and the next day a Hamas suicide bomber detonated a large bomb on municipal bus number 4 at the corner of Allenby and Rothschild streets in Tel Aviv, killing 6 and injuring 70. Furious, Prime Minister Sharon decided to go after his old foe Arafat again. He blamed Arafat for failing to stop suicide bombers, and led his Cabinet in giving the green light to the military to execute 'Operation Question of Time' – to reoccupy Ramallah and attack the *muqata*, Arafat's headquarters.

'GET IN THE BUILDING! ABANDON THE CAR!'

That Thursday afternoon, 19 September 2002, unaware that Israeli tanks were bearing down on Ramallah, the Palestinian Minister of Finance, Dr Salam Fayyad, had just arrived at the *muqata* for a routine meeting. When he found that Arafat was busy, Fayyad decided to come back later. He recalls, 'I was about to leave. My car was right by the gates. Then I started to hear shooting. I got in the car, a bit worried. There was a burst of heavy machine-gun fire. Everybody looked baffled, scared. I realized that leaving through the gates was not a good idea. I shouted [to the taxi driver], "Abandon the car!" There was another burst of heavy gunfire. I said, "Get in the building! Abandon the car!"'

Minister of Labour Ghassan Khatib, also waiting to see Arafat, remembers: 'One of the guards was shot in the leg and we dragged him inside the *muqata* . . . It was one of the most horrible and frightening moments in my life.'[1] When everyone was inside, the guards shut the gates. Two hundred Palestinians were locked inside.

This second siege of the *muqata* was to be even more aggressive than the one that April. Tanks and bulldozers rapidly surrounded the compound and began razing the various ministries to the ground, tightening the noose on Arafat. The Israelis demanded that Arafat extradite fifty wanted militants lodged with him in the *muqata* – men, Israel claimed, with 'blood on their hands'.[2]

'COWARDS! COWARDS!'

As the tanks and bulldozers deployed outside, the trapped Palestinians were peeping through cracks in the hastily barricaded windows. Minister Ghassan Khatib recalls:

The Israelis were not only shooting continuously, they were blowing up the buildings around the main building we were in. They were demolishing one room after another. Constantly. It was very close, so when you heard the explosion you closed your eyes and only when you opened them do you realize it was actually next door and you are not dead. The sound of the Israeli tanks driving over cars was terrifying. The metal being crushed makes a horrible sound.

Arafat stayed calm. Khatib asked him, 'How can you stay so calm and continue working?' Arafat laughed. 'It comes back to my experience,' he said. 'We had difficult periods like this often in the siege of Beirut [in 1982]. The experience was tougher, and the situation more serious, more terrifying than this one.'

But even Arafat had moments when he lost control. When a guard rushed in to report that an Israeli tank was crashing through the metal gates of the compound, Arafat, as Khatib recalls, 'was suddenly enraged . . . he stood up . . . took his little sub-machine gun . . . and rushed down the stairs shouting, "Cowards! Cowards!"' His guards managed to catch up with him at the bottom of the stairs before he burst out into the courtyard, and brought him back upstairs into the room. Arafat carried on yelling: 'This is a cowardly action! Why do they destroy the building? Why do they crash vehicles? Why do they destroy the gates? This is a cowardly action.'

The Israelis, meanwhile, crept closer and closer to the main building housing Arafat and the other Palestinians. At around 4 a.m. on Friday, 20 September, a message came through from the Israelis, telling them to evacuate the room as the army was about to blow up the adjacent building. The almighty explosion at 5.30 a.m. shattered the windows and doors in Arafat's office.

'CALL US IF YOU NEED ANYTHING!'

The Israelis sent a list of names to Arafat; those on it were free to go. 'My name was the first on the list,' Ghassan Khatib recalls. 'I said [to Arafat], "I don't want to leave! I want to remain." Arafat said: "You should leave. You'll be more useful outside than inside."' Khatib then asked, 'What about Salam Fayyad [whose name was also on the list]?' Arafat replied 'He's asleep. Let's not disturb him.' In fact, Fayyad was sitting right next to Arafat, but this was Arafat's way of saying that Salam Fayyad, his Finance Minister, would have to stay with him inside the *muqata*. Fayyad had good links with the Americans, so Arafat felt it advisable to keep Fayyad with him.

Fayyad sent out a Mayday signal, phoning NSC Senior Director Flynt Leverett in Washington. Leverett recalls his conversation with the Palestinian minister: 'Fayyad said to me that he wanted [National Security Advisor Condoleezza] Rice to know that he was really fearing for his life. He believed that there was a very serious chance that the Israelis would storm the compound and that he and others would be killed . . . and that only the United States could keep it from happening.' Leverett said he would report immediately to his superiors. He ended the conversation by saying to Fayyad, 'Here is the direct number for the White House Situation Room. If you need anything, do call us.' Fayyad recalls what he thought at the time: 'Call us if you need anything?! We are about to get blown off the face of the earth, and all the great Americans can say is "Call us if you need anything!"' '

'WE CAN'T HAVE YOU ROCK THE BOAT'

The message got through. Later that day, Condoleezza Rice phoned Prime Minister Sharon's Chief of Staff, Dov Weisglass, to protest. And the next day, the US ambassador to Israel, Dan Kurtzer, flew from Tel Aviv to see Sharon at his farm in the Negev. Kurtzer was blunt. He said to the Prime Minister that the US never raised its voice when Israel took an action which was clearly needed for her security, even when innocent Palestinian civilians were killed. But the US was now in big trouble over Iraq and 'we can't have you rock the boat'. The US would support Israel in any action against a clear and present danger, Kurtzer continued, 'even if the Middle East shivered all over'. However, this siege was going too far, the ambassador said; Arafat himself clearly did not present an immediate threat. 'So please,' said Kurtzer, 'take this into account.'[3] The Prime Minister listened, polite as ever, but promised nothing. That night, Secretary of State Colin Powell phoned Sharon to tell him that his non-committal response to Ambassador Kurtzer was 'unsatisfying'.[4]

In Washington, the President was livid. Powell explains: 'Every time we put Arafat in his place and started to move him to the sidelines, [Sharon would do something and] suddenly Arafat is right dead back in the centre of everything . . . and rather than isolating him, [Sharon would] just bring him right back into the game.'[5] This was not the only reason why the President was aghast. Just a few days before, on 12 September, he had gone to the United Nations General Assembly to challenge the world to enforce previous Security Council resolutions on Iraq. He went out of his way to commit the US to the future of the Palestinians ('America stands committed to an independent and democratic Palestine'), knowing that this could help persuade Europeans and Arabs to join him in his proposed war on Iraq.[6] Now, Arafat was once again all over the TV news networks, with Israeli tanks inches from him, apparently threatening his life. Prime Minister Sharon was bringing world attention back to the Palestinian issue, and making a mockery of Bush's promises. At a Situation Room meeting, Bush said that this episode 'really calls into question [Prime Minister] Sharon's commitment to a peaceful resolution of this conflict'.[7]

To divert the growing criticism, Sharon now gave instructions to open negotiations with the Palestinians about lifting the siege on Arafat. But he also made it clear that there was no need to hurry: talks could be protracted. According to General Eival Gilady, who was appointed to talk to the chief Palestinian negotiator, Saeb Erekat, 'I didn't feel that I was under pressure of time [to conclude a deal to lift the siege], so [myself and Saeb Erekat] were both playing a game.'[8]

In New York, on Tuesday, 24 September, the UN Security Council adopted resolution 1435 (2002), which called on Israel to halt its operations in Ramallah, 'including the destruction of Palestinian civilian and security infrastructure'. Deeply upset with the Israelis, Washington refrained from using its customary veto on resolutions condemning the Israelis. It also made a blunt criticism of Israel. President Bush warned that the five-day-old blockade on Arafat was 'not helpful'. National Security Advisor Condoleezza Rice told Israel that the US expected a speedy resolution of the siege, because it 'doesn't help' US efforts to galvanize support for the campaign against Iraq.[9]

Careful not to go too far, Prime Minister Sharon informed Ambassador Kurtzer that he would send his Chief of Staff Dov Weisglass to Washington to discuss the siege.

'ARAFAT HAD HIDDEN IT'

As the Israelis tightened their grip on the *muqata*, conditions inside rapidly deteriorated. 'There was no water, the toilets were swimming and there were maggots', Fayyad recalls.[10] He shared a room with Arafat, Nabil Abu Rudeineh and Hani al-Hassan, which posed its own particular problems.

Abu Ammar [Arafat] does not like air conditioning. And he covers himself in blankets. It was hot. I cannot stand it when it's hot, and Nabil is like me. But the President is the President! So Nabil and I had to cheat a bit. If the President went out for a stroll, we turned the air conditioning on. He'd come back and turn it off again. He'd fall asleep, and we'd turn it on. Then he'd wake up and turn it off again. We kept doing this – but none of us spoke about it! One night, Nabil and I got out our little torch to find the remote control for the air conditioning. This was normally on the table. But it had disappeared. We looked everywhere for it, sneaking about, using our little torch. Then we realized that the only place it could be was under Abu Ammar's pillow. Arafat had hidden it![11]

Outside the *muqata*, meanwhile, rumours were circulating that the Israelis intended to bomb or storm the building Arafat was in. An Israeli tank had recently shelled the bridge connecting that building to some adjacent offices – one shell was off target and actually struck the wall of Arafat's room. He could have been killed. The ordinary Palestinians of Ramallah poured into the streets, banging saucepans in support of their besieged leader. Similar protests took place in Nablus, Gaza City, Qalqilya, Tulkarm, Hebron, Bethlehem, Jericho, in the Israeli prisons holding Palestinians, and in refugee camps in Lebanon.

'YOU'RE GOING TO HAVE THAT SERIOUS
PROBLEM WITH ME'

Meanwhile, Sharon's Chief of Staff, Dov Weisglass, had arrived in Washington. Accompanied by the Israeli ambassador, Danny Ayalon, he went to see National Security Advisor Rice. She was livid. Flynt Leverett of the NSC recalls what she said to her Israeli guests:

'Israel has had no better friend in the White House than this Administration, and you've had no better friend in this Administration than me, but I am telling you, if you do not end this siege in Ramallah, if you don't withdraw your forces from the compound, you are going to have a public rift with this President. This needs to end *now*. If you and I are having this same conversation a week from now, you are going to have a serious problem in this building, and you're going to have that serious problem with me.'[12]

Rice added: 'Don't turn Arafat into a martyr. You should consider also the other results. What are the ramifications on public opinion . . . Arab public opinion and the world public opinion?' 'We got the message, a bit late maybe, but we got it', Ambassador Ayalon admits. Then, Leverett recalls, '[Rice] put [Assistant Secretary of State] William Burns and me in the Roosevelt Room with Weisglass and Danny Ayalon to work out the timetable upon which Israeli forces would pull back from the compound in Ramallah.'

At noon on Sunday, 29 September, Prime Minister Sharon gave instructions to end the ten-day stand-off. General Giora Eiland of the IDF's Planning Division phoned the UN envoy in the Middle East, Terje Roed-Larsen, to say, 'We're going to lift the siege.' Larsen jumped into his car and drove straight to Ramallah, where he was the first to enter the *muqata*. 'Everybody was colossally relieved,' Larsen recalls. 'Everybody hugged me . . . some were even in tears.' But not Arafat. 'Why did they leave?' he said. 'I needed them to stay longer!' Larsen remembers that Arafat was 'in a foul mood while everybody else was jubilant'.[13]

Briefly emerging from his sandbagged building – one of only three still standing in the government complex – Arafat blew kisses to his supporters and flashed a V-for-victory sign. But he still would not leave the *muqata*, lest Sharon in his absence should order it to be stormed and so prevent Arafat from returning to his headquarters.

In Washington, White House spokesman Gordon Johndroe pronounced the President pleased with the development.[14] With the siege over, Bush could refocus on Iraq and on releasing the roadmap – the plan that would provide much-needed cover on the Palestinian issue for his Arab and European allies in the Iraq war. However, before the roadmap could be published, an unexpected obstacle emerged – a domestic upheaval in Israel.

22

Dead Ends and Back Alleys on the Roadmap

'NO, WE CAN'T GO THROUGH WITH IT'

On 30 October 2002, Sharon's fragile coalition government collapsed after the Labour Party walked out when the Prime Minister rejected its demand to divert $147 million, earmarked for expanding Jewish settlements on Palestinian land, to fund social services. Unable to patch together a new coalition government, Sharon called a general election for 28 January 2003. He then instructed his ambassador in Washington, Danny Ayalon, to urge the Americans to postpone the publication of the roadmap until after the Israeli election. Releasing such a controversial document during the election campaign would inevitably affect not only the outcome of the vote, the Israelis argued, but also Sharon's ability to embrace the peace plan in such a politically sensitive period.

The neoconservatives in the Bush Administration, including Condoleezza Rice and Vice President Dick Cheney, bought the Israeli's logic. Rice said to Flynt Leverett, chief drafter of the roadmap, 'We can't go through with it', insisting that releasing the plan would amount to US intervention in Israeli politics.[1] Leverett argued back, 'If we pull the roadmap simply because Ariel Sharon has called for an early election, and we don't want to make life politically difficult for him, then we *are* intervening in Israeli politics. We're just intervening in a different direction.' But the President was persuaded, and the roadmap was put on hold.

'A BETRAYAL'

News of the postponement did not go down well in the Arab world. The Jordanians, the driving force behind the roadmap, felt that the failure of the US to provide some kind of cover on the Palestinian issue was 'a betrayal', as Jordanian Foreign Minister Muasher recalls. Muasher told Flynt Leverett 'the US is leaving me and others who had supported the Administration out in the cold'. Referring to rumours that, in addition to postponement, Washington was also working behind the scenes on a language more palatable to Israel's tastes, Muasher added, 'You can rest assured, if the language [of the roadmap] is not accepted by Jordan, there will not be one Arab state that accepts it.'

Worse was to come. National Security Advisor Condoleezza Rice appointed a new official as her Middle East co-ordinator on the NSC, over Flynt Leverett – the hawkish neoconservative Elliott Abrams. He did not see eye to eye with Leverett on the roadmap.

The roadmap, we should recall, was officially the work of the 'Quartet' – Russia, the UN, the European Union and America. However, Abrams was deeply suspicious of the Quartet, particularly its European component, which he regarded as anti-Israeli, if not anti-Semitic. He asked Leverett, 'Why do we need to do the roadmap with the Quartet at all? Why couldn't we just get together and say, "Well, there are a lot of differences that we still have to work out and, you know, now we've got a war to go fight in Iraq." And we may get back to this, and maybe we'll just never get back to it?'[2] Abrams also found sympathy with a list of objections to the roadmap sent to him by AIPAC, the American Israel Public Affairs Committee, a powerful lobbyist group, which argued that the roadmap was inconsistent with the President's 24 June speech, that it did not reflect Bush's intent.[3] Leverett disagreed. He told Abrams that when he and Assistant Secretary of State William Burns had been working on the roadmap, 'there was one document that we had in front of us every minute ... and that was the June 24th speech'.[4]

'YOU KNOW, I READ THE ROADMAP LAST NIGHT'

On the morning of 18 December 2002, Elliott Abrams and Flynt Leverett went over to the Oval Office to brief the President on the roadmap. Bush said: 'I keep hearing that the roadmap is not consistent with the June 24th speech. Elliott, what do you think about that?' Abrams replied: 'Well, we're working on it, Mr President, to try and make it more consistent, but there are some serious problems with it.' The President then turned to Flynt Leverett, who said, 'Mr President, I really think you should make the judgement, is it consistent with the June 24th speech or not.' The President said, 'Well, I guess I am going to get a chance to read the roadmap at some point, won't I?' Leverett responded, 'Mr President, we can send it over to the residence tonight.'

The next day, Abrams and Leverett returned, with Secretary of State Powell, National Security Advisor Rice and the other principal officials for a briefing before a Quartet meeting. The President said, 'You know, I read the roadmap last night, and I think it's perfectly consistent with the June 24th speech. All the elements are there.' Turning to Abrams, the President said, 'Elliott, why aren't we getting our message out on this? Why are people only hearing from AIPAC and the Israeli embassy on this subject?' Abrams blustered: 'Well, Mr President, we'll get right to work on that.'

The roadmap was approaching its final form. At the heart of the plan was a performance-based approach – making the two parties act in parallel. It had three phases. The first called on the Palestinians to undertake comprehensive political reform – to appoint a prime minister, draft a constitution and hold democratic elections. Most importantly, they had to dismantle terrorist infrastructures and declare 'an unequivocal end to violence and terrorism', and end incitement against Israel. At the same time, Israel had to withdraw from those Palestinian areas occupied since the beginning of the intifada, dismantle settlement outposts and freeze all settlement expansion – including ending the widely used 'natural growth' loophole.[5] In the second phase, the provisional borders of a Palestinian state were to be established. The final phase would deal with the thorny macro issues – the status of

Jerusalem, the borders of the future Palestinian state, the right of return of Palestinian refugees, and the fate of existing Israeli settlements.

'I ACCEPT'

The emerging roadmap draft made it clear that the Palestinians had to appoint an 'empowered' prime minister – one with real authority. This was intended to sideline Arafat, with whom the US and Israel refused to deal. It also had to be done *before* the roadmap was released. But Arafat had held the reins for the Palestinian people for decades, and giving up his power was going to be painful. Minister Nabil Shaath, a close ally of Arafat, who was working on a new Palestinian constitution, took it upon himself to convince the Palestinian leader. Shaath recalls their meeting:

[Arafat] listened to all the things that were being taken away from him and said, 'What is left for me, what will protect my authority?' And I said, 'First, you will remain the elected President of the Palestinian people, you will be elected by the people and not by the parliament, which gives you an edge. Second, you will nominate the prime minister, and you will [have the power to] dismiss the prime minister. And third, you will remain the supreme leader of the armed forces . . . all the security forces. Everything else will go to the prime minister.[6]

It was not an easy conversation, but, Shaath recalls, 'I had the surprise of my life. Arafat said, "I accept."'

'LISTEN, THIS IS SOMETHING BIG'

The Palestinians now needed a credible messenger to convince President Bush that Arafat was serious, and that the new prime minister would have real power. They turned to the British. Chief Palestinian negotiator Saeb Erekat and minister Yasser Abed Rabbo contacted Lord Levy, Tony Blair's roving ambassador to the Middle East. They said it would be 'beneficial and interesting' for him to come to Ramallah.[7] After consulting Number 10, Levy set off for the West Bank, accompanied by an official from the Foreign and Commonwealth Office and the British Consul-General in Jerusalem, Geoffrey Adams.

On 23 January 2003, the three Britons had a long conference with Abed Rabbo, Erekat and other prominent Palestinians, who told them that they had a letter, signed by Arafat, undertaking to appoint a prime minister. They wanted Prime Minister Blair to show this letter to President Bush in their meeting scheduled for the end of January.

Abed Rabbo and Erekat were not quite telling the truth. Even as they were talking, elsewhere in the *muqata* discussions were still under way about the exact wording of the letter. Arafat – manoeuvring to retain as much authority as he could – was still trying to modify the letter. He wanted it to say that he accepted the idea of appointing a prime minister 'in principle' and 'in due course'.[8] However, he was eventually convinced that such qualifications were unlikely to impress the Americans.

With the letter – promising an empowered prime minister – finally signed, it was given to Lord Levy, who then asked for a break to consult. In a side room he opened the envelope and found two copies of the letter – one in Arabic, the other in English. The British guests realized that what they had obtained was significant but they had already foreseen potential problems, and wanted to know more.[9] They reconvened with the Palestinians and Lord Levy said, 'Can we go into what the role of the prime minister is going to be? How there is going to be the interaction between the prime minister and the President? What the relationships are going to be? What the powers for this newly appointed prime minister are going to be? How is the prime minister going to be appointed? How is all this going to work?'[10] Erekat replied: 'Listen, this is something big in your hand . . .'[11] Lord Levy recalls that 'the answer was pretty plainly and bluntly, "You have got something very important and historic in your hand." '[12] Realizing that he was not going to get any more in terms of specifics (probably because those specifics had not even been worked out yet), Levy thanked his hosts and departed.

On 31 January, Prime Minister Blair met President Bush, showed him the letter and urged him that with Arafat agreeing to appoint a prime minister and step aside, and with the election in Israel over and Sharon reinstalled as Prime Minister, it was time to release the roadmap. Blair, of course, had his own reasons for wanting the Americans to publish the roadmap. He needed to persuade a sceptical parliament and public at home that his support for Bush over Iraq would pay dividends and result in tangible gains for the Middle East peace process. According to Secretary of State Colin Powell, 'Mr Blair made the case that if Iraq is now heating up and we're going to have to [go to war], we really need to have this roadmap out to give some comfort to the Palestinians and to the Arab world ... [to show] that we're dealing with this other crisis ... the Israeli–Palestinian crisis.' But, in spite of Arafat's letter and Blair's pressure, the President still held the roadmap back, apparently to give Sharon time to form a new coalition government.

'ARAFAT, COME ALONG, THIS IS YOUR BROTHER, GIVE HIM A CHANCE'

The question was, however, who would be the new Palestinian prime minister? Arafat first offered the job to Munib Masri, a Palestinian billionaire and scion of a prominent and successful family from Nablus. But Masri was almost unknown beyond the West Bank, and there was pressure on Arafat to nominate Abu Mazen, a moderate and a critic of the violent intifada. Egypt played a leading role in persuading Arafat to select Abu Mazen for the job. According to Nabil Shaath, 'It was basically Omar Suleiman [the Egyptian head of Intelligence], who came [to Ramallah] with messages from Mubarak, and Mubarak himself was on the phone all the time ... Very brief conversations [with Arafat], three or four sentences. "Arafat, come along, this is your brother, give him a chance, he will protect you, he will stand up for you." Three or four times a day!'[13]

On 7 March, Arafat relented. He publicly invited Abu Mazen to become Prime Minister, which the latter accepted on 19 March. The following day the American- and British-led invasion of Iraq began.

Tony Blair increased the pressure on President Bush to publish the roadmap. However, Bush now placed another hurdle in the way, announcing he would publish the roadmap as soon as Abu Mazen had appointed a working cabinet. Clearly, Bush was reluctant to issue his own roadmap, and was trying to put it off as long as possible. The Israelis were not happy about it, but also, as Secretary of State Powell explains, 'there was still a little bit of reluctance to publicly release it because the US then takes on additional obligations and commitments'.

However, Abu Mazen found that appointing a working cabinet, as Bush was now demanding, was easier said than done. Disagreement focused on one name: Mohammed Dahlan, the 42-year-old Gazan, whom Abu Mazen wanted as Interior Minister – in charge of security and therefore the most important job in government. Arafat, however, did not want Dahlan. The two had fallen out during the Israeli Defensive Shield operation in April 2002, when Arafat felt that Dahlan was not supportive enough. And in Arafat's eyes, Dahlan was also too close to the Israelis and the Americans, and a threat to his own popularity. 'President Arafat', Dahlan comments in an interview for *Elusive Peace*, 'felt the danger of having me and Abu Mazen in one government. [Arafat] . . . was not interested in anything other than his own position.'

With Arafat standing firm, the Jordanians – keen to see the roadmap released – weighed in. They sent a secret message to Arafat to say that if he did not back down and let Mohammed Dahlan into the cabinet, Arafat would lose the support of all the Arab states. Egypt's President Mubarak intervened as well, sending his Chief of Intelligence, Omar Suleiman, to mediate between Arafat and Abu Mazen and smooth over the difficulties.[14] On 23 April, a compromise was reached: Abu Mazen would be Prime Minister *and* Interior Minister, whereas Dahlan would be made a Minister of State: Dahlan was in charge of security in all but name. Nevertheless, real control of the various security forces remained in Arafat's hands. As Abu Mazen recalls in an interview for *Elusive Peace*, 'Abu Ammar [Arafat] said he cannot give up security, it has to be affiliated to him . . . I had to accept that. There was no choice.'[15]

In Washington, on 30 April 2003, hours after Abu Mazen and his new Cabinet were sworn in, President Bush finally gave the green light to the Quartet to release the roadmap.

The effect on the ground was by no means instant. Violence continued. The Israeli army tightened its grip over the occupied territories, and the Palestinians hit back. On 17 May 2003, a suicide bomb in Hebron killed 2 Israelis, and the next day, the suicide bombing of a number 6 bus in Jerusalem killed 7 and wounded 20. To save the roadmap from dying before it had even got off the ground, Washington asked Prime Minister Abu Mazen to dispatch a trusted emissary to discuss the situation.

On 21 May, Finance Minister Salam Fayyad met with Condoleezza Rice and her aides. During the meeting, as Fayyad recalls, 'the phone rings and Condi [Rice] says to me, "You and I need to go somewhere alone." She takes me by the hand and sits me down on a sofa in another room. Suddenly I realize I'm in the Oval Office, and there is George W. Bush pacing around, and he makes the Texas Longhorns [hand] sign at me, and I make it back.'[16]

The two had a long talk. Fayyad said that the Palestinians had a right to their own state and that 'we just want to be left alone'. Bush told Fayyad he was planning to go to the region to launch the roadmap, and he let him know that before this could happen the Palestinians had to stop terror attacks on Israel. This requirement was clearly spelled out in the first phase of the roadmap, and the message the President wished Fayyad to convey to his Prime Minister in Ramallah was that Palestinian violence *had* to be stopped, otherwise the roadmap was doomed.

'I WANT YOU TO BE PARTNERS'

Abu Mazen needed no reminder of that. On 22 May 2003, he asked minister Ziad Abu Amr, who had good contacts with Hamas, to set up a meeting with the group's leaders – Abdel Aziz al-Rantissi, Mahmoud Zahar and Ismail Hanieh. They met in Abu Mazen's Gaza office. 'We all made our introductions,' Ziad Abu Amr recalls; 'the atmosphere was pretty friendly. Abu Mazen was very straight with them – and this added to the trust.'[17] Abu Mazen reported on his talks with President Bush, National Security Advisor Condoleezza Rice and Prime Minister Sharon. He then added, 'I want you to be *partners*.'[18] He explained, as he recalls in an interview for *Elusive Peace*: 'I have to end armed intifada. The intifada can be applied in peaceful manners, demonstrations, protests, meetings but not by militant operations [against the Israelis].'[19] He then added, 'I don't want to achieve that through bloodshed ... through civil war. We need a truce ... A ceasefire ... a *hudna*.'[20] Ziad Abu Amr took over. 'I started telling them what this would entail,' he recalls. 'Hamas was to stop acts of violence ... I mentioned a timeframe – three months [of truce]. No violence anywhere. So Hanieh said at the end of the meeting: "OK. We'll go back and check with everyone."'

After leaving the ninety-minute-long meeting, Hamas spokesman Ismail Hanieh talked to the press. He praised Prime Minister Abu Mazen, saying that he had talked to them as equals, something Arafat have never done, adding, 'We are dealing here with a different kind of leadership.' Abu Amr recalls how, 'on the next day I was with Arafat in Ramallah and I noticed him underlining those words in a press report, over and over again. He was furious.'

'IT ASKS THAT THE PALESTINIANS BECOME BLUE-EYED SCANDINAVIANS'

The Palestinians accepted the roadmap immediately – after all, it contained a promise of an independent state. The Israelis were more hesitant – they would be the ones who had to give up tangible assets. Prime Minister Sharon was reluctant to deal with a Palestinian leadership under Arafat's umbrella. He also disliked the roadmap's idea of a Palestinian state in three years' time, preferring instead a long-term interim agreement and a transitional state that would last longer. Above all, he was reluctant to make any move – the roadmap called for parallel actions by both sides – before Palestinian terror attacks on Israel ceased.

Sharon sent his Chief of Staff, Dov Weisglass, to Washington, where he complained to the Americans that the roadmap asked Israel to give up too much, and for what? Elliott Abrams – not a fan of the roadmap – said, 'Look, ask yourself what the roadmap is. It is moving towards a Palestinian state in stages. OK? Now, the very first thing that has to happen is that the Palestinians fight terrorism. So what are you worried about?' Abrams' reading of the roadmap – that it was sequential after all, and Israel need do nothing until the Palestinians eradicated terror, which, as he argued, they were certain not to do – persuaded Weisglass to accept the roadmap. In a later interview Weisglass commented, 'Phase one [of the roadmap] requires the Palestinians to control terrorists ... it asks that the Palestinians become blue-eyed Scandinavians ... when they become blue-eyed Scandinavians, we'll move on to phase two.'[21]

The Israelis still had specific reservations – initially around one hundred – which were eventually whittled down to fourteen. Sharon told the Americans he would bring the roadmap before his government for consideration only if Washington agreed to include *all* fourteen amendments in the roadmap.[22] The amendments were uncompromising. The first, for instance, said among other things:

In the first phase of the plan and as a condition for progress to the second phase, the Palestinians will complete the dismantling of terrorist organizations (Hamas, Islamic Jihad, the Popular Front, the Democratic Front, Al-Aqsa Brigades and other apparatuses) and their infrastructure; collection of all illegal weapons and their transfer to a third party for the sake of being removed from the area and destroyed; cessation of weapons smuggling and weapons production inside the Palestinian Authority; activation of the full prevention apparatus and cessation of incitement ...

After months of intifada, in which their security forces had been systematically destroyed by the Israeli army, the Palestinians were hardly in a position to dismantle all terrorist organizations as now requested by the Israelis. Even with their full security capability, this demand would have taken months if not years for the Palestinian Authority to fulfil, as it amounted to undertaking an all-out war against the militants. And this was just the first of fourteen equally tough amendments.

The Americans told the Israelis that it was too late to change the text of the roadmap, but they would take the objections on board and deal with each of them as and when they actually occurred.[23] The Israelis insisted on a public and written pledge to this effect, and the Americans accepted. On 23 May 2003, Secretary of State Colin Powell and National Security Advisor Condoleezza Rice issued the following statement:

The roadmap was presented to the Government of Israel with a request from the President that it respond with contributions to this document to advance true peace. The United States Government received a response from the Government of Israel, explaining its significant concerns about the roadmap. The United States shares the view of the Government of Israel that these are real concerns, and will address them fully and seriously in the implementation of the roadmap to fulfill the President's vision of June 24, 2002.

This declaration enabled the Prime Minister to say to his right-wing ministers and other objectors that he had not fully endorsed the roadmap. It also ensured, as minister Benjamin Netanyahu explains in an interview for *Elusive Peace*, 'that the Palestinians do their part before we do our part'.

'LET'S LEAVE THE BULLSHIT'

Two days later, Sharon brought the roadmap before his sceptical government for approval. It was not going to get an easy ride. An Israeli official recalls how 'some ministers were trying to put in additions, and turning up with dictionaries'. After several hours of battling, the Minister of Justice, Yoseph Lapid, banged his fist on the table. 'Listen guys,' he said, 'let's leave the bullshit. Those among us who support the peace process are *for* the roadmap; those who are against the peace process are *against* the roadmap, and let's stop this stupid meeting.'

Finally, after a heated debate, the government accepted the roadmap and issued a statement. It went: 'The Government, by a majority vote, resolved ... based on the 23 May 2003 statement of the United States Government, in which the United States committed to fully and seriously address Israel's comments to the roadmap during the implementation phase ... to accept it.'

23

Summits at Sharm and Aqaba

President Bush and his team wanted to officially launch the roadmap with some fanfare at a well-publicized regional summit. As many Arab leaders would not attend a summit with Israelis present, two separate meetings were arranged. The first, at Sharm el-Sheikh in Egypt, where President Bush would meet Arab heads of state with no Israelis; the second, at Aqaba in Jordan the following day, where Prime Ministers Sharon and Abu Mazen and President Bush would meet and deliver their speeches.[1]

Ahead of the arrival of President Bush and the Arab heads of state, Secretary of State Colin Powell held preparatory talks with Arab Foreign Ministers in Sharm on 2 June. He tried to get assurances that they would make some gestures of reconciliation towards Israel, so that the roadmap could mark a new dawn not only for the Israeli–Palestinian conflict, but also for the entire region. According to Jordan's Foreign Minister Marwan Muasher, 'Secretary Powell pushed hard for confidence-building measures. [For Arab] meetings with Israelis, opening of trade missions . . .' But, as Muasher relates, 'The Saudis would not have anything of this. And Prince Saud [al-Faisal Bin Abdul Aziz al-Saud] on behalf of Crown Prince Abdullah made clear . . . it was very difficult for Saudi Arabia to take such measures. The discussion became heated at times.' Not budging, Powell insisted that his President needed something on this issue, and he went as far as hinting that Bush might not come if the Arabs failed to compromise.

According to Muasher: 'We kept on arguing until about three o'clock in the morning. And Prince Saud [of Saudi Arabia] said, "We won't be pressured on this."' Powell, in an interview for *Elusive Peace*, recalls how 'they just would not go along ... the Saudis would not come forward.' Faced with such stiff resistance, Powell backed down; he phoned the President to report that this would not fly and they decided to drop the matter altogether and, instead, to focus on getting the Arab leaders to support Abu Mazen.

When President Bush arrived at Sharm, he met King Abdullah II of Jordan, Crown Prince Abdullah of Saudi Arabia, Hosni Mubarak of Egypt and King Hamad al Khalifa of Bahrain, among others. He did his best to gain these leaders' support for the roadmap and, particularly, for Abu Mazen. A participant told *Elusive Peace*: 'Bush was bustling about ... slapping all these dignified Arabs on the back and putting his arm round Abu Mazen and joshing him along. He said to those leaders, "You have to help this man."' It was also an opportunity for these Arab leaders to get to know the President better. The official recalls how 'Bush kept spinning round on his chair, like a child ... Spinning round and round in front of all these Arab leaders. It was embarrassing. He was saying things like, "You have got to kick their asses!" of Palestinian terrorists, and "We are gonna get those bastards" of Al Qaeda.'

No doubt Bush's support was a great boost for Abu Mazen, but it did nothing for the new Prime Minister's relationship with Arafat, who was feeling increasingly marginalized. Nabil Shaath explains that, 'Sharm was a matter of grave jealousy for Arafat. Here for the first time the upfront representative of Palestinians meeting the President of the US was not Arafat [but Abu Mazen] ... it was weighing heavily on Arafat's heart.'[2]

'I FEEL GOD'S WORDS COMING TO ME'

The next day, in Aqaba, President Bush met the Palestinians first. 'Bush was effusive ... very ebullient ... supportive of Abu Mazen ... very optimistic', Nabil Shaath recalls.[3] The President, as witnesses describe, was particularly interested in the man whose job it was to deal with security, Mohammed Dahlan. 'Bush suddenly looked at Dahlan,' Shaath recalls, 'and said to him "Dahlan, I want to hear your security plan."' Dahlan began describing his plan, but after just a minute the President cut him short. 'Don't say any more,' the President said; 'all I wanted was to look into your eyes, and I trust you. It's exactly the way I trusted Mr Sharon, I looked into his eyes and I believed that he was honest and serious in getting us along . . . it's trust that is very important.' Dahlan liked that. An American official recalls that the President was very direct with the Palestinians. 'You have a failed leader [Arafat], who brought you nothing but blood!' he said. The Palestinians replied, 'We are what the West wants in the Middle East – we are secular, we are democratic, we are exactly what you are always saying you want!' Bush said, 'Look, I agree with you. And it's remarkable how little anyone else has done for you, how little your Arab "brothers" have done for you.' The Palestinians were also to learn at first hand what drove Bush as he told them,

I'm driven with a mission from God. God would tell me, 'George, go fight those terrorists in Afghanistan.' And I did, and I was able to vanquish them, to end terrorism. And then God would tell me, 'George, go and end the tyranny in Iraq.' And I did. And now again I feel God's words coming to me, 'Go get the Palestinians their state, and the Israelis their security, and get peace in the Middle East.' And by God, I'm gonna do it.[4]

The President then met the Israelis. In this meeting, according to an American official, 'Sharon was nervous . . . he isn't normally. He was less self-assured with the President than I've seen him. The President was direct about the need for the Israelis to take action to help Abu Mazen.'

The President then brought the Israelis and Palestinians together at a round table. Secretary of State Colin Powell recalls Bush's opening words: 'We have a historic opportunity before us. The Palestinians have come forward with new leadership as we had hoped they would. They have a Prime Minister; he is saying the right things, he is prepared to do the right things.'

Security was at the top of the agenda – at Sharon's request – so

Bush asked Mohammed Dahlan to give a briefing. Dahlan gave a five-minute synopsis of the situation on the ground, and his plan to deal with it, concluding, 'There are some things we can do and some things we cannot. We will do our best. But we will need help', by which he meant Israeli help.[5] However, Israeli Defence Minister Shaul Mofaz was not impressed. He burst in at the end of Dahlan's presentation: 'Well, they won't be getting any help from us,' he said. 'They have their own security service.' This irritated the President and he turned on Mofaz angrily: 'Their own security service? But you have destroyed their security service.' Mofaz said, 'I do not think that we can help them, Mr President.' Bush replied, 'Oh, but I think that you can. And I think that you will.' Bush added, according to the Palestinian Yasser Abed Rabbo, 'I heard what you want *from* the Palestinians but I did not hear from you what you want to do *for* the Palestinians.' Mofaz went very quiet. Bush turned to Sharon and asked him, 'Who are these?' Sharon replied, 'My ministers.' 'No, I mean what do they represent?' 'These are my doves.' 'Your doves! My God, if these are your doves, God preserve us from your hawks!'[6]

Bush then turned to Abu Mazen. 'Mr Prime Minister,' he said, 'perhaps you could give an overview of the situation in the West Bank and Gaza.' Abu Mazen outlined the increasingly dire situation in the territories. He said that the humanitarian crisis was deepening and 'new funding was necessary' (Israel, which controlled the tax revenue of the Palestinian areas, had frozen the flow of cash to the Palestinian Authority since the beginning of the intifada). Sharon maintained that 'the insertion of new funding must be dependent on your good behaviour'. This remark visibly irritated President Bush: 'You should release their money as soon as possible. This will help the situation.' Sharon: 'We have to deal with security first and we will condition the release of their monies on this alone.' Bush: 'But it is their money . . .' Sharon: 'Nevertheless, Mr President . . .' 'It is their money, so give it to them.'

Then, turning to the Palestinians again, Bush said, 'I will not accept Palestinians killing Israelis. Don't ever tell me that killing Israelis is legitimate resistance. Don't tell me you cannot control the streets. If you can't control the streets, you don't deserve a state.'[7]

According to Secretary of State Powell, 'The President said both sides will have to take action and it begins with Palestinians fighting terror ... because bombs will destroy this process just as it has destroyed every other effort that we have made since the beginning of the Administration. He also made it clear to the Israeli side that they would have to take action as well – prisoner release, [ending] the delays at the checkpoints – all of that would have to be dealt with.'

At the end of the meeting, Bush pointed at Prime Minister Abu Mazen and said to the Israelis, 'If you cannot make peace with him, you cannot make peace with anybody else. Therefore, do not convince me that either he works or he doesn't, give him the opportunity to work, give him the necessary help to succeed, and I will give him the necessary help to succeed.'[8]

As they were leaving the room, Bush turned to National Security Advisor Condoleezza Rice: 'We have a problem with Sharon,' he said, 'but I like that young man [Mohammed Dahlan] and I think their Prime Minister [Abu Mazen] is incapable of lying. I hope that [the Palestinians] will be successful. We can work with them.'[9]

Bush had delivered his message to the teams – it was now time for the leaders to deliver *theirs* to their people.

'I ALMOST FELL FROM MY CHAIR'

Designed as it was to trumpet President Bush's engagement with the Palestinian issue, the Aqaba summit was a highly choreographed affair, not least in the leaders' speeches. It was important that Sharon and Abu Mazen should say the right thing. The NSC's Elliott Abrams and Assistant Secretary of State William Burns had been in the region during the previous two weeks, working with both sides – and particularly with the Palestinians – to ensure just that. William Burns explains, 'The big thing was to get Abu Mazen to call for the end of the armed intifada. And on the Israeli side it was more the language to do with the Palestinian state – with territorial contiguity.' The Americans were in no mood to compromise with the Palestinians on this. As Diana Buttu, who was a member of the Palestinian team drafting Abu

Mazen's speech, explains, 'The US pretty much wrote our statement . . . Elliott Abrams was constantly calling the office . . . Pretty much all the elements were laid out by the Americans. Drafts were given to them and they edited things out.'

Prime Minister Abu Mazen accepted the US wording, but his colleagues objected. Nabil Shaath describes how, 'Abu Mazen called me to a small room, and said, "I want you to have a look at it." ' When he finished reading the speech Nabil Shaath recalls how he 'almost fell from my chair'.[10] The speech did not even touch on the historic grievances of the Palestinian people. It read like an Israeli wishlist of Palestinian actions. Shaath said to Abu Mazen, 'This speech will be the incitement for people to assassinate you and possibly to assassinate me as well . . . it does not address anything positive to the Palestinian people.' Abu Mazen replied, 'I was promised by the Americans that Sharon will say exactly something reciprocal, that if I say what *we* need to do, he will say what *Israelis* need to do.' Shaath responded, 'I bet you a million dollars to one that Sharon will never say anything like this.'[11] He went on to say: 'Abu Mazen . . . rewrite that speech!'[12] But Abu Mazen was adamant: 'If we want to get the full support of the President of the United States,' he said, 'then we cannot change a word of this speech.' Nabil Shaath advised that it should, at least, mention Europe, 'our strategic ally'. But Abu Mazen would not, explaining that '[Elliott Abrams] would not allow that'. The debate within the Palestinian team continued until 3 a.m. the night before the summit.

As the leaders approached their podiums the next day to deliver their speeches, it felt like a historic moment. The Israeli minister Yoseph Lapid described the scene: 'You sit there on the grass, on the shore of the Red Sea, which is shining in the background, and between yourself and the water is the President of the United States, the King of Jordan, the leader of the Palestinians and the Prime Minister of Israel – the scene is a photograph for history.' They were on Jordanian soil but it was clear who was running the affair: 'The sound system was all made by the Americans and those who introduced everything were American Arabs with thick Texas or Chicago accents!' as Nabil Shaath recalls.[13] Abu Mazen spoke first. He said, among other things:

We do not ignore the suffering of the Jews throughout history. It is time to bring all this suffering to an end ... we repeat our renunciation of terror against the Israelis wherever they might be. Such methods are inconsistent with our religious and moral traditions and are dangerous obstacles to the achievement of an independent, sovereign state we seek. These methods also conflict with the kind of state we wish to build, based on human rights and the rule of law. The armed intifada must end ... a complete end to violence and terrorism ... We will also act vigorously against incitement and violence and hatred [towards Israelis].

Then it was Sharon's turn:

My paramount responsibility is the security of the people of Israel and of the State of Israel. There can be no compromise with terror, and Israel, together with all free nations, will continue fighting terrorism until its final defeat ... There can be no peace ... without the abandonment and elimination of terrorism, violence and incitement.

One of Abu Mazen's aides recalls how 'Each party was supposed to speak only about *their* own commitments ... We were shocked at Sharon's speech – he was talking about things the *Palestinians* had to do, he was breaking the rules.'[14] As Diana Buttu says, 'Sharon was meant to say certain things ... reciprocally ... He was supposed to call for a complete end to violence from *both* sides. He didn't say that. He was supposed to call for an *independent* sovereign Palestinian state ... They promised us ... that it would be said. Acknowledging the suffering of the Palestinian people, all that stuff, and he didn't say it.'[15]

There was an extremely negative reaction to Abu Mazen's speech back on the streets of Gaza and the West Bank. As an American official who was involved in preparing the speeches admits, 'what we wanted Abu Mazen to say probably stretched the limits more than what Sharon had to say. He stuck his neck out, and was widely criticized for it in the Palestinian street.' More importantly, it was not just the ordinary Palestinians who felt betrayed.

'YOU HAVE TO HELP – AND IT DOESN'T HURT!'

Before the Aqaba summit Abu Mazen had persuaded Hamas to seriously consider accepting a ceasefire, or *hudna*. But on 5 June 2003, as minister Ziad Abu Amr, Abu Mazen's main contact with the militants, remembers, 'I got a phone call from one of the Hamas leaders who said, "This speech is a stab in the back ... and this is going to undermine the dialogue for the *hudna*." '[16] Alarmed, Abu Mazen went to Gaza to talk with Hamas once more. He said: 'You know perhaps I was fooled [at Aqaba] ... I did what I did because I was asked to by the Americans ... Sharon did not do what he was asked to do ... I thought he would do the same as me ... he did not.' He added, 'Look, we have a roadmap, we have committed ourselves to a roadmap, there are certain obligations on us, we have to have a ceasefire, a halt of violence.' The Hamas leaders maintained that 'This roadmap is no good ... We are worried that if you implement the roadmap to the letter you will be arresting us and you will be collecting our weapons and you will be dismantling our infrastructure. This is what the roadmap stipulates.' Abu Mazen replied that 'We don't have to necessarily do it that way ... If we agree amongst ourselves on putting a halt on violence, then we can go to the Israelis and the Americans and the rest of the world and say, "Look, we have fulfilled our obligations ... there is no violence on the Palestinian side, and now we want to see Israel delivering on its obligations in the roadmap." ' He added: 'You have to help – and it doesn't hurt! Why don't you try it? And if you don't like the outcome, you are free then to change your minds.'

The Hamas leaders asked whether Israel would stop targeting them for assassination (this was, according to Ziad Abu Amr, 'the only thing that really mattered to Hamas'). Abu Mazen responded: 'I have no guarantees.' Hamas asked whether Israel would release Palestinian prisoners. Again, Abu Mazen replied, 'I don't have any guarantees.' They asked about the building of Jewish settlements on occupied land. Abu Mazen replied, 'Look, I know all of these demands, and they are not only your demands, they are our own demands too. We are engaging the Israelis ... we are involving third parties – the Americans, the Europeans, the Quartet. But I don't have any guarantees from the Sharon government.' So, as Abu Amr recalls, 'Abu Mazen was very clear. He did not sell them any dreams.' The Hamas leaders went away to think about what they had heard. They were not yet convinced, but they promised to keep talking to Abu Mazen.

Although Abu Mazen thought he could get a ceasefire from Hamas, he needed to know if the Israelis would sign up to one too. He sent Mohammed Dahlan to talk to General Giora Eiland. 'All I am asking you', Dahlan said, 'is to try a truce for a month or two, you have got nothing to lose and if there are excesses from any of the Palestinian factions, tell us, and we will take our actions.' The Israelis, however, were reluctant. They wanted Dahlan to dismantle the militant organizations physically – by destroying them, not by reaching agreements with them. General Eiland recalls what Dahlan said: ' "I'll make sure there is a ceasefire. How do I do it, it's not your problem, whether I persuade them to stop, whether I gather their weapons, whether I dismantle them, whether I put them in jail, what business is it of yours? This is an internal Palestinian matter." ' Dahlan knew he could not take on the militants directly. To do so would risk being seen as Israel's enforcer and could lead to Palestinians killing Palestinians. Eventually, despite their concerns that the militants would simply use a truce to regroup and rearm, the Israelis went along with Dahlan.

The negotiations between Abu Mazen's aides and Hamas continued. Those negotiations, however, were about to become a lot more dangerous. The Israeli army had its own ideas about how to force the leaders of Hamas to accept a ceasefire. 'We decided', explains the Defence Minister's Military Secretary, Mike Herzog, 'to hit the [militants'] political leaders. In a week we got four of them.' On 10 June 2003, Israeli helicopters fired on Abdel Aziz al-Rantissi, the number 2 in the Hamas leadership, as he drove through Gaza City. He survived. 'We failed,' General Eiland admits, 'but to a large extent we got the results . . . The leaders of the terrorist organizations were very happy to sacrifice everyone else's lives, but when it came to their own lives . . .'

24

First Steps on the Roadmap

The Americans dispatched an envoy to the region, tasked with monitoring implementation of the roadmap. He was a diplomat with no previous experience in the region – John Wolf. When he landed at Ben-Gurion Airport on 15 June 2003, Wolf was taken straight to US ambassador Dan Kurtzer's residence, where he met the Israelis – the Prime Minister's Chief of Staff Dov Weisglass, Director of Shin Bet Avi Dichter, and others. 'The Israelis', Wolf recalls, 'just kept going on about their expectations of me, and of the Palestinians. I don't think I recall them mentioning anything *they* had to do. They said they expected us to be tough with the Palestinians and make sure they comply fully with their obligations . . . they have to deal with terrorism, and if they don't the process can't go forward.' When Wolf went to see Prime Minister Sharon the next day he got the same message. He remembers, 'Sharon was unrelenting . . . he had a point to make, and he would have three or four pages of talking points, read the first page which was on terrorism, then read something on page three, then go back to page one which was on terrorism, then a little bit from page three, then back to page one again, then a bit from three, then back to page one. He was Prime Minister of Israel – I had to listen! I told him that my role is to watch each side, and to report fully to Washington.'[1]

'THAT SUCKER WAS GOING TO DIVE INTO
THE MEDITERRANEAN'

One of Wolf's aims was to reach an agreement on the transfer of responsibility for security in the Gaza Strip and the Bethlehem area from Israel to the Palestinian Authority. This was intended to be the first step in the Israeli withdrawal from the areas reoccupied during the intifada, as long as the Palestinians could prove themselves able to maintain security and curb attacks on Israel. Thus two of the requirements of the first phase of the roadmap – Israeli withdrawal and a Palestinian clampdown on terror – could be met.

On Thursday, 26 June, Wolf brought Israeli and Palestinian negotiators together in a hotel in Tel Aviv to try to strike a deal. They started fairly early in the evening, 7 or 8 p.m., but they went on until nearly 3 a.m. before they had what they thought was an agreement in principle for an Israeli disengagement from the Gaza Strip and Bethlehem areas. This included: the creation of free passage for Palestinians up and down the main road in the Gaza Strip, a full withdrawal of Israeli troops, except around the Jewish settlements, and the collecting by Palestinians of illegal weapons. 'So,' John Wolf recalls, 'we were actually quite ebullient.'[2]

Wolf phoned the NSC in Washington to report. 'I think', he said to Condoleezza Rice's deputy, Stephen Hadley, 'that we have an agreement in principle and we are pulling the group back together Friday afternoon to dot the i's and cross the t's, and we've got our fingers crossed.'

Before the Friday meeting, Wolf and his team wrote up the substance of the previous day's deal in a formal document. Wolf decided not to hand the script over to either side, but instead to read it to them and get their nodding approval. He would then use the document as the benchmark by which he would monitor progress: have the Israelis withdrawn from this or that junction? Have the Palestinians started collecting illegal weapons? Can the Palestinians move freely across the Gaza Strip? Have the Israelis evacuated agreed areas in the Bethlehem area?

Wolf brought the parties together again on the afternoon of the 27th. He recalls what happened:

I read from the computer, paragraph by paragraph, 'you agree, you agree', move on. Well, we didn't make it through the first paragraph, when I said that the Palestinians would have full sovereignty over the main road [the Salah el-Din main road, the only road that connects the south and north of the Gaza Strip] and it was like somebody pushed a whoopee cushion because [Israeli General] Eiland shot up out of his seat and said, 'We never agreed to turn over sovereignty for the crossroads.'[3]

A heated discussion followed as the parties tried to agree on what exactly they had agreed the night before. Giora Eiland was certain there were things in what Wolf was reading that he would never have agreed to, never did agree to in the past, and was not going to agree to in the future. He insisted on full Israeli control and sovereignty over the Salah el-Din road so that the army could block all traffic when Jewish settlers were moving to minimize the risk of confrontation. Mohammed Dahlan interrupted: 'Of course you did agree to that.' Eiland retorted, 'You know quite well that we didn't agree to it last night.'[4] With the battle of words raging, Wolf decided it would be better to have the Palestinians in one room and the Israelis in another. He and his aides started shuttling between the rooms, trying to salvage the talks.

The discussions dragged on. General Eiland eventually persuaded Wolf that there had been a major misunderstanding over the main road in Gaza, and that he was negotiating in good faith. The American diplomat then spoke to Mohammed Dahlan. 'You can have all or nothing,' he said, 'or you can have something . . . Having negotiated with Israel and achieved a substantial liberalization of their current fist-like control over Gaza, you will have achieved something that will have a real impact on the street. If you try for the perfect outcome, you risk getting nothing, which won't do much for you economically or politically.'

Wolf began to worry, as the talks were up against a hard deadline – the Friday Sabbath. Everything would stop at sunset, deal or no deal. As Wolf describes,

Since the window of the hotel faced west, we had a sun clock that was kind of absolute. When the sun went below the Mediterranean we were going to run out of negotiating time. And that sucker was going to dive into the Mediterranean and that was going to be the end, and that seemed to have concentrated the minds, and we got a lot more work done in the last ninety minutes . . . We went through the last two-thirds of my written text in less time than it took to do the first paragraph.[5]

At sunset they shook hands. They had a deal. They called it 'The Gaza Agreement'.

'YOU ARE HAMAS!'

However, would Hamas and the other militants accept a ceasefire with Israel? Would they stop their suicide bombers? Abu Mazen faced other problems in his talks with Hamas – Arafat was trying to push himself back into the centre of events. According to minister Ziad Abu Amr, 'I got a call from Abu Mazen, who said there is definitely some foul play here. People – he meant Arafat – are trying to jeopardize [talks to achieve a ceasefire with Hamas].'[6] The minister phoned one of Hamas' leaders Ismail Hanieh. 'Look,' he said, 'the only person who can give you commitments is the Prime Minister [Abu Mazen]. You have been doing these spectacular attacks [against Israel]. You are feared the world over. You are Hamas! You will be seen as more of a threat if you go very quiet. It is a sign of strength.' It worked.

On Saturday, 28 June 2003, the Palestinians got security responsibility for the Gaza Strip and Bethlehem area. Prime Minister Abu Mazen was on his way to meet US National Security Advisor Condoleezza Rice in the West Bank town of Jericho[7] when he received a call telling him that Hamas, Islamic Jihad and Fatah's Tanzim (though not the Al-Aqsa Martyrs Brigade) had all agreed to suspend military operations against Israel, for an initial period of three months. Abu Mazen had good news to report to his visitor. It was an encouraging day at the end of a bloody month that had seen 81 Israelis and Palestinians killed.

The effects of the ceasefire were felt almost immediately. According to John Wolf:

Tensions were reduced, quality of life in Gaza and metropolitan Israel went up sharply. The Gaza Agreement enabled Palestinians to move freely [in the Strip], people could go to the beach. We had an informal indicator . . . quality of life indicator . . . how late are the stores open [in the occupied territories] – and stores which had hardly been open at all were staying open until ten or eleven at night . . . So this was a moment of opportunity, it got people's hopes up.

Eliciting a ninety-day truce from the militants was a tremendous achievement for Abu Mazen. He was rewarded with an invitation to the White House, something which had been denied to Arafat since George W. Bush became President.

'A WALL SNAKING THROUGH THE WEST BANK'

Abu Mazen arrived in Washington on 25 July with one aim in mind – to persuade the President to condemn Israel's Security Fence – what the Palestinians called The Wall. It was, in fact, a network of concrete walls, electronic fences, ditches and guard towers, stretching hundreds of miles around the West Bank to stop suicide bombers from crossing into Israel. Even though it was still under construction, the barrier's effectiveness on that score could not be denied – the number of suicide bombers getting through was decreasing. But it also caused immense upheaval in the lives of thousands of Palestinians living nearby and, crucially, it deviated from the Green Line, the internationally accepted border between Palestinian and Israeli land.

Inside the Oval Office, where he was given thirty minutes to present his case, Abu Mazen spread a big map on the table in front of the President. It showed how the barrier, combined with the expansion of Jewish settlements and bypass roads, mutilated the West Bank, cutting it up into a series of cantons. Abu Mazen explained that, with a wall like that, there could be no Palestinian state; with a map like that there could never be a viable Palestinian state. Secretary of State Colin

Powell explains: 'Abu Mazen's case was simply that the wall was more than a wall that ran along the Green Line; it was a wall that was [running deep in Palestinian land] taking in farmland, it was taking in communities, splitting communities, and it was difficult for him to do what he needed to do within the roadmap context if his people could see this kind of thing taking place.'

The map also showed Israeli checkpoints on the West Bank, which surprised the President. According to Nabil Shaath,

[It was] a detailed map [showing] the two hundred-odd checkpoints that Israel has created almost every five miles . . . it's totally separated a village from a village and town from town and made it look like a medieval sort of setting where you would move from one enclave to the other, from one little statelet to the other. And that was really very surprising to him. He said, 'I thought that these checkpoints protected Israel from the Palestinian territory, and I find that they are suffocating every Palestinian town and village.'[8]

At the press conference in the Rose Garden afterwards, Abu Mazen's press man, Hadar Abu Saya, planted a question about the wall. The President replied, 'I think the wall is a problem . . . It is very difficult to develop confidence between the Palestinians and the Israelis with a wall snaking through the West Bank.'[9] With that answer, as one of Abu Mazen's aides recalls, 'We were on cloud nine! This was a huge success, a huge coup.'

Following the press conference, as Nabil Shaath recalls, 'There was a magnificent luncheon, way above the typical food presented by the White House . . . we've had so many lunches and dinners in the White House before. White House food stinks usually. But this was a superb lunch.' The American envoy John Wolf, who had come back from Israel for the occasion, recalls how 'the luncheon discussion . . . probably two-thirds of it was a two-way discussion between the President and Mohammed Dahlan [the minister in charge of security], and the President was pressing very hard, "Take action, are you going to take action, what actions are you going to take?" and Dahlan kept saying, "Of course I'm going to take action, I know how to do this, I've done it before, and I have a plan". It was a vintage Dahlan.'[10] Secretary of

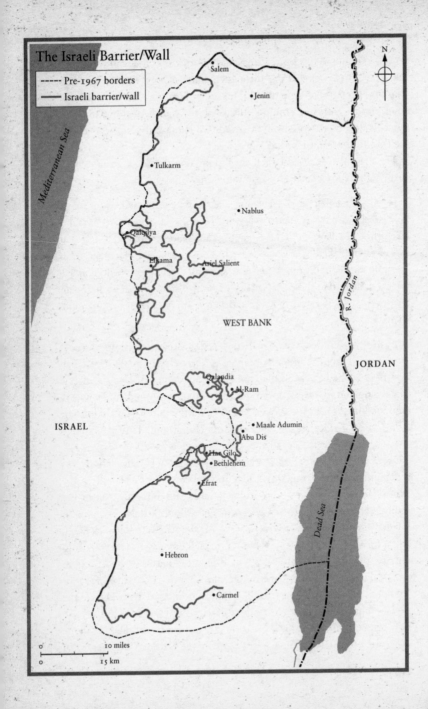

The Israeli Barrier/Wall

- - - - - Pre-1967 borders
———— Israeli barrier/wall

Mediterranean Sea

N

Salem

Jenin

Tulkarm

Nablus

Qalqilya

Elkama

Ariel Salient

WEST BANK

R. Jordan

Qalandia

Al-Ram

JORDAN

ISRAEL

Maale Adumin

Abu Dis

Har Gilo

Bethlehem

Efrat

Dead Sea

Hebron

Carmel

0   10 miles
0   15 km

State Powell, who was also present, recalls what he said to Dahlan: 'It isn't enough to have a plan ... the President is expecting and I'm expecting, specific, concrete action to get the security forces under control and to get them into action. Go after some of the militants, start doing something, so that we can make the case to the Israelis that we are seeing progress.'[11]

'WHAT DO YOU WANT?'

On 29 July, it was Prime Minister Sharon's turn to visit the White House. After the Palestinian presentation the security fence was top on the President's agenda. However, Sharon was immovable; he would not stop the building of the barrier. He told the President that it was necessary for Israel's security – the numbers spoke for themselves, the barrier was stopping suicide bombers from crossing into Israel. But although the President had been quite enraged about the fence in his talk with Abu Mazen a few days before, he did not press Sharon. He just said, 'I would hope that in the long term, a fence would be irrelevant.'[12] Colin Powell explains the President's thinking: 'It's hard to argue when you're under attack that you shouldn't protect yourself, and if one way to protect yourself is with a fence, that's fine ... [Sharon's] counter-argument was a fence can go up, a fence can come down, so we're not making a final judgement as to where the line will be.'

The Prime Minister was off the hook. When the Palestinians protested to the Americans, they were told, as a leading member of the NSC recalls, 'What do you want the Israelis to do? You don't want them to come into your territories and take out terrorists, and you don't want a passive fence that prevents those terrorists from getting into Israel. What do you want?'

'HE WAS A BAD MAN'

On 12 August 2003, the Israelis decided to extend the agreement with the Palestinians, to hand over more West Bank cities to their control in addition to the Gaza Strip and Bethlehem areas. Israel would hand over security responsibility for Qalqilya and Jericho, and then, two weeks later, Tulkarm and the flagship Ramallah, where the *muqata*, Arafat's headquarters, was situated. This arrangement had still to be finalized by Defence Minister Shaul Mofaz and Mohammed Dahlan, before the plan was brought before the Israeli government for final approval.

This was the carrot – the stick came two days later, when, in spite of the ceasefire, which was holding, the Israelis assassinated Mohammed Seder, the head of Islamic Jihad's armed wing in Hebron. He had long been on the Israelis' wanted list, as he was responsible for the killing of 12 Israelis in Hebron on 15 November 2002. According to the Defence Minister's Military Secretary, Mike Herzog, 'We knew Seder was planning an attack [on us]. So we sent our special forces to arrest him, and in the exchange of fire he was killed. He was a bad man.'[13] Abu Mazen, using the good contacts his minister Ziad Abu Amr had with the militants, urged them not to respond to the killing. Abu Amr said to them: 'Look, don't play into Israel's hands. Retaliation is exactly what they want you to do. Are you better off with this *hudna* or not?' But the killing of Seder was too great a provocation for the militants to ignore. 'They kept saying,' Abu Amr recalls, ' "We don't want our people to say we are weak [by not responding]." '

The Israelis had not played by the rules and had broken a ceasefire, so the angry militants decided to hit back. The assassinated Seder was Islamic Jihad, but it was Hamas that was planning revenge.

'GOODBYE AND SEE YOU IN PARADISE'

On 19 August, Majd Zaatri, a painter from Gaza and Hamas member, collected 29-year-old Raed Abdel Hamid Mask and they drove to the centre of Jerusalem. Hamid Mask was on a suicide mission to blow himself up in a bus and kill as many Israelis as possible.

Zaatri recalls how 'The bomber was dressed up [as an orthodox Jew] in a white shirt and black pants [and I] put a hat on him . . . I was dealing with the [explosive] belt. I was setting up the batteries.'[14] In the car on the way to downtown Jerusalem, Zaatri explained to Hamid Mask how to operate the belt: 'I showed him the switch to cause the explosion. And I showed him how not to mess it up . . . that he shouldn't put on the belt backwards . . . I showed him how to put it on so the switch would be on the outside . . . So that he wouldn't make a mistake.' The would-be bomber was in a good mood, as Zaatri recalls: 'He was happy. He was laughing . . . he was a guy who had finished university. He had an MA. He wasn't a young kid. He had studied in Amman – Islamic law. He knew [what he was doing]. He was an educated man. Not just a stupid guy. He's got two sons and there was a third on the way.'

They stopped at a bus stop in a religious neighbourhood in Jerusalem. The bomber got out of the car. 'I said to him God be with you,' Zaatri recalls; 'goodbye and see you in paradise.'

Elsewhere in Jerusalem, around the same time, Sharon's Cabinet was meeting to discuss the transfer of security responsibility to the Palestinians in the four West Bank cities. During the meeting, a messenger came in holding a piece of paper. He handed it over to the Prime Minister's Military Secretary, who glanced at it and said, 'Gentlemen, I'm sorry . . . I hate to tell you this but a few minutes ago a terrible thing happened.'

Hamid Mask had set off his device, causing a massive explosion on the number 2 bus. He killed 23 – 7 of them children and infants – and injured more than 100. Minister Yoseph Lapid recalls how, 'Sharon went out to see the place . . . he saw the bodies in plastic bags. He came back with the feeling . . . that this cannot be tolerated.'[15] Two days later, on 21 August, Israel launched a helicopter strike in Gaza, killing Hamas official Ismail Abu Shanab. There was no American rebuke for Israel's action. White House spokesman Scott McClellan said: 'Israel has a right to defend herself.' US Secretary of State Colin Powell called on Yasser Arafat to help Abu Mazen crack down on Palestinian militants, and urged Israelis and Palestinians not to abandon the roadmap. 'The end of the roadmap is a cliff that both sides will fall off of', he warned. But it was to no avail – Hamas and Islamic Jihad called off their ceasefire; the intifada started once again.

'DO SOMETHING'

That same day, John Wolf, the American diplomat charged with monitoring the implementation of the roadmap, met Mohammed Dahlan, the Palestinian minister responsible for security, at the Erez Crossing in Gaza. He said, 'History is about to stop, in terms of the roadmap, if you don't act.' Wolf added, 'Do something, take out a factory, make some arrests. We need to see progress, pragmatic steps, and very fast.' They worked out a package of measures which Dahlan agreed to take. 'I'll do it, I'll do it,' Dahlan said. 'I'll start tonight. I've got my men, I'm all ready . . .'[16]

On his way back to Jerusalem, Wolf reported what he had agreed with Dahlan to the Prime Minister's office. One of Sharon's aides remembers Wolf's words: 'Dahlan spoke to me, from his car, from his cell phone. I could hear the sirens of his security forces.' The Israelis agreed to hold back their forces for the night, to allow Dahlan to prove himself capable of cracking down on the militants. John Wolf recalls how 'All night on the one hand I was getting calls from Palestinians saying "Our guys are on the move", and I was getting calls from the Israelis saying "Nothing is happening, we are watching and there is nobody moving"'.[17] The light of morning brought American and Israeli intelligence reports saying that very little had been done by Dahlan's security forces. Wolf called Dahlan's office to complain. 'Is Dahlan there?' he asked. He heard Dahlan's secretary saying to him, 'It's the Israeli army, or it's Shin Bet.' When Dahlan came on the phone, Wolf said, 'Mohammed, I am not the Shin Bet, and I'm not the Israeli army, I'm your worst nightmare, I am the representative of the last remaining superpower.'[18] Dahlan explained his lack of results: 'Well, you know, I only have two cars, and we only have a few guns, so I did what I could, but that's all I could do.' Dahlan promised he would continue to act against the militants. He did, as Wolf remembers, 'move against a couple of tunnels [used to smuggle weapons] and he poured some concrete down a few holes, and that was it'.

However, Dahlan's power to deal with security matters was very limited. His real problem was Yasser Arafat, who had insisted on retaining personal control of the security forces when he appointed Abu Mazen as Prime Minister. Now, Arafat would simply not allow Dahlan to use his troops against fellow Palestinians.

The 19 August bus bombing in Jerusalem was a turning point. After that bombing, explains John Wolf, 'the whole process [of roadmap implementation] was constipated'. The spiral of violence worsened. On 29 August, following a shooting attack on a Jewish family near Ramallah, Sharon and his Cabinet decided to end all contact with the Palestinian Authority.

'WHOEVER IS KILLED IS KILLED AND WHOEVER ISN'T WE'LL GET HIM LATER'

A few days later, Israeli intelligence learned that the founder and spiritual leader of Hamas, Sheikh Ahmed Yassin, would attend a meeting in Gaza on 6 September. With him, went the intelligence report, would be the entire Hamas leadership in one building. 'It was clear to us', Israeli General Giora Eiland comments, 'we could hit a large group of leaders at that moment, and as a result cause real damage to Hamas and perhaps scare the others ... [it was] ... such a perfect opportunity, [a] once in a lifetime chance!'[19] But opinion was divided within the Israeli political-military establishment about whether it was wise to assassinate the Sheikh. Those who were opposed said that Yassin 'may be the leader of Hamas but he is not the operational and tactical leader, let's concentrate on the tactical guys'.[20] There was also concern that killing a senior leader such as Yassin might lead to a strong Hamas reaction. Those in favour of killing Yassin said that the distinction between military and political in an organization such as Hamas was non-existent. Defence Minister Shaul Mofaz was in favour of killing him. He said, 'Yassin is a terrorist for all intents and purposes ... he is leading this organization with incitement ... many of the suicide attackers come [to Israel] on his directions ... Yassin sends them ... he gives them the instructions ... it is right to act against him.' Eventually they agreed to kill the Sheikh – it only remained to be decided how.

The dilemma, as Mofaz recalls, was 'what weight of explosives should we drop from the air on the building [where the meeting was to take place]'. The military planners recommended a one-tonne bomb, which would be certain to kill Yassin and his associates, but it would also cause substantial damage to surrounding buildings and could kill innocent people. But any smaller bomb might mean Yassin would escape. Convinced that only a big bomb would do the job properly, but aware it would cause colossal damage, Defence Minister Mofaz decided to cancel the operation. He said to the Prime Minister, 'Arik, I've decided not to go for it.'[21] However, new information was received showing that a 500-kilogram bomb would be enough to destroy the top floor of the building, where the intelligence reports indicated the Hamas leaders would be meeting. Mofaz agreed to proceed, saying: 'Whoever is killed is killed and whoever isn't we'll get him later.'

With the green light given, as the Defence Minister's Military Secretary, Mike Herzog, recalls, 'we came quietly to the office – Mofaz, myself and a very small team of people, and we followed up closely the turning of this operation'.[22] An air force jet dropped a 500-kilogram bomb on the building. The third floor was completely destroyed. But the Israeli intelligence was wrong. The Hamas leaders had met on the ground floor, perhaps because Yassin was in a wheelchair. The Sheikh was slightly injured, along with fourteen others. He later gave a warning: 'Israel will pay a high price for this crime.'

25

Unilateral Disengagement

'THIS WILL BE MUSIC TO YOUR EARS'

A few hours after the bungled Israeli attempt to assassinate the Hamas leadership, Prime Minister Abu Mazen called Saeb Erekat into his Ramallah office. He showed him a piece of paper. It was a letter of resignation addressed to Arafat. Erekat said: 'Don't! Don't do it. Don't do it, please. Be patient. Please weigh the consequences of such a step.' But it was to no avail – Abu Mazen was determined to resign. He had had enough. Arafat had put obstacles in his path at every step ('Arafat was playing his dirty tricks' as a leading Palestinian put it) and had not given him real powers, particularly over the security services. Abu Mazen also blamed the Israelis for not making real the concessions on the ground – stopping the assassinations, releasing Palestinian prisoners, removing checkpoints, dismantling settlement outposts – which would have bolstered his position. And he blamed Washington for not pressing Sharon to make these goodwill gestures towards the Palestinians.

Abu Mazen's letter of resignation was taken to Arafat by Yasser Abed Rabbo. He recalls: 'I was careful to carry it myself because up to the last minute I was trying to have Abu Ammar [Arafat] reject the resignation. When I entered Yasser Arafat's office, he asked me: "What are you carrying?" I said, "This will be music to your ears."'[1] Arafat, as Abed Rabbo describes, 'started reading the letter in a loud voice ... and in his reading you could see a kind of sarcasm ... he was pleased that Abu Mazen had resigned'. Arafat's campaign to undermine his own Prime Minister had worked.

That day Abu Mazen had to present a 100-day report to the Palestinian Legislative Council (PLC) on the achievements of his government. When he reached the parliament building, accompanied by Mohammed Dahlan and Yasser Abed Rabbo, he found himself confronted by a large and violent demonstration. 'The demonstrators got very close to me', Abu Mazen recalls in an interview for *Elusive Peace*. 'They even pushed me ... they used aggression against me.'[2] The crowd was shouting slogans: 'Where are the prisoners [jailed in Israel]?' 'Why does the Wall continue [to be built by the Israelis]?' 'Why do settlements continue [to be built on Palestinian land]?' Abu Mazen was pushed and shoved as he made his way inside.

In the hall, Abu Mazen started delivering his speech but, as Abed Rabbo recalls, 'some of [the crowd] started breaking glass ... [the demonstrators] tried to create some sort of tension and psychological pressure on him'. Minister Nabil Shaath recalls that '[Abu Mazen] felt that his life was at risk. For him, that was the end of his mission ... nothing was going to stop him from resigning.'[3] Abu Mazen ended his speech by saying, 'Today I sent the letter of my resignation to Brother Abu Ammar.' And with that, after just six months as the first Palestinian Prime Minister, he left the stage.

'I THINK THEY WILL KILL YOU'

By then, Israel was engaged in an all-out war with the Palestinian militant groups. On 7 September an Israeli helicopter gunship attacked the home of a Hamas member, Abdul Salem Abu Musa, in the southern Gaza Strip, injuring at least 12 people. Two days later, two separate suicide attacks left at least 15 people dead and scores wounded in Tel Aviv and Jerusalem. Israel struck again on 10 September, firing missiles at the Gaza City home of Mahmoud Zahar, a senior Hamas member, killing his son and a bodyguard and leaving about 25 people wounded – Zahar himself escaped with minor injuries. Prime Minister Sharon, as usual, blamed his old foe Arafat for the escalation of the violence. On 11 September, he called Arafat a 'complete obstacle to peace' and led his Cabinet in a decision to 'remove this obstacle in the manner, and time, of our choosing'.

The few visitors Arafat still received at the *muqata* warned him he was facing a real danger – he was likely to be eliminated. Alastair Crooke, working for the EU, recalls his last meeting with Arafat:

I went in alone just to say goodbye and I said to him, 'You know, if there is another big attack [on the Israelis], I think they will kill you. There are no red lights.' And he said, 'Alastair. They are *green* lights. This is more serious than Beirut [in 1982].' I've never ever heard him say something is more serious than Beirut. He normally says, 'I've seen off Sharon, Beirut was worse than this.' He said to me at that last meeting, 'You'll understand, I'd normally see you off but I won't come down today.'

On 22 September Arafat had another visitor – a top British envoy – who said to him: 'We cannot protect you any more, we cannot guarantee your survival.'

'ABU ALA, SHMABU ALA'

Arafat appointed a new Prime Minister, his loyal lieutenant Abu Ala, a veteran PLO leader and experienced negotiator with Israel. Once again, however, Arafat retained control of the security forces, though he did grant Abu Ala a seat on his Security Council. But Arafat held the chair, which meant that he had more influence than his new Prime Minister on the direction of events on the ground. The Israelis were not impressed with the gesture.

Prime Minister Sharon dispatched his Chief of Staff Dov Weisglass to Washington to let the Americans know what he thought of the new Palestinian Prime Minister. Weisglass told National Security Advisor Condoleezza Rice, 'Look, it's clear Abu Ala is not Winston Churchill. We are very disappointed . . . We see the political set-up he's agreed to – he agreed to start functioning without any authority on security issues.' Rice said, 'Well, give him a chance', but Weisglass replied, 'Nothing will happen with these guys.'

On 5 October, a female suicide bomber killed 19 and injured 50 in a Haifa restaurant. The Israelis said to themselves, as one official says in an interview, 'Abu Ala, Shmabu Ala – they are all the same and we should look after ourselves.'

'I DO NOT INTEND TO WAIT FOR THEM INDEFINITELY'

By now, the suggestion of a unilateral Israeli disengagement from the Gaza Strip – a pull-out on the Israelis' own terms, rather than negotiated with the Palestinians – had been circulating in the Israeli press for some time. The idea was not new. In the 2001 general election, Labour Party Prime Minister Ehud Barak campaigned under the slogan: 'We are here, they are there.' He called for the country to complete construction of the security barrier along a route which would annex 7 to 8 per cent of the West Bank to Israel – retaining the big blocs of Jewish settlements under Israeli control – and to unilaterally withdraw from the rest of the land. This was the first time a leading Israeli politician called for unilateral withdrawal from land occupied in 1967. Barak lost the election to Sharon. In the 2003 general election, Labour leader Amram Mitzna called for unilateral withdrawal from the Gaza Strip. Again, he lost to Sharon.

Now, however, Sharon was convinced he had no one to negotiate with on the Palestinian side, and he was also getting flak from his political rivals for not having a coherent plan to deal with the Israeli–Palestinian crisis. So he adopted the Labour idea of a unilateral disengagement from the Palestinians. Before presenting it to the Israeli public, Sharon first ran the idea past the Americans.

In Rome, on 19 November 2003, the Prime Minister, accompanied by his Chief of Staff Dov Weisglass and a few aides, met secretly with the NSC's specialist, Elliott Abrams. An American official at this meeting recalls the atmosphere:

It was at dinner . . . we were at Sharon's hotel, the Hilton. And then they bring food. Jeez. And it's big slabs of meat, and they absolutely do not look kosher! And Dov [Weisglass] goes ahead and cuts out a big slice, and I'm thinking it's very pink . . . it might be ham, and I said to Sharon, 'OK, what kind of meat do you think that is?' And Sharon said, 'It is better not to ask.'

Having demonstrated his credentials as a pragmatist over the menu, Sharon then told his guests, 'We will have to think about some unilateral steps.' The Americans liked the sound of Sharon's proposals.

On 18 December at a conference in Herzliya, the Prime Minister announced his Disengagement Plan to the Israeli public. 'Like all Israeli citizens, I yearn for peace,' he said, '[however,] if the Palestinians do not make a similar effort towards a solution of the conflict – I do not intend to wait for them indefinitely.' Sharon said that the roadmap was the 'best way to achieve true peace', but added, 'the terrorist organizations joined with Yasser Arafat and sabotaged the process with a series of the most brutal terror attacks we have ever known . . . if in a few months the Palestinians still continue to disregard their part in implementing the roadmap, then Israel will initiate the unilateral . . . disengagement from the Palestinians . . . fully co-ordinated with the United States'. He explained that he intended to remove all Jewish settlements from the Gaza Strip, and redeploy the IDF along new security lines. This would reduce the number of Israelis located in the heart of the Palestinian population, and reduce friction. However, Sharon explained, 'At the same time . . . Israel will strengthen its control over those same areas in the Land of Israel which will constitute an inseparable part of the State of Israel in any future agreement.' It was, in other words, a plan to trade off the Gaza Strip – a 'nest of snakes' as then Defence Minister Moshe Dayan described it in 1967 – for the West Bank, the cradle of Jewish history.

'LET'S WEAKEN HAMAS'

Before withdrawing from the Gaza Strip, the Prime Minister wanted to decapitate its militants. It was particularly important to show a victory over Hamas, in order to prevent a repeat of the Israeli withdrawal from Lebanon in 2000, which Hezbollah claimed as a victory for their terror tactics. Sharon did not want to appear to be caving in to terror. Weakening Hamas would also give the Palestinian Authority and Mohammed Dahlan a chance to control Gaza when the Israelis were gone. An Israeli official explains: '[We said] if we are going to leave Gaza, let's weaken Hamas.' The military embarked on a systematic campaign to wipe out the Hamas leadership, and not only the operational level but also the top leadership.

Israel's collaborators in the Gaza Strip kept the army informed on the whereabouts of Hamas operatives, and they also kept an eye on the spiritual leader of Hamas, the elderly quadriplegic, Sheikh Ahmed Yassin. But to get Yassin, the Israelis needed a lot of patience. 'There were several nights during which we followed him', Defence Minister Shaul Mofaz recalls, 'and I waited every night until around one or two to know if there was a chance [of assassinating him].' The Defence Minister did not have to wait much longer. On 22 March 2004, at 5.30 a.m., Military Secretary Mike Herzog woke him up at home to say that the Sheikh had been assassinated as he left a mosque in Gaza.

'WE WANT SOMETHING IN RETURN'

The Prime Minister thought the US ought to reward him for his readiness to pull out unilaterally from occupied territories. He wanted a written guarantee, a letter from President Bush, saying that in the event of a final settlement, none of the millions of Palestinian refugees would be allowed to return to Israel – that the so-called 'right of return' would not apply. He also wanted US recognition that the final border between Israel and any future Palestinian state would not be the internationally recognized Green Line, but a boundary further to the east, allowing Israel to annex the big blocs of Jewish settlements on the West Bank. An American pledge to support Israel on these two crucial issues would help Sharon sell unilateral disengagement to his sceptical public.[4]

Weeks of tough negotiations took place in Washington between the Prime Minister's envoys and American officials. The Israelis said: 'We are going to evacuate [the] Gaza [Strip] so we are beginning to paint the map in two colours – Israeli and Palestinian . . . we are beginning to implement the President's vision [expressed in his 24 June 2002 speech]. It's only a beginning, but it is a beginning . . .' And they insisted: 'We want something in return.'[5]

However, for America publicly to throw its lot behind Israel, supporting the annexation of West Bank land, and closing the door on the Palestinian right of return, would be a red rag to the Arab world – these two issues touched upon the very heart of the Israeli–Palestinian conflict. US Deputy National Security Advisor Stephen Hadley, the NSC's Elliott Abrams and Assistant Secretary of State William Burns set out to Amman, Jordan to test the water with their closest Arab ally. There, on 31 March, they presented Sharon's ideas to the Jordanian Foreign Minister, Marwan Muasher. He was appalled. Jordan would agree only to language implying that there would be 'minor changes to the 1967 borders'.[6] As for the idea of abolishing the Palestinian right of return, the Jordanian Foreign Minister was clear: 'No Arab state is going to accept this. Period.'[7] The Jordanian also feared that Sharon intended to disengage only from the over-populated Gaza Strip, a thorn in the side of the IDF, but not from the West Bank.

The US pressed Sharon to demonstrate, even if only symbolically, that this was not his intention. Secretary of State Colin Powell recalls what he said to Sharon. ' "You've got to do something in the West Bank as well. It's gotta be seen as part of a comprehensive approach to the problem and not just [a withdrawal from the Gaza Strip]." And we talked about how many settlements in the West Bank [will be evacuated], and the number went up and down, and finally it settled out at four.' The Prime Minister agreed to evacuate the small Jewish settlements of Kadim, Ganim, Sa-Nur and Chomesh, all in the northern West Bank.

Sharon was scheduled to visit Washington on 14 April, when he expected to receive his written guarantee from the President. King Abdullah of Jordan sent the President a letter on 8 April. 'I'm writing to share with you some of Jordan's thoughts ahead of Sharon's visit to Washington', it said.

I fear the concessions asked for by Israel on final status issues will undermine both our efforts. In particular we hope that no concessions on borders will be given that would suggest any major deviations from [the] 1967 [Green Line]. The solution to the refugee issue should also leave the door open for an agreed solution by both sides.[8]

Two days later, over the Easter weekend, ahead of Sharon's visit, the Israelis arrived in Washington. Negotiators met Hadley, Abrams and other US officials at the Hay-Adams Hotel, to thrash out the final details of the American guarantee on borders and refugees.

The Israelis knew how to bargain. Upping the ante, they insisted that the American guarantee on borders should specify – in writing and by name – each and every settlement east of the Green Line that Israel would be allowed to keep in any future agreement with the Palestinians. The Americans baulked at this – it would enrage the Arab world. Instead, Stephen Hadley came up with a masterpiece of ambiguity: 'In light of new realities on the ground, including already existing major Israeli population centres, *it is unrealistic* to expect that the outcome of final status negotiations will be a full and complete [Israeli] return to the [1967 Green Line].' The Americans had folded, and the Israelis had the guarantee they wanted – the big blocs of settlements were safe. Next up, the Palestinian refugees' right of return.

The Israelis demanded a guarantee that Palestinian refugees would be settled in the future Palestinian state, but 'not in Israel'. The Americans refused, preferring instead to adhere to a positive formula – that the refugees would be absorbed in the Palestinian state with no mention of Israel at all. This would be far less sensitive to the Arab world. However, the Israelis insisted on the words 'not in Israel'. The Americans suggested a new formula: the refugees will be absorbed in the Palestinian state 'rather than in Israel'. The Israeli negotiators pored over dictionaries to see what the difference was between 'not in Israel' and 'rather than in Israel'. The Israeli Giora Eiland recalls: 'We needed to consult with experts in Israel about the different meanings ... whether there was a difference or not. We had to find experts who were good at English, who were also legal experts, and, most important, whose opinion was accepted by the Prime Minister.'[9] They concluded that 'rather than in Israel' meant exactly the same as 'not in Israel'. The Israelis were satisfied; they had got what they wanted on both borders and refugees.

The Americans decided to run the text by their Jordanian friends once again. Secretary of State Powell phoned Foreign Minister Muasher and read him the text. Muasher was not happy with it, particularly with the idea that there would be no right of return. So, shortly before Sharon was due to arrive in Washington, the Americans tried to open the matter again with the Israelis, meeting over dinner. The Israeli ambassador to the US, Danny Ayalon, recalls, 'We thought that the letters are agreed upon and the formula is closed and we will spend a pleasant evening of a nice dinner together.' National Security Advisor Condoleezza Rice asked the Israelis to consider inserting the word 'generally' into the wording on refugees: that in any future agreement Palestinian refugees would 'generally' return to Palestine. This would keep the option open for some of them to return to Israel. The Israelis rejected the idea. A heated debate followed, while Prime Minister Sharon sat in his jet waiting to take off for Washington. He would not leave Israel until the matter was sorted out. Eventually, as Ambassador Ayalon recalls, the Americans gave up and 'we thought we had sealed everything and the Prime Minister was on his way'.[10]

The night before the summit, Prime Minister Sharon had dinner with Condoleezza Rice in his hotel. During dinner, as Ambassador Ayalon recalls, Rice surprised the Israelis by again trying to make Sharon agree to the word 'generally' being introduced into the text of the letters. But Sharon would not move. 'He was prepared to let the whole exchange fall rather than accept this word', recalls Ayalon.[11] Rice asked her guests to think about it, but with the Israelis still refusing to give up the next morning, Rice conceded: 'OK, we can live without the word "generally".'[12] Sharon had got what he wanted. President Bush's guarantee letter said that any agreement would be based upon 'the establishment of a Palestinian state, and the settling of Palestinian refugees there, *rather than* in Israel'.[13]

At the press conference after their meeting on 14 April, the President described what Sharon had promised to do – 'to remove certain military installations and all settlements from Gaza, and certain military installations and settlements from the West Bank'. Then he added,

In an exchange of letters today and in a statement I will release later today, I'm repeating to the Prime Minister my commitment to Israel's security. The United States will not prejudice the outcome of final status negotiations. That matter is for the parties. But the realities on the ground and in the region have changed greatly over the last several decades, and any final settlement must take into account those realities.

It was a remarkable victory for Sharon. President Bush, leader of the most powerful country in the world, had moved even closer to Israel, and declared that the two most dearly held principles of the Palestinian people – Israeli withdrawal to the 1967 borders and the right of return – were null and void. The rules of the peace process had been rewritten.

Epilogue

'DR CHIRAC WILL LOOK AFTER ME'

In Ramallah, by the second half of 2004, Yasser Arafat was ill, suffering from a mysterious blood disorder. Rumours were rife that he had been poisoned by the Israelis. In October, his doctors advised that he should leave Ramallah, where medical facilities were limited, to receive treatment abroad. Arafat resisted, apprehensive that, once he had left, Ariel Sharon would not allow him to return. Minister Yasser Abed Rabbo was one of many close to Arafat who were urging him to take his doctors' advice. 'I hadn't seen Arafat for a few days,' Abed Rabbo recalls, '[and when I now saw him] he was a totally different person, he was extremely weak, his face had red spots because of the blood problem he had. We were prevented from kissing him as we were used to, but he smiled very happily when he saw us.'[1] Abed Rabbo managed to talk Arafat round, and at the end of the short visit Arafat said, 'God willing we'll do it.' He agreed to travel to a hospital in France.

Soon after Abed Rabbo had seen him, Arafat was visited by his close associate Mohammed Rashid. When Rashid entered the room Arafat was praying. He recalls: 'At the end of the prayer we say, "Peace be upon you", and we turn to the left, and to the right. When Arafat looked to the right he saw me. He smiled, and he waved me to come in, but he was frail, he was weak, I leaned to him, I kissed him, and he said, "Stay away, I don't want to contaminate you." '[2] Prime Minister Sharon had promised he would let Arafat return to the West Bank after any medical treatment abroad. Arafat now asked Rashid, 'Do you think that [Sharon's] promises are real?' Rashid replied: 'Well, the only guarantee that is being asked for, is to save your life and to be reassured about your health, and the rest will come later.'[3]

Rashid had brought with him another visitor – Mohammed Dahlan. Dahlan had fallen out with Arafat back in 2002, when he became increasingly critical of Arafat who, in turn, felt threatened by Dahlan's popularity. But now, as Rashid recalls, 'they shook hands'. Though forgiven, Dahlan's ambitions were not forgotten, and Rashid suggested to Arafat that Dahlan should go with them to France, lest he take advantage of Arafat's absence to move against him. Arafat replied, 'Yes, let's take him with us to Paris.'[4]

On 29 October 2004, a Jordanian helicopter carried Arafat from Ramallah to Marka Airport in Amman, where a French plane was waiting to transfer him to the Percy Military Hospital in the Paris suburb of Clamart. The Palestinian Foreign Minister, Nabil Shaath, happened to land in Amman at around the same time, on his way back to Ramallah from Switzerland. He recalls:

I saw Arafat's helicopter touch down and I rushed over to greet him. We walked together about fifty metres to the French plane. I was on his right side supporting him a little, but he was walking and talking. He said: 'Dr Hissam [one of Arafat's doctors] says I'll be fine, because Hissam himself had had similar symptoms as me and he's fine and well . . . I'll be fine. And Dr Chirac (as Arafat called the French President) will look after me. He cares for me.'[5]

As the world watched and waited, Arafat's condition rapidly deteriorated. He lost consciousness, sank into a coma and was moved into intensive care. He died on 11 November 2004, at 3.30 a.m. Paris time. The precise cause of his death remains unclear.[6]

Egypt stepped in to provide a venue for an official military funeral – it would have been politically difficult for Arab leaders to travel to the Israeli-controlled Palestinian territories for any ceremony. As world leaders gathered in Egypt to pay their respects, Arafat's coffin, draped in the black, white, red and green Palestinian flag, arrived from Paris. After a 25-minute funeral at a military base near the airport, Arafat's coffin was flown to Al Arish, near Egypt's border with Israel, and from there by helicopter to Ramallah, where it was met by vast crowds of ordinary Palestinians. Yasser Abed Rabbo was among those on the helicopter. He remembers:

It was a very small number of people with him in that helicopter that landed in the mess, the sea of confusion in Ramallah ... I opened the door after half an hour of waiting and shooting in the air ... I was worried because one shot could blow up the whole helicopter. I carried the coffin ... there was a big wave of people ... and it pushed me away after I got down to the ground ... and this was the last time that I was in direct contact with Yasser Arafat.

Arafat had long stated his wish to be buried in the Haram al-Sharif in Jerusalem's Old City, but Sharon had vowed that 'Arafat won't be buried in Jerusalem as long as I'm Prime Minister.'[7] So Arafat was buried in the *muqata* under soil from the Haram, brought for the purpose by Ikrima Sabri, the mufti of Jerusalem. His coffin was of stone, rather than wood, to allow for his re-interment in Jerusalem at some point in the future, when it was the capital of a Palestinian state.

'THIS IS A NEW HISTORIC OPPORTUNITY'

Arafat, adorned with his trademark chequered *keffiyya* carefully folded to form the shape of historic Palestine, had led the stateless Palestinian people for more than thirty-five years. He was the face and symbol of Palestine. Though awarded the Nobel Prize for peace in 1994, in truth he never quite made the transition from revolutionary to statesman. He was not, as Prime Minister Sharon often claimed, behind all attacks against Israel, but he did flirt with violence. He did not use his full authority and status in the Palestinian street to rein in attacks on Israel. Now, his exit from the stage seemed an opportunity to start a new chapter, and re-embark on the peace process. US Secretary of State Colin Powell flew to the region, and talked to the leading Palestinians. 'This is a new historic opportunity,' he said:

You no longer have Arafat as an excuse not to do things. This is your moment to really do something about terror once and for all ... everybody is expecting you to speak clearly against terrorism and to begin to take the actions necessary to demonstrate to the world that terrorism is going to be ended and the roadmap can get going.

Abu Mazen was quickly elected as Arafat's successor. One of the few surviving founders of the PLO, he had been close to Arafat for more than three decades. He was a leading negotiator with Israel, and had been the short-lived first prime minister of the Palestinian people. A man of few words, he believed in reason and logic and was guided by a deep sense of ethics. Crucially, he was against the violent intifada and the existence of armed militias.

However, stepping into Arafat's shoes would be no easy task. To succeed, Abu Mazen needed Prime Minister Sharon's help. Easing the tight grip the Israeli army had on the Palestinians would bolster Abu Mazen's position. Secretary of State Colin Powell talked to Sharon. 'You know,' he said, 'you have got to give him some room . . .'

Sharon, however, offered little. His eyes were fixed on his plan to disengage unilaterally from the Palestinians, and he was reluctant to offer concessions which would upset his political opponents even further. So, in spite of his plan to withdraw from some occupied lands, elsewhere, particularly around Jerusalem, he continued building settlements and erecting the security fence across the West Bank. And the Israeli army continued its harsh treatment of the Palestinians, imposing strict curfews, searches and checkpoints.

At the time of writing, final preparations are under way in Israel to implement Sharon's unilateral disengagement plan, and withdraw from the Gaza Strip and four settlements in the northern West Bank. It is due to start in August 2005.

Will this – if it is implemented – be the first step for further Israeli withdrawals from occupied lands? Could a viable Palestinian state emerge on the evacuated lands? Is this the beginning of the end of the 57-year-war between Israelis and Palestinians? It is too early to tell. For now, peace in the Middle East seems as elusive as ever.

Notes on Sources

This is the list of people we talked to and some of whom we filmed.

Israelis

Ami Ayalon, Danny Ayalon, Ehud Barak, Yossi Beilin, Shlomo Ben-Ami, Binyamin Ben-Eliezer, Uzi Dayan, Giora Eiland, Eival Gilady, Gidi Grinstein, Israel Hasson, Mike Herzog, Yoseph (Tommy) Lapid, Amnon Lipkin-Shahak, Pini Medan-Shani, Dan Meridor, Shaul Mofaz, Benjamin Netanyahu, Shimon Peres, Uri Saguie, Silvan Shalom, Omri Sharon, Gilead Sher, Moshe (Chicho) Tamir, Ahmed Tibi, Dov Weisglass, Danny Yatom.

Palestinians

Mahmoud Abbas (Abu Mazen), Ziad Abu Amr, Hassan Asfour, Diana Buttu, Mohammed Dahlan, Mohammed al-Daya, Saeb Erekat, Salam Fayyad, Mohammed Abu Hamid, Hani al-Hassan, Ala Hosni, Mazzin Hussein, Hak Kamil, Umm Khaled, Ahmed Khalidi, Ghassan Khatib, Stephanie Koury, Mohamed al-Madani, Ghaith al-Omari, Ahmed Qurei (Abu Ala), Yasser Abed Rabbo, Jibril Rajoub, Mohammed Rashid, Anton Salman, Maia Saraf, Mustafa Sayyad, Nabil Shaath, Rami Shehadeh, Salah Tamari.

Jordanians

Marwan Muasher.

Syrians

Bouthaina Shaaban.

Americans

Edward Abington, Elliott Abrams, Madeleine Albright, Richard Armitage, Samuel (Sandy) Berger, William Burns, Bill Clinton, Gamal Helal, Martin Indyk, Flynt Leverett, Robert Malley, Aaron Miller, Mark Perry, John Podesta, Colin Powell, Bill Smullen, John Wolf, Anthony Zinni.

British

Geoffrey Adams, Chris Cobb Smith, Sherard Cowper-Coles, Andrew Coyle, Alastair Crooke, Lord Levy.

French

Hubert Vedrine.

Others

Terje Roed-Larsen.

Select Bibliography

Mahmoud Abbas (Abu Mazen), *Through Secret Channels* (Reading, 1995)

Madeleine Albright, *Madam Secretary, A Memoir* (New York, 2003)

Hanan Ashrawi, *This Side of Peace* (New York, 1995)

James Baker, *The Politics of Diplomacy: Revolution, War and Peace, 1989–1992* (New York, 1995)

Eytan Bentsur, *A First-Hand Account of the Arab-Israeli Peace Process* (Westport, 2001)

Ahron Bregman, *Israel's Wars: A History since 1947* (London, 2002)

Ahron Bregman and Jihan el-Tahri, *The Fifty Years War: Israel and the Arabs* (London, 1998)

Christopher Cerf and Micah L. Sifry, *The Iraq War Reader* (New York, 2003)

Tom Clancy with General Tony Zinni (Ret.) and Tony Koltz, *Battle Ready* (New York, 2004)

Bill Clinton, *My Life* (New York, 2004)

Charles Enderlin, *Shattered Dreams: The Failure of the Peace Process in the Middle East 1995–2002* (New York, 2002)

Amira Hass, *Drinking the Sea at Gaza: Days and Nights in a Land under Siege* (New York, 1999)

Martin Indyk, *Best of Intentions: The Successes, Failures and Unintended Consequences of Clinton's Middle East Diplomacy* (New York, forthcoming)

John Kampfner, *Blair's Wars* (London, 2003)

Shaul Mishal and Avraham Sela, *The Palestinian Hamas* (New York, 2000)

Shimon Peres, *Battling for Peace: Memoirs* (London, 1995)

Itamar Rabinovich, *Waging Peace: Israel and the Arabs, 1948–2003* (Princeton, 2004)

Dennis Ross, *The Missing Peace: The Inside Story of the Fight for Middle East Peace* (New York, 2004)

Edward W. Said, *The End of the Peace Process: Oslo and After* (New York, 2000)

Uri Savir, *The Process* (New York, 1998)

Ariel Sharon (with David Chanoff), *Warrior: The Autobiography of Ariel Sharon* (New York, 1989)

Avi Shlaim, *The Iron Wall: Israel and the Arab World* (London, 2000)

Peter Stothard, *30 Days: A Month at the Heart of Blair's War* (London, 2003)

Clayton E. Swisher, *The Truth About Camp David: The Untold Story About the Collapse of the Middle East Peace Process* (New York, 2004)

Bernard Wasserstein, *Israel and Palestine: Why They Fight and Can They Stop* (London, 2003)

Bob Woodward, *Bush at War* (New York, 2002)

In Hebrew

Yossi Beilin, *From Hachula to Geneva* (Tel Aviv, 2004)

Shlomo Ben-Ami, *A Front Without a Rearguard* (Tel Aviv, 2004)

Ronen Bergman, *Authority Given* (Tel Aviv, 2002)

Raviv Drucker, *Harakiri, Ehud Barak: The Failure* (Tel Aviv, 2002)

Ran Edelist, *Ehud Barak: Fighting the Demons* (Tel Aviv, 2003)

Amos Harel and Avi Isacharoff, *The Seventh War* (Tel Aviv, 2004)

Ben Kaspit and Ilan Kfir, *Ehud Barak: Israel's Number 1 Soldier* (Tel Aviv, 1998)

Dan Naveh, *Executive Secrets* (Tel Aviv, 1999)

Uri Saguie, *Lights Within the Fog* (Tel Aviv, 1998)

Gilead Sher, *Just Beyond Reach: The Israeli–Palestinian Peace Negotiations 1999–2001* (Tel Aviv, 2001)

Idith Zertal and Akiva Eldar, *Lords of the Land: The Settlers and the State of Israel 1967–2004* (Tel Aviv, 2004)

Notes

This book is based mainly on filmed interviews for the BBC television series *Elusive Peace*, conducted with the chief participants in the events described – Israelis, Palestinians, Jordanians, Syrians, Americans, Europeans and others. I have also drawn on interviews which cannot be directly attributed, and have used 'Anonymous' to indicate these sources.

Introduction

1. Ahron Bregman and Jihan el-Tahri, *The Fifty Years War: Israel and the Arabs* (London, 1998).
2. For the full text of the Wye River Memorandum see, Walter Laqueur and Barry Rubin, *The Israel-Arab Reader* (London, 2001), p. 529.
3. The 13 per cent of land was to be transferred from the so-called Area C, where Israel managed all security and civil affairs. One per cent was to go to Area A, where the PA was in charge of security control and civil administration and 12 per cent to Area B, where the Israeli military had responsibility for security and the PA controlled some civil administration.
4. The relevant articles are: 6–10, 15, 19–23 and 30. There are also parts in articles 1–5, 11–14, 16–18, 25–7 and 29. For the letter see, 'Letter from Yasser Arafat to President Clinton', 13 January 1998, www.miftah.org.
5. Interview with Yossi Beilin, 24 January 2005, Tel Aviv.
6. Interview with Saeb Erekat, 28 May 2004, Jericho.
7. Yossi Beilin, *Manual for a Wounded Dove* (Tel Aviv, 2001), p. 36 (in Hebrew); interview with Yossi Beilin.
8. It was a decisive victory for Barak – he won by a 56 per cent majority.
9. Interview with Hassan Asfour, 29 May 2004, Gaza City.

1 Barak's Grand Plan

1. Ben Kaspit and Ilan Kfir, *Ehud Barak: Israel's Number 1 Soldier* (Tel Aviv, 1998), p. 11 (in Hebrew).

2. As cited in Deborah Sontag, 'Peace Period', *New York Times Magazine*, 19 December 1999; Madeleine Albright, *Madam Secretary, A Memoir* (New York, 2003), p. 483.

3. Interview with Ehud Barak, 1 November 2004, Tel Aviv.

4. Interview with Ehud Barak, 30 June 2004, Tel Aviv; interview with Danny Yatom, 12 September 2004, Kochav Yair.

5. Interview with Bill Clinton, 20 June 2005, Little Rock.

6. This quote appears in the *Jerusalem Post*, 30 August 2000.

7. Ahron Bregman, telephone interview with Ehud Barak, 17 November 1997, Tel Aviv.

8. Dennis Ross, *The Missing Peace: The Inside Story of the Fight for Middle East Peace* (New York, 2004), p. 111; Ahron Bregman, interview with Warren Christopher, 23 January 1998, Los Angeles; Ze'ev Schiff, 'What did Rabin promise the Syrians?', *Haaretz*, 29 August 1997 (in Hebrew).

9. This is according to Ehud Barak, interview, 30 June 2004, Tel Aviv; interview with Danny Yatom, 18 May 2004, Jerusalem.

10. Syria also rejected the international 1923 border as a creation of Western imperialism. See for example, President Assad's interview with CNN, 29 September 1996.

11. Ran Edelist, *Ehud Barak: Fighting the Demons* (Tel Aviv, 2003), p. 90 (in Hebrew).

12. Interview with Ami Ayalon, 11 August 2004, Ramat Gan.

13. Interview with Ami Ayalon.

14. In August 1999, according to Shin Bet, Israel held 1,894 Palestinian prisoners. Of them 1,714 were West Bankers and Gazans, while the rest were from East Jerusalem.

15. Interview with Mohammed Dahlan, 27 October 2004, Gaza.

16. Based on interviews with Mohammed Dahlan and other participants.

17. Interview with Saeb Erekat, 9 September 2004, Jericho.

18. 'Remarks by the President at Florida Democratic Party Dinner', Private Residence, Coral Gables, Florida, 13 July 1999.

19. Lisa Beyer, 'Love at First Wonk', *Time*, 19 July 1999.

20. 'Remarks by the President and Prime Minister Ehud Barak of Israel in Press Conference', Rose Garden, The White House, Office of the Press Secretary, 15 July 1999.

21. Ahron Bregman, interview with Danny Yatom, 31 March 2000, Tel Aviv and 12 September 2004, Kochav Yair.

22. As cited in Deborah Sontag, 'Peace Period'.

23. Bill Clinton, *My Life* (New York, 2004), p. 867.

24. Interview with Bill Clinton.

25. The National Security Council (NSC) is the President's principal forum for considering national security and foreign policy matters. It is chaired by the President, and its regular attendees include, among others, the Vice President, the Secretary of State, the Secretary of the Treasury, the Secretary of Defense and the Assistant to the President for National Security Affairs. The Chairman of the Joint Chiefs of Staff is the statutory military adviser to the Council, and the Director of Central Intelligence is the intelligence adviser. The Chief of Staff to the President, Counsel to the President and the Assistant to the President for Economic Policy are invited to attend any NSC meeting. The Attorney General and the Director of the Office of Management and Budget are invited to attend meetings pertaining to their responsibilities. The heads of other executive departments and agencies, as well as other senior officials, are invited to attend meetings of the NSC when appropriate.

26. Interview with Robert Malley, 13 October 2004, Washington.

27. The following is based mainly on interviews with Samuel (Sandy) Berger, 18 April 2005, Washington, and Robert Malley.

28. Interview with Sandy Berger.

29. 'Joint Press Conference with Prime Minister Barak', The White House, Office of the Press Secretary, 19 July 1999; interview with Danny Yatom, 12 September 2004, Kochav Yair.

30. Dennis Ross, *The Missing Peace: The Inside Story of the Fight for Middle East Peace* (original pre-publication manuscript), p. 498.

2 From Wye to Sharm

1. Interview with Danny Yatom, 18 May 2004, Jerusalem; interview with Saeb Erekat, 9 September 2004, Jericho.

2. Interview with Mohammed Dahlan, 27 May 2004, Gaza; interview with Gilead Sher, 21 September 2004, Tel Aviv.

3. Interview with Yasser Abed Rabbo, 6 June 2004, Ramallah.

4. As cited in Deborah Sontag, 'Peace Period'.

3 Talking to 'the mistress'

1. Interview with Martin Indyk, 6 December 2004, Washington.
2. Interview with Martin Indyk, 27 June 2004, Jerusalem.
3. The above is based on Dennis Ross, *The Missing Peace*, p. 513.
4. Interview with Uri Saguie, 23 May 2004, Herzliya.
5. Dennis Ross, *The Missing Peace*, p. 514.
6. Much of the above is based on Dennis Ross, *The Missing Peace*, pp. 520–21.
7. Dennis Ross, *The Missing Peace*, p. 524.
8. Bill Clinton, *My Life*, p. 884.
9. Eran was joined by General Shlomo Yanai, Daniel Reisner, Allan Baker, a lawyer from the Foreign Ministry and Pini Medan-Shani, formerly of Mossad. The Palestinian delegation was nominated by Arafat on 16 September 1999. In addition to Yasser Abed Rabbo, it also included Nabil Shaath, Faisal Husseini, the minister in charge of Jerusalem affairs, Nabil Kassis and Akram Hanieh, a close associate of Arafat.
10. The above is based on an interview with Yasser Abed Rabbo, 6 June 2004, Ramallah.
11. Bill Clinton, *My Life*, p. 884.
12. Interview with Robert Malley, 13 October 2004, Washington.
13. Interview with Bouthaina Shaaban, 20 December 2004, Damascus.
14. Interview with Lord Levy, 15 November 2004, London.
15. Interview with Lord Levy.
16. Interview with Martin Indyk, 6 December 2004, Washington.
17. Dennis Ross, *The Missing Peace*, p. 532.
18. Interview with Madeleine Albright, 19 January 2005, Washington.
19. Madeleine Albright, *Madam Secretary*, p. 475; interview with Martin Indyk, 27 June 2004, Jerusalem.
20. Dennis Ross, *The Missing Peace*, p. 533; interview with Danny Yatom, 12 September 2004, Kochav Yair.
21. Letter from Aaron Miller to *Elusive Peace*, 17 September 2004 and interview on 16 June 2004, Washington.
22. 'West Bank: Land for Peace Negotiations Resume', Israel Broadcasting Authority, 9 December 1999.
23. As cited in Charles Enderlin, *Shattered Dreams* (New York, 2002), p. 127.
24. Raviv Drucker, *Harakiri, Ehud Barak: The Failure* (Tel Aviv, 2002), pp. 71–2 (in Hebrew).

25. Dennis Ross, *The Missing Peace*, p. 534.

26. 'Remarks by President Clinton, Prime Minister Barak of Israel and Foreign Minister Shara of Syria', Rose Garden, The White House, Office of the Press Secretary, 15 December 1999.

27. Interview with Anonymous, 27 June 2004, Jerusalem.

28. According to Secretary of State Madeleine Albright, it was in fact Foreign Minister Shara who had insisted on giving a speech; see interview with Madeleine Albright.

29. Interview with Danny Yatom, 18 May 2004, Jerusalem; interview with Martin Indyk, 6 December 2004, Jerusalem.

30. See also Bill Clinton, *My Life*, p. 885.

31. Interview with Robert Malley, 13 October 2004, Washington.

32. Dennis Ross, *The Missing Peace*, p. 536; interview with Madeleine Albright.

33. Ahron Bregman, interview with Danny Yatom, 31 March 2000, Tel Aviv.

34. Ahron Bregman and Jihan el-Tahri, *Israel and the Arabs: An Eyewitness Account of War and Peace in the Middle East* (New York, 2000), p. 352.

35. Interview with Ehud Barak, 30 June 2004, Tel Aviv; Dennis Ross, *The Missing Peace*, p. 537; Bill Clinton, *My Life*, p. 885; interview with Robert Malley; interview with Danny Yatom, 12 September 2004, Kochav Yair.

36. Interview with Robert Malley; Dennis Ross, *The Missing Peace*, p. 537.

37. Prince Bandar has served under four American presidents and was the senior Saudi diplomat in Washington for many years with unprecedented access to each president.

38. 'Statement by the President', The White House, Office of the Press Secretary, 16 December 1999.

39. Interview with Danny Yatom, 29 September 2004, Kochav Yair.

40. Interview with Ehud Barak.

41. Dennis Ross, *The Missing Peace*, p. 539.

42. Bill Clinton, *My Life*, p. 885. A forensic team was dispatched to Syria to recover the bodies, but they were not found where the Israelis thought they should be.

43. Interview with Ehud Barak.

44. Dennis Ross, *The Missing Peace*, p. 546.

45. Interview with Bouthaina Shaaban.

46. Dennis Ross, *The Missing Peace*, p. 554.

47. Dennis Ross, *The Missing Peace*, p. 558.

48. *Haaretz*, 10 January 2000 (in Hebrew); Ran Edelist, *Ehud Barak: Fighting the Demons*, p. 220 (in Hebrew).

49. Interview with Amnon Lipkin-Shahak, 24 May 2004, Tel Aviv.

50. Interview with Uri Saguie; Alex Fishman, 'We have Missed Peace with Syria – It's unforgivable', *Yediot Aharonot*, 24 September 2004 (in Hebrew).

51. Interview with Robert Malley.

52. For the full text see, 'A Framework for Peace between Israel and Syria: The Draft Peace Treaty Presented by Clinton's Administration to Jerusalem and Damascus', *Haaretz*, 13 January 2000 (in Hebrew).

53. As cited in Dennis Ross, *The Missing Peace*, p. 595.

4 The Lion Comes to Geneva

1. Elsa Walsh, 'The Prince', *The New Yorker*, 24 March 2003, p. 54.

2. Interview with Robert Malley, 13 October 2004, Washington; interview with Madeleine Albright, 19 January 2005, Washington; and interview with Martin Indyk, 6 December 2004, Washington. According to Indyk the Syrian statement was made as early as the Daoudi–Saguie talks, which took place even before Shepherdstown.

3. This, as it later emerged, was either a mistake or a misunderstanding and indeed it is odd that the Americans took it so seriously given that it was so much at odds with everything the Syrians had been saying, and was a major departure from the longstanding Syrian insistence on access to the water. See, for example, Farouk al-Shara, interview in *Newsweek*, 11 October 1999.

4. Clinton's line is based on the following story: George Bernard Shaw is at dinner, and asks the rather attractive woman next to him, 'Would you go to bed with me for a million pounds?' She says 'Absolutely.' He then asks 'Would you go to bed with me for sixpence?' to which she replies, 'Of course not, what do you take me for?' 'Madam, we have established what you are, we are merely haggling over the price.'

5. Dennis Ross, *The Missing Peace*, p. 571.

6. Dennis Ross, *The Missing Peace*, p. 573.

7. Much of the above is based on Dennis Ross, *The Missing Peace*, pp. 572–3.

8. Interview with Martin Indyk, 27 June 2004, Jerusalem.

9. Madeleine Albright, *Madam Secretary*, p. 480.

10. Interview with Danny Yatom, 12 September 2004, Kochav Yair.

11. See interviews with Robert Malley, 13 October 2004, Washington and with Sandy Berger, 18 April 2005, Washington.

12. Interview with Bouthaina Shaaban, 20 December 2004, Damascus.

13. As cited in Ahron Bregman and Jihan el-Tahri, *Israel and the Arabs: An Eyewitness Account of War and Peace in the Middle East*, p. 354.

14. Interview with Robert Malley, 13 October 2004, Washington.

15. Assad's optimism can also be seen by the fact that he was willing to travel to Geneva at all. He hated travelling and, in private, Prime Minister Barak would call him the President of Albania, because he disliked leaving home so much.

16. Interview with Bouthaina Shaaban.

17. Clinton was ill. He had gone to Pakistan and had meetings with Perrez Musharraf. The Pakistanis insisted the President stay for a state lunch, as he had a dinner in India. The food sat out in the sun while the meetings continued. Two hours later they sat down. The first course was shrimp cocktail with mayonnaise.

18. Interview with Bouthaina Shaaban.

19. As cited in Ahron Bregman and Jihan el-Tahri, *Israel and the Arabs: An Eyewitness Account of War and Peace in the Middle East*, p. 356.

20. Interview with Bill Clinton, 20 June 2005, Little Rock.

21. Interview with Bouthaina Shaaban; interview with Robert Malley, 13 October 2004, Washington; Dennis Ross, *The Missing Peace*, p. 581; interview with Gamal Helal, 14 October 2004, Washington.

22. This is according to interviews with Madeleine Albright and Sandy Berger.

23. Copy of note in the author's archive; see also Bill Clinton, *My Life*, p. 903.

24. Interview with Robert Malley, 13 October 2004, Washington.

25. Interview with Bill Clinton.

26. Dennis Ross, *The Missing Peace*, p. 582.

27. Interview with Madeleine Albright.

28. Dennis Ross, *The Missing Peace*, p. 583.

29. Interviews with Sandy Berger and Robert Malley.

30. Dennis Ross, *The Missing Peace*, p. 584.

31. Madeleine Albright, *Madam Secretary*, p. 481.

32. Dennis Ross, *The Missing Peace*, p. 585.

5 Stockholm Calling

1. Interview with Saeb Erekat, 9 September 2004, Jericho.

2. Interview with Shlomo Ben-Ami, 4 May 2004, Kfar Saba.

3. Interview with Anonymous, 27 June 2004, Jerusalem.

4. Gilead Sher, *Just Beyond Reach* (Frank Cass, 2005), p. 19 (original pre-publication manuscript).

5. Interview with Shlomo Ben-Ami, 13 September 2004, Kfar Saba.

6. Interview with Hassan Asfour, 29 May 2004, Gaza City.

7. Interview with Shlomo Ben-Ami, 4 May 2004, Kfar Saba.

8. Interview with Shlomo Ben-Ami, 4 May 2004, Kfar Saba.

9. Interview with Aaron Miller, 3 January 2004, Washington.

10. About the leak see, Raviv Drucker, *Harakiri*, p. 193 (in Hebrew).

11. Dennis Ross, *The Missing Peace*, p. 615; interview with Shlomo Ben-Ami, 13 September 2004, Kfar Saba.

12. Interview with Giora Eiland, 28 September 2004, Ramat Ha'Sharon.

6 Farewell Lebanon

1. Middle East Historic Documents, UN resolution 425, 19 March 1978, www.lebanonwire.com.

2. Interview with Giora Eiland, 1 June 2004, Ramat Ha'Sharon; interview with Anonymous, 14 June 2004, Washington.

3. Interview with Terje Roed-Larsen, 29 June 2004, Herzliya.

4. Interview with Giora Eiland, 28 September 2004, Ramat Ha'Sharon.

5. Interview with Giora Eiland, 1 June 2004, Ramat Ha'Sharon.

6. Interview with Giora Eiland, 1 June 2004, Ramat Ha'Sharon.

7. Interview with Mohammed Dahlan, 27 October 2004, Gaza.

8. Interview with Gilead Sher, 21 September 2004, Tel Aviv.

7 Dragging Arafat to Camp David

1. Interview with Shlomo Ben-Ami, 13 September 2004, Kfar Saba.

2. Interview with Gidi Grinstein, 23 May 2004, Tel Aviv.

3. Akram Hanieh, series of articles published in *Al Ayyam* from 29 July to 10 August 2000.

4. Interview with Saeb Erekat, 9 September 2004, Jericho; interviews with Mohammed Rashid, 3 and 4 November 2004, Paris and 6 September 2004, London.

5. Interview with Gilead Sher, 21 September 2004, Tel Aviv.

6. Abu Ammar is Arafat's *nom de guerre*.

7. Interview with Shlomo Ben-Ami.

8. Interview with Gilead Sher; interview with Abu Ala, 22 September 2004, Abu Dis.

9. Interview with Shlomo Ben-Ami.

10. The *muqata* was built as a British police fort, then served as a Jordanian base and an Israeli military camp before the Palestinians took it over in 1996, turning it into Arafat's headquarters in the West Bank.

11. Akram Hanieh, articles in *Al Ayyam*, from 29 July to 10 August 2000.

12. Interview with Bill Clinton, 20 June 2005, Little Rock.

13. Interview with Robert Malley, 13 October 2004, Washington.

14. Interview with Saeb Erekat.

15. Interview with Saeb Erekat.

8 Showdown at Camp David

1. Dennis Ross, *The Missing Peace*, p. 649.

2. Dennis Ross, *The Missing Peace*, p. 652; Madeleine Albright, *Madam Secretary*, pp. 484–5.

3. Gilead Sher, *Just Beyond Reach*, pp. 157–8; Shlomo Ben-Ami, *A Front Without a Rearguard* (Tel Aviv, 2004), p. 140 (in Hebrew); Charles Enderlin, *Shattered Dreams*, pp. 179–81.

4. Although there was a complete media blackout, the public back home would know about events inside Camp David through information leaked from inside the camp.

5. Madeleine Albright, *Madam Secretary*, p. 485.

6. Madeleine Albright, *Madam Secretary*, p. 485; Dennis Ross, *The Missing Peace*, p. 661.

7. Madeleine Albright, *Madam Secretary*, pp. 485–6.

8. Dennis Ross, *The Missing Peace*, p. 664.

9. The hill is identified with the biblical Mount Moriah, where Abraham set up the altar on which to sacrifice his son Isaac. The First Temple was built on the Mount in the middle of the tenth century BCE and was destroyed in 586 BCE. The Second Temple was built on the same location, completed around 515 BCE and destroyed in 70 CE by the Romans.

10. Dennis Ross, *The Missing Peace*, p. 664.

11. Interviews with Mohammed Rashid, 3 and 4 November 2004, Paris and London; Shlomo Ben-Ami's Camp David Diaries, *Maariv*, 6 April 2001 (in Hebrew).

12. Dennis Ross, *The Missing Peace*, p. 667.

13. Madeleine Albright, *Madam Secretary*, p. 488.

14. Interview with Robert Malley, 13 October 2004, Washington.

15. Interviews with Mohammed Rashid, 3, 4 and 6 November 2004, Paris and London.

16. Interview with Gilead Sher, 21 September 2004, Tel Aviv.

17. Dennis Ross, *The Missing Peace*, p. 672.

18. Interview with Gidi Grinstein.

19. Dennis Ross, *The Missing Peace*, p. 673.

20. Interview with Shlomo Ben-Ami, 13 September 2004, Kfar Saba; interview with Ehud Barak, 1 November 2004, Tel Aviv.

21. Dennis Ross, *The Missing Peace*, p. 673.

22. Dennis Ross, *The Missing Peace*, p. 673.

23. Bill Clinton, *My Life*, p. 913 (my emphasis).

24. Dennis Ross, *The Missing Peace*, p. 676; interview with Ehud Barak.

25. Yatom dictated rather than just handed over Barak's letter to Indyk in order to avoid leaving a paper trail.

26. Interview with Saeb Erekat, 14 September 2004, Jericho.

27. Interview with Robert Malley; see also Dennis Ross, *The Missing Peace*, p. 675.

28. Interview with Saeb Erekat, 14 September 2004, Jericho.

29. Bill Clinton, *My Life*, p. 914.

30. Interview with Israel Hasson, 7 October 2004, London.

31. Interview with Ehud Barak, 1 November 2004, Tel Aviv, and other testimonies including Anonymous, 'The Diaries of Camp David' (unpublished manuscript).

32. Interview with Danny Yatom, 12 September 2004, Kochav Yair; interview with Martin Indyk, 6 December 2004, Washington.

33. As told by Israel Hasson in his interview.

34. Dennis Ross, *The Missing Peace*, p. 683; according to Berger, Clinton said: ' "You know, you pressed me to go to Geneva, to negotiate with Assad, and then you cut the rug out from under me hours before the meeting, and I'm not going to have that happen here again." And I think Barak was somewhat stunned by the President's conviction here.'

35. Interview with Sandy Berger, 18 April 2005, Washington.

36. Bill Clinton, *My Life*, p. 914.

37. Dennis Ross, *The Missing Peace*, p. 683.

38. Interview with Martin Indyk.

39. Bill Clinton, *My Life*, p. 914; interview with Sandy Berger.

40. Dennis Ross, *The Missing Peace*, p. 686.

41. It was similar to Rabin's 1993 'deposit', to be kept in the President's back pocket and tried on Arafat as an American offer.

42. According to Dennis Ross: 'With [us] leaning up against the swinging door, I had the image of the Marx Brothers movie where people keep going into a tiny stateroom on a ship and suddenly the door crashes open and they all pour out of the room. I whispered this and we all smiled.' See Dennis Ross, *The Missing Peace*, p. 688.

43. Dennis Ross, *The Missing Peace*, p. 689.

44. Interview with Israel Hasson.

45. The Prime Minister refused to meet Arafat personally to discuss things lest the Palestinian leader record his positions and pocket them for further haggling, as he was prone to do. The two, in fact, had only one face-to-face meeting at Camp David, when Barak invited himself to Birch Cabin for a cup of tea, but the conversation focused on non-political issues – on 'small talk' as Barak later referred to it. See, for example, Benny Morris, 'Camp David and After: An Exchange (1. An interview with Ehud Barak)', *The New York Review of Books*, 49, no. 10, 13 June 2002.

46. Madeleine Albright, *Madam Secretary*, p. 490.

47. Akram Hanieh, 'The Sixth Paper: A Long American Movie', *Al Ayyam*, series of articles published from 29 July to 10 August 2000.

48. Bill Clinton, *My Life*, p. 915.

49. Anonymous, 'The Diaries of Camp David'.

50. Anonymous, 'The Diaries of Camp David'.

51. Interview with Gilead Sher.

52. Madeleine Albright, *Madam Secretary*, p. 491.

53. Anonymous, 'The Diaries of Camp David'.

54. Anonymous, 'The Diaries of Camp David'; Madeleine Albright, *Madam Secretary*, p. 490.

55. Interview with Major Mohammed al-Daya, 29 January 2005, Ramallah.

56. On this and more see Dennis Ross, *The Missing Peace*, p. 701.

57. Dennis Ross, *The Missing Peace*, p. 706.

58. Dennis Ross, *The Missing Peace*, p. 706.

59. Akram Hanieh, 'The Seventh Paper: Areas of Failure ... Limits of Accomplishment', *Al Ayyam*, series of articles published from 29 July to 10 August 2000.

60. Interview with Saeb Erekat.

61. Dennis Ross, *The Missing Peace*, p. 707.

62. See also interview with Bill Clinton, 20 June 2005, Little Rock.

63. Anonymous, 'The Diaries of Camp David'.

9 Picking Up the Pieces

1. Interview with Israel Hasson, 7 October 2004, London.

2. Interview with Ehud Barak, 1 November 2004, Tel Aviv; also interview with Yassar Arafat, 11 November 2004, Ramallah, by Next Century Foundation.

3. Interview with Danny Yatom, 18 May 2004, Jerusalem.

4. Interviews with Gilead Sher and Danny Yatom, 18 May 2004, Jerusalem.

5. About the renewal of Israeli–Palestinian talks in Washington see, Amira Hass and Aluf Ben, 'Barak meets Arafat, talks in the US are resumed', *Haaretz*, 26 September 2000 (in Hebrew).

6. On the Israeli side Foreign Minister Shlomo Ben-Ami, Israel Hasson, Barak's loyal aide Gilead Sher and his deputy Gidi Grinstein. On the Palestinian side Saeb Erekat, Mohammed Dahlan and a few other aides. Clinton was represented by his special Middle East envoy Dennis Ross, Aaron Miller and Gamal Helal.

7. Interview with Mohammed Dahlan, 10 June 2004, Gaza.

8. Interview with Israel Hasson.

9. Interview with Shlomo Ben-Ami, 13 September 2004, Kfar Saba; see also, Nina Gilbert and Lamia Lahoud, 'Ben-Ami: Rajoub accepted Sharon's Temple Mount Visit', *Jerusalem Post*, 4 October 2000.

10 Death at the Mosque

1. Interview with Ehud Barak, 4 November 2004, Tel Aviv; see also Benny Morris, 'Camp David and After: An Exchange (1. An interview with Ehud Barak)', *The New York Review of Books*, 49, no.10, 13 June 2002, where Barak says: 'Sharon's visit . . . was directed against me, not the Palestinians, to show that the Likud cared more about Jerusalem than I did.'

2. Polls showed that more than two-thirds of Likud members preferred to see Netanyahu as their leader, see Yossi Verter, 'Sharon will climb down the tree and will get the second place', *Haaretz*, 28 September 2000 (in Hebrew), and Sara Leibovitz-Dar, 'An intimate opponent', *Haaretz*, 23 January 2004 (in Hebrew).

3. The visit also coincided with the fifth anniversary of the signing of the Oslo 2 Agreement between Israel and the Palestinians.

4. About the visit see, www.CNN.com, 28 September 2000.

5. Interview with Mohammed Dahlan, 27 May 2004, Gaza.

6. Idith Zertal and Akiva Eldar, *Lords of the Land: The Settlers and the State of Israel 1967–2004* (Tel Aviv, 2004), p. 534 (in Hebrew).

7. Interview with Hubert Vedrine, 13 January 2005, Paris.

8. Gilead Sher, *Just Beyond Reach*, p. 292.

9. Interview with Hubert Vedrine.

10. Interview with Hubert Vedrine.

11. Gilead Sher, *Just Beyond Reach*, pp. 294–7 and Charles Enderlin, *Shattered Dreams*, pp. 301–5.

12. Charles Enderlin, *Shattered Dreams*, pp. 305–6.

13. Interview with Nabil Shaath, 7 September 2004, Ramallah.

14. Interview with Robert Malley, 13 October 2004, Washington.

15. Interview with Gamal Helal, 14 October 2004, Washington.

16. Interview with Robert Malley.

17. Interview with Gamal Helal.

18. Interview with Saeb Erekat, 14 September 2004, Jericho.

19. Interviews with Saeb Erekat and Robert Malley.

20. Interviews with Terje Roed-Larsen, 29 June 2004, Herzliya, Robert Malley and Hubert Vedrine. See also, Charles Enderlin, *Shattered Dreams*, p. 309.

21. Charles Enderlin, *Shattered Dreams*, p. 309.

22. Interview with Robert Malley.

23. The above is based on an interview with Nabil Shaath.

24. Interview with Gamal Helal.

25. Interview with Gilead Sher, 21 September 2004, Tel Aviv.

26. As cited in Amos Harel and Avi Isacharoff, *The Seventh War* (Tel Aviv, 2004), p. 38 (in Hebrew).

27. Interview with Mohammed Dahlan.

28. As cited in Lisa Beyer, 'Breaking Point', *Time Europe*, 156, no. 17, 23 October 2000.

29. Interview with Gamal Helal.

30. It was called the Mitchell Commission after its Chairman, former US Senator George Mitchell, who had brokered a Northern Irish peace plan two years before.

11 Clinton's Last Stand

1. Interview with Ehud Barak, 9 March 2005, Tel Aviv.

2. Prince Bandar, the Saudi ambassador, picked Arafat up at Andrews Air Force Base. He pressed him to accept the 'Clinton Parameters'. Bandar said

to Arafat: 'Since 1948, every time we've had something on the table we say no. Then we say yes. When we say yes, it's not on the table any more. Then we have to deal with something less. Isn't it about time we say yes? If you take this deal, we will all throw our weight behind you.' Elsa Walsh, 'The Prince', *The New Yorker*, 24 March 2003, p. 55.

3. Dennis Ross, *The Missing Peace*, p. 11.

4. The Western Wall is 485 metres long, the Wailing Wall 58 metres.

5. Bill Clinton, *My Life*, p. 944. The call probably took place on 18 or 19 January, according to John Podesta. The parameters, although rejected by both sides, laid the foundation for yet another round of Israeli–Palestinian talks at Taba, from 21 to 27 January 2001. But with Clinton out of office, the US not involved, Barak deep in his election campaign and Arafat nowhere there, they stood no chance of any success.

12 Enter Sharon

1. Interview with Danny Ayalon, 12 September 2004, Washington.

2. Interview with Anonymous, 16 June 2004, Washington.

3. Amos Harel and Avi Isacharoff, *The Seventh War*, p. 109.

4. Amos Harel and Avi Isacharoff, *The Seventh War*, p. 110.

5. 'Remarks by the President and Prime Minister Ariel Sharon of Israel in Photo Opportunity', The Oval Office, The White House, 20 March 2001.

6. Interview with Anonymous, 1 September 2004, London. Another indication that the Administration was reluctant to intervene in the conflict was its failure to appoint a replacement to Dennis Ross, Middle East special envoy, when he left office in January 2001.

7. Suzanne Goldenberg, 'Upset at Sharon son's visit to Arafat', *Guardian*, 17 April 2001; interview with Omri Sharon, 1 June 2004, Jerusalem.

8. Suzanne Goldenberg, 'War jets attack West Bank after mall bomb carnage', *Guardian*, 19 May 2001.

9. As cited in Amos Harel and Avi Isacharoff, *The Seventh War*, p. 115.

10. The attack on Sbarro was Hamas's retaliation for the Israeli assassination of two senior Hamas operators in Nablus – Sheikhs Gamal Mansur and Gamal Salim.

11. Interview with Anonymous, 1 June 2004, Tel Aviv.

12. Jane Perlez, 'U.S. says killings by Israel inflame Middle East conflict', *New York Times*, 28 August 2001. However, the Bush Administration was divided about the Israeli assassination policy. Vice President Dick Cheney told Fox Television, 'If you've got an organization that had plotted, or is

plotting, some kind of suicide bomber attack ... and [the Israelis] have hard evidence of who it is and where they're located, I think there's some justification in their trying to protect themselves by pre-empting.' See also Mark Lavie, 'Cheney backs Israel assassination policy', *Sydney Morning Herald*, 4–5 August 2001.

13. In 2001 Israel assassinated at least 33 Palestinians, 37 in 2002.

14. Interviews with Jibril Rajoub, 25 May 2004, 4 June 2004 and 13 October 2004, Jericho and Ramallah.

15. Interview with Anonymous, 16 June 2004, Washington.

13 The Long Shadow of 9/11

1. Interview with Yasser Abed Rabbo, 3 January 2005, Ramallah.

2. As cited in Amos Harel and Avi Isacharoff, *The Seventh War*, p. 166.

3. Interview with Yasser Abed Rabbo.

4. Interview with Anonymous, 16 June 2004, Washington.

5. Interview with Anonymous, 1 June 2004, Tel Aviv.

6. Interview with Anonymous, 1 June 2004, Tel Aviv.

7. The above conversation between the Prime Minister and Ambassador Kurtzer is based on an interview with Anonymous, 1 June 2004, Tel Aviv.

8. Interview with Shimon Peres, 17 October 2004, Tel Aviv.

9. On 18 October 2001 the Israelis assassinated Atef Abayat.

10. 'Bush: Palestinian State "part of a vision" if Israel respected', CNN, 2 October 2001, 17.49 GMT.

11. On 10 November 2001 President Bush would repeat the same idea in a speech to the UN General Assembly. He would commit to establishing a Palestinian state. The objective of the peace process, Bush would tell delegates, is to have two states, Israel and Palestine, living side by side.

12. Interview with Anonymous, 1 June 2004, Tel Aviv.

13. Interview with Anonymous, 22 August 2004, Washington.

14. Aluf Benn, 'Sharon calls Powell after White House blasts PM comments', *Haaretz*, 5 October 2001 (English edition).

14 Spiralling Violence

1. Interview with Shimon Peres, 17 October 2004, Tel Aviv.

2. Sharon's speech in a special session of the Knesset, 18 October 2001 (in Hebrew).

3. Interview with Anonymous, 16 June 2004, Washington.

4. Interview with Anonymous, 22 August 2004, Washington.

5. Interview with Gamal Helal, 14 October 2004, Washington.

6. Interview with Alastair Crooke, 8 June 2004, London.

7. Avi Machlis, 'Israeli bus blast casts shadow on peace process', *Financial Times*, 30 November 2001.

8. Interview with Aaron Miller, 15 October 2004, Washington.

9. James Bennet and Joel Greenberg, 'Israel breaks with Arafat after Palestinian assault on bus in West Bank kills 10', *New York Times*, 13 December 2001.

10. Arafat's declaration in Gaza, Palestine Satellite Channel Television, 16 December 2001, at 16.00 GMT. On that same day in Gaza the leader of Hamas, Sheikh Ahmed Yassin, also declared a ceasefire: interview with Diana Buttu, 26 May 2004, Ramallah.

11. Amos Harel and Avi Isacharoff, *The Seventh War*, Appendix.

12. A flag of convenience is a foreign flag under which a ship is registered for tax avoidance purposes.

13. Interview with Shaul Mofaz, 31 February 2005, Tel Aviv.

14. Interview with Mike Herzog, 11 October 2004, Washington.

15. Interview with Anthony Zinni, 19 October 2004, Washington; see also Tom Clancy with General Tony Zinni (Ret.) and Tony Koltz, *Battle Ready* (New York, 2004), p. 394.

16. Interview with Aaron Miller.

17. Tom Clancy with General Tony Zinni (Ret.) and Tony Koltz, *Battle Ready*, p. 395.

18. Interview with Shaul Mofaz.

19. Also interview with Richard Armitage, 20 June 2005, Washington.

20. Interview with Anonymous, 22 August 2004, Washington.

21. Interview with Binyamin Ben-Eliezer, 27 September 2004, Tel Aviv.

22. Interview with Binyamin Ben-Eliezer.

23. During the first year of Sharon's government, the people involved in deciding who would be assassinated were Prime Minister Sharon, Defence Minister Ben-Eliezer and Foreign Minister Peres. Gradually the moderate Peres was pushed out of this circle of decision makers, leaving the task effectively in Sharon's hands. Also involved were deputy head of Shin Bet, Yuval Diskin and the deputy Chief of Staff, Moshe ('Boogie') Yaalon. From November 2000 to April 2003, Israel conducted 175 targeted killings, which killed 235 people and wounded 310. Of those killed, only 156 were the targets of the strikes; of those wounded, only 5 were so defined. Source: Uzi Benziman, 'Attention Dan Haluz', *Haaretz*, 2 December 2004.

24. See: http://www.guardian.co.uk/israel/Story/0,2763,633643,00.htm.

25. Interview with Mohammed Rashid, 7 October 2004, London.

15 Operation Defensive Shield

1. Tom Clancy with General Tony Zinni (Ret.) and Tony Koltz, *Battle Ready*, p. 365.

2. Tom Clancy with General Tony Zinni (Ret.), and Tony Koltz, *Battle Ready*, pp. 397–8.

3. Interview with Eival Gilady, 28 January 2005, Acre; interview with Saeb Erekat, 22 September 2004, Jericho; interview with Anthony Zinni, 19 October 2004, Washington.

4. Interview with Mohammed Rashid, 7 October 2004, London.

5. Interview with Saeb Erekat; see also Tom Clancy with General Tony Zinni (Ret.) and Tony Koltz, *Battle Ready*, p. 401.

6. Interview with Saeb Erekat.

7. Interview with Giora Eiland, 28 September 2004, Ramat Ha'Sharon; interview with Eival Gilady.

8. Interviews with Giora Eiland and Eival Gilady.

9. Interviews with Eival Gilady and Anthony Zinni.

10. Interview with Anthony Zinni; interview with Aaron Miller, 15 October 2004, Washington.

11. Interview with Aaron Miller.

12. Interview with Anthony Zinni.

13. Interview with Abbas Bin Muhammad al-Sayyid, 31 January 2005. The interview was conducted in an Israeli jail where al-Sayyid is imprisoned for his involvement in the Park Hotel bombing.

14. According to the recruiter, Muammar Shahrouri, the explosive belts were prepared in Nablus by Muhammad Taher and Ali Khudeiri and were hidden by Shahrouri himself until the moment came to give them to the suicide bombers.

15. Interview with Fathi Khatib, 31 January 2005. The interview was conducted in the Beersheva jail where Fathi Khatib is imprisoned for his involvement in the Park Hotel bombing.

16. Interview with Fathi Khatib.

17. Interview with Binyamin Ben-Eliezer, 2 June 2004, Jerusalem.

18. Interview with Binyamin Ben-Eliezer.

19. Interview with Giora Eiland.

20. Interview with Anonymous, 14 June 2004, Washington.

21. That day, the Arab summit meeting in Beirut issued the historic Beirut Declaration. It said that in return for a full Israeli withdrawal from the occupied territories, the Arabs would consider the Arab–Israeli conflict over, sign a peace agreement with Israel and establish normal relations with her. This important announcement, however, was overshadowed by the Park Hotel bombing and the subsequent Israeli operation.

22. Interview with Saeb Erekat.

23. Interview with Saeb Erekat.

24. Interview with Saeb Erekat.

25. Interview with Mohammed Rashid.

26. Interview with Mazzin Hussein, 30 May 2004, Gaza.

27. Craig Whitlock, 'A Sanctuary under Siege', *Washington Post*, 20 April 2001.

28. Interview with Ala Hosni, 20 May 2004, Ramallah.

16 The Holy Land Defeats America

1. Interview with Colin Powell, 22 February 2005, Alexandria, Virginia. Also interview with Richard Armitage, 20 June 2005, Washington.

2. Interview with Flynt Leverett, 15 October 2004, Washington.

3. Interview with Colin Powell.

4. Bob Woodward, *Bush at War* (New York, 2002), pp. 323–4.

5. 'President to Send Secretary Powell to the Middle East', Speech by President Bush at the Rose Garden, The White House, 4 April 2002; Bob Woodward, *Bush at War*, p. 34.

6. Interview with Anonymous, 1 June 2004, Tel Aviv.

7. *Haaretz*, 9 April 2002 (in Hebrew).

8. John Kampfner, *Blair's Wars* (London, 2003), p. 185.

9. This description of the situation in Ramallah and the *muqata* is based on an interview with Yasser Abed Rabbo, 26 June 2004, Ramallah.

10. Interview with Anthony Zinni, 19 October 2004, Washington.

11. Interview with Aaron Miller, 15 October 2004, Washington.

12. Interview with Gamal Helal, 14 October 2004, Washington.

13. Interview with Colin Powell.

14. The above conversation is based on an interview with Anonymous, 14 June 2004, Washington and with Danny Ayalon, 12 September 2004, Washington.

15. Interview with Flynt Leverett.

16. See too, interview with Colin Powell.

17. Interview with Flynt Leverett.
18. On 2 July 1972, Indira Gandhi, the Prime Minister of India, and Zulfikar Ali Bhutto, President of Pakistan, signed the Simla Accord, committing their warring nations to respect a ceasefire line called the Line of Control.
19. Interview with Gamal Helal.
20. Interview with Flynt Leverett.
21. Interview with Saeb Erekat, 22 September 2004, Jericho.
22. Interview with Colin Powell.
23. Interview with Anonymous, 14 June 2004, Washington.
24. Interview with Flynt Leverett.
25. Interview with Richard Armitage.

17 Massacre in Jenin?

1. Interview with Binyamin Ben-Eliezer and Mike Herzog, 11 October 2004, Washington.
2. In an interview given to CNN on 17 April Erekat said to Wolf Blitzer: 'We have 1,600 missing men in this refugee camp. Mostly women and children, husbands and wives ... how many people were massacred? We say the number will not be less than 500.'
3. Interview with Terje Roed-Larsen, 29 June 2004, Herzliya.
4. BBC News online, 18 April 2002; also interview with Terje Roed-Larsen.
5. Interview with Hani al-Hassan, 9 June 2004, Ramallah.
6. Tenth emergency special session, Agenda item 5, 'Illegal Israeli actions in Occupied East Jerusalem and the rest of the Occupied Palestinian Territory, Report of the Secretary-General prepared pursuant to General Assembly resolution ES-10/10'.
7. Interview with Giora Eiland, 28 September 2004 and 30 June 2004, Ramat Ha'Sharon.
8. Interviews with Terje Roed-Larsen and Giora Eiland. The Israeli Cabinet announced that, 'Israel has raised essential issues before the United Nations for a fair examination. As long as these terms have not been met, it will not be possible for the clarification process to begin.'
9. The above is based on an interview with Flynt Leverett, 15 October 2004, Washington, and Elsa Walsh, 'The Prince', *The New Yorker*, 24 March 2003.
10. Interview with Colin Powell, 22 February 2005, Alexandria, Virginia; interview with Flynt Leverett; Elsa Walsh, 'The Prince'.
11. Interview with Colin Powell.
12. Elsa Walsh, 'The Prince'.

18 Double-dealing in Ramallah and Bethlehem

1. Interview with Anonymous, 14 June 2004, Washington.
2. Interview with Sir Sherard Cowper-Coles, 26 November 2004, London.
3. Interview with Geoffrey Adams, 2 June 2005, London.
4. Interview with Andrew Coyle, 16 November 2004, London.
5. Interview with Anonymous, 30 June 2004, Tel Aviv, and with Sir Sherard Cowper-Coles.
6. Interview with Sir Sherard Cowper-Coles.
7. On 28 April 2003, Geoffrey Adams and the US Consul-General Ron Schlicher met Arafat for two and a half hours in the evening. This was the first time the proposal to transfer the prisoners was put to him in very general terms. He agreed in principle, sending the diplomats to talk to Yasser Abed Rabbo.
8. Interview with Geoffrey Adams.
9. 'Secretary-General Disbanding Jenin Fact-Finding Team', 2 May 2002, Press Release, Department of Public Information, News Coverage Service, New York, SG/SM/8220.
10. Arafat was caught by surprise. Here is an interview he gave to ABC news on 2 May. Interviewer: 'You are free to leave now, the Israelis have gone. What are you going to do now?' Arafat: 'If they will permit me to go out. But I don't know how they had accepted for you to come in?' Interviewer: 'There's nobody out there any more.' Arafat. 'That means they have . . . oh. OK.'
11. Interviews with Mohammed Rashid, 3 and 4 November 2004, Paris; interview with Eival Gilady, 28 January and 23 January 2005, Acre.
12. Interviews with Eival Gilady.
13. Interview with Mazzin Hussein, 30 May 2004, Gaza.

19 Dumping Arafat

1. Interview with Flynt Leverett, 15 October 2004, Washington.
2. Interview with Anonymous, 2 July 2004, Tel Aviv.
3. Interview with Colin Powell, 22 February 2005, Alexandria, Virginia.
4. Interview with Anonymous, 30 June 2004, Tel Aviv.
5. Interview with Anonymous, 30 June 2004, Tel Aviv.
6. Interview with Flynt Leverett.
7. Interview with Flynt Leverett.

8. For the text of Bush's 24 June speech, see *Washington Post*, 25 June 2002.

9. Interview with Nabil Shaath, 7 September 2004, Ramallah.

10. Interview with Diana Buttu, 26 May 2004, Ramallah.

11. The following reconstruction is based on interviews with Binyamin Ben-Eliezer, 27 September 2004, Tel Aviv, and Mike Herzog, 11 October 2004 and 2 December 2004, Washington.

12. According to Ben-Eliezer: 'His wife, we knew, was a terrorist just like him.'

13. Interview with Binyamin Ben-Eliezer. Fingers were pointed at Shin Bet for failing to provide accurate information.

14. Interview with Chief Commander of Israeli Air Force General Dan Haluz, *Haaretz*, 23 August 2002 (in Hebrew).

20 The King, the President and the Roadmap

1. Ten official Palestinian refugee camps are located in Jordan. They accommodate 307,785 registered refugees, or 17 per cent of the 1.7 million refugees registered with the UN Relief and Works Agency in Jordan. Four of the camps were set up on the east bank of the Jordan River after the 1948 Arab–Israeli war, and six after the 1967 war. In addition, there are three neighbourhoods in Amman, Zarqa and Madaba that are considered refugee camps by the government of Jordan and as 'unofficial' camps by UNRWA.

2. Interview with Marwan Muasher, 12 December 2004, Amman.

3. Interview with Flynt Leverett, 15 October 2004, Washington.

4. The Germans often claim credit for the roadmap because their Foreign Minister, Yoshke Fischer, had set out a kind of bare-bones peace plan that he referred to as the roadmap. But history should record that it was the Jordanians who really sold President Bush on the idea of having a roadmap for peace to show how to get to the two-state solution expressed in the President's 24 June 2002 speech.

5. Interview with Flynt Leverett.

6. Interview with Marwan Muasher.

7. The minutes of the conversation are published here for the first time. Source: Anonymous.

8. Interview with Flynt Leverett.

9. There was no need to start from scratch on the roadmap as there had been a State Department paper in existence for a while, which set out what each side (Israel, Palestinians, other Arab states) would need to do to put the peace process back on track. It was a one-page document at first, then

two, and was drawn up by Don Bloom and David Satterfield for internal State Department use. It was this that evolved into the roadmap. Source: Anonymous.

10. This body served a useful purpose as it was the means by which the US kept the European Union, Russia and the United Nations linked up with US efforts, thus preventing a bunch of random ideas and peace programmes floating around. See, interview with Colin Powell, 22 February 2005, Washington.

11. Interview with Flynt Leverett.

21 Locking Arafat Up Again

1. Interview with Ghassan Khatib, 26 September 2004, Ramallah.

2. Top of the Israeli list were Tawfiq al-Tirawi, Head of General Intelligence in the West Bank, who Israel claimed had transferred money and weapons for terrorist purposes, and had been personally involved in terror action; Amin al-Halo, head of Special Forces of General Intelligence in the West Bank, who Israel alleged had assisted terror operation cells in the West Bank, and had contacts with terrorists and activists; Abu Awad, also known as Mahmoud Damra, head of Arafat's Security Force 17, accused of activating attacks on Israeli communities; and Khalid Shawish, a senior activist in the presidential security forces, who Israel believed had aided terror attacks.

3. This is based on an interview with Anonymous, 30 June 2004, Tel Aviv.

4. Amos Harel and Avi Isacharoff, *The Seventh War*, p. 286 and interview with Colin Powell, 22 February 2005, Washington.

5. See also, interview with William Burns, 18 April 2005, Washington.

6. 'A Grave and Gathering Danger', Speech by President George W. Bush to the UN, 12 September 2002, in Christopher Cerf and Micah L. Sifry, *The Iraq War Reader* (New York, 2003), pp. 313–14.

7. Interview with Flynt Leverett, 15 October 2004, Washington.

8. Interview with Eival Gilady, 28 January 2005, Acre.

9. Aluf Benn, 'US telling PM that the Muqata siege undermining plans for Iraq', *Haaretz*, 29 September 2002.

10. Interview with Salam Fayyad, 8 March 2005, Ramallah.

11. Interview with Salam Fayyad, 27 September 2004, Ramallah.

12. Interview with Flynt Leverett.

13. Interview with Terje Roed-Larsen, 29 June 2004, Herzliya.

14. *New York Times*, 29 September 2002.

22 Dead Ends and Back Alleys on the Roadmap

1. Interview with Flynt Leverett, 15 October 2004, Washington.

2. Interview with Flynt Leverett; Abrams would often say his concern was not the intricacies of the language in the roadmap, but what in essence the European role should be.

3. In that, Abrams was also supported by 88 US senators, who attacked the document saying it did not take a strong enough position against Palestinian terrorism when compared with Bush's approach as reflected in his speech. For the text of the letter of these senators, see *Journal of Palestine Studies*, 32, no. 4 (Summer), 2003, p. 185.

4. Interview with Flynt Leverett.

5. For the text of the roadmap see US Department of State website, 30 April 2003.

6. Interview with Nabil Shaath, 7 September 2004, Ramallah.

7. Interview with Lord Levy, 15 November 2004, London.

8. Interview with Yasser Abed Rabbo, 3 January 2005, Ramallah.

9. Interview with Lord Levy.

10. Interview with Lord Levy.

11. Interview with Saeb Erekat, 27 September 2004, Jericho.

12. Interview with Lord Levy.

13. Interview with Nabil Shaath.

14. Interview with Yasser Abed Rabbo.

15. Interview with Abu Mazen, 10 June 2005, Gaza.

16. Interview with Salam Fayyad, 8 March 2005, Ramallah.

17. Interview with Ziad Abu Amr, 28 October 2004, Gaza.

18. This is according to Ziad Abu Amr.

19. Interview with Abu Mazen.

20. *Hudna* has a distinct meaning to Islamic fundamentalists, and should be regarded as a temporary, non-lasting truce. The prophet Muhammad struck a legendary, ten-year *hudna* with the Quraysh tribe that controlled Mecca in the seventh century. Over the following two years, Muhammad rearmed, broke the *hudna* and launched the full conquest of Mecca.

21. As cited in Connie Bruck, 'Back Roads', *The New Yorker*, 15 December 2003.

22. For Israel's fourteen roadmap reservations, see *Haaretz*, 27 April 2004.

23. According to Assistant Secretary of State William Burns, who said in an interview with *Elusive Peace*: 'Our position . . . was that we weren't in the

market for any further negotiation of the text . . . we were not interested in fiddling with the text any further', 18 April 2005, Washington.

23 Summits at Sharm and Aqaba

1. A leading American official involved in organizing the summits explains: 'Of course, we would have to have two summits, as you weren't going to get the Saudis in the same city as Sharon without giving them all heart attacks. And we put them in different places for logistical reasons. Otherwise we'd be telling some Saudi prince he can't land his plane yet because Sharon is still in town and if they are in the same town at the same time they will all melt or something; so we opted for Sharm and Aqaba.'
2. Interview with Nabil Shaath, 7 September 2004, Ramallah.
3. Interview with Nabil Shaath.
4. Interview with Nabil Shaath; interview with Mohammed Dahlan, 27 October 2004, Gaza.
5. The following is based on, among other sources, Akiva Eldar, 'Bush Likes Dahlan, Believes Abbas, and has "a problem with Sharon"', *Haaretz*, 10 June 2003.
6. Interviews with Nabil Shaath and Mohammed Dahlan.
7. Interview with Gamal Helal, 14 October 2004, Washington.
8. Interview with Mohammed Dahlan.
9. Akiva Eldar, 'Bush Likes Dahlan, Believes Abbas, and has "a problem with Sharon"'.
10. Interview with Nabil Shaath.
11. Interview with Nabil Shaath.
12. Interview with Nabil Shaath.
13. Interview with Nabil Shaath.
14. Interview with Anonymous, 18 August 2004, Ramallah.
15. Interview with Diana Buttu, 1 June 2004, Ramallah.
16. Interview with Ziad Abu Amr, 28 October 2004, Gaza.

24 First Steps on the Roadmap

1. Interview with John Wolf, 18 October 2004, Philadelphia.
2. Interview with John Wolf.
3. Interview with John Wolf; interview with Giora Eiland, 28 September 2004, Ramat Ha'Sharon.

4. Interview with John Wolf.

5. Interview with John Wolf.

6. Interview with Ziad Abu Amr, 28 October 2004, Gaza.

7. The meeting with Rice took place in Jericho because the Israelis would not accept a Palestinian–American meeting taking place in (Arab) East Jerusalem, because of the symbolism of it – it might acknowledge East Jerusalem as the Palestinian capital. The Israelis would only allow the meeting to take place in Israeli West Jerusalem. With Abu Mazen insisting that it should not take place in West Jerusalem, they settled on Jericho.

8. Interview with Nabil Shaath, 7 September 2004, Ramallah.

9. The Israelis were irritated that the President called the barrier a 'wall'. Within two hours of the press conference, they sent pictures to the Americans showing that, in fact, 90 per cent of the barrier was a fence, not a wall. By the next day the President was not calling it a wall any more.

10. Interview with John Wolf.

11. Interview with Diana Buttu, 1 June 2004, Ramallah; see also Elaine Monaghan, 'Bush praises Palestinian leader's courage', The Times, 26 July 2003.

12. Guy Dunmore, 'Bush attacks Israelis for building of West Bank wall', Financial Times, 26 July 2003; Brian Knowlton, 'Sharon meets with Bush but says security fence will still go up', International Herald Tribune, 30 July 2003.

13. Interviews with Mike Herzog, 11 October and 2 December 2004, Washington, and Giora Eiland, 10 August 2004, Ramat Ha'Sharon.

14. The following is based on an interview with Majd Zaatri, 1 February 2005, Beersheva Prison.

15. During July 2003, which was the main month of the ceasefire, the number of casualties on both sides dropped dramatically: only 10 were killed – 3 Israelis and 7 Palestinians. This was the lowest number of killed since the beginning of the intifada.

16. Interview with John Wolf.

17. Interview with John Wolf.

18. Interview with John Wolf.

19. Interview with Giora Eiland.

20. Interviews with Mike Herzog.

21. Interviews with Mike Herzog and Giora Eiland.

22. Interview with Mike Herzog.

25 Unilateral Disengagement

1. Interview with Yasser Abed Rabbo, 3 January 2005, Ramallah.
2. Interview with Abu Mazen, 10 June 2005, Gaza.
3. Interview with Nabil Shaath, 7 September 2004, Ramallah.
4. Interview with Colin Powell, 25 February 2005, Washington.
5. Interview with Giora Eiland, 28 September 2004, Ramat Ha'Sharon.
6. Interview with Marwan Muasher, 12 December 2004, Amman.
7. Interview with Marwan Muasher.
8. Source: Anonymous.
9. Interview with Giora Eiland.
10. Interview with Danny Ayalon, 12 September 2004, Washington.
11. Interview with Danny Ayalon.
12. Interview with Danny Ayalon.
13. See 'Exchange of letters between Prime Minister Sharon and President Bush', 14 April 2004, Israel Ministry of Foreign Affairs, www.mfa.gov.il.

Epilogue

1. Interview with Yasser Abed Rabbo, 3 January 2005, Ramallah.
2. Interview with Mohammed Rashid, 3 November 2004, Paris.
3. Interview with Mohammed Rashid.
4. Interview with Mohammed Rashid.
5. Telephone interview with Nabil Shaath, 15 April 2005, Tel Aviv.
6. Arafat's Jordanian doctor has called for an autopsy, citing possible poisoning. Tayeb Abdul Rahim, the Secretary-General of the Palestinian Authority, also raised the possibility of poisoning, saying that Palestinians deserved to know what had caused Arafat's death. See, for example, John Ward Anderson, 'Conspiracy Theories Persist on Arafat's Death', *Washington Post*, 18 November 2004.
7. Tovah Lazaroff, 'Sharon: "Arafat won't be buried in Jerusalem"', *Jerusalem Post*, 27 October 2004.

Index

PENGUIN HISTORY/CURRENT EVENTS

THE FIFTY YEARS WAR: ISRAEL AND THE ARABS
AHRON BREGMAN & JIHAN EL-TAHRI

'Often reads more as a thriller than a well documented work of history, with plans, alliances, conspiracies and counter-conspiracies chasing each other from chapter to chapter ... an excellent book of diplomatic history' *Financial Times*

Since the creation of the state of Israel in 1948, the region has been the scene of fierce power struggles, of injustice and of tragic events. Now, for the first time, a unique Israeli–Arab author collaboration is tackling the fifty years of conflict in one of the worlds most complex and controversial situations – from both sides of the enemy lines.

This ground-breaking book exposes some of the long-held myths about events in the Middle East. Drawing on candid in-depth interviews with key figures in the struggles – from both Israel and Arab neighbours, many of whom have never spoken out before – this book unearths some startling new insights. It is the first balanced account of behind-the-scenes negotiations and intrigues.

Covering the main events between Israel and its Arab neighbours during the past fifty years – from its earliest attempts to establish itself, through the Six Day War in 1967 and the Lebanon War in 1982 to the peace negotiations of the 1990s – this is the definitive insiders' account of war and peace in the Middle East.

'A fascinating book full of new insights ... Anyone who wants to understand the Middle East conflict will be both enlightened and stimulated by *The Fifty Years War*' *Jewish Chronicle*